Lay Down with Dogs

Byron Woodfin

Lay Down with Dogs

The Story of
Hugh Otis Bynum
and the Scottsboro
First Monday Bombing

The University of Alabama Press

TUSCALOOSA & LONDON

Library of Congress Cataloging-in-Publication Data

Woodfin, Byron
    Lay Down with dogs : Hugh Otis Bynum and the
Scottsboro First Monday Bombing / Byron Woodfin.
            p.   cm.
    Includes index.
    ISBN 0-8173-0845-8 (cloth : alk. paper)
    1. Bynum, Hugh Otis—Trials, litigation, etc.   2. Trials
(Attempted murder)—Alabama—Scottsboro.   3. Bombings—
Alabama—Scottsboro.   I. Title.
    KF224.B96W66   1997
    345.73′02523′0976195—dc20
    [347.30525230976195]   96-8068

British Library
Cataloguing-in-Publication
Data available

To Johnnie Hale,
the lady who taught me the true value of being a good reporter,
and to the memory of George Tubbs,
the carpenter-turned-investigator who helped build this case.

If you lay down with dogs, you get fleas,
and Hugh Otis Bynum has been laying
with the biggest dogs in this county.

—Bill Baxley, closing arguments,
   29 March 1975

Evil is a mystery we will not understand
this side of Eternity.

—Rev. Billy Graham
   23 April 1995
   Oklahoma City, Oklahoma

Contents

Prologue

Many of the people who were in Scottsboro on the morning of 4 December 1972 thought the explosion they heard was a sonic boom caused by an airplane passing overhead. Within a few hours the town learned that the sound was that of a car bomb that critically injured a popular attorney. The investigation of the bombing lasted more than two years and eventually led to the arrest of one of the town's wealthiest and most prominent landowners.

The case is filled with some of the most eccentric characters imaginable and it brought together some of the state's brightest legal minds. The state's young and idealistic attorney general was pitted against the best defense team in Alabama. Many of those who took part in the criminal investigation and subsequent trial went on to earn notoriety in their own right.

But beyond being an example of a fascinating investigation and trial, the case symbolizes the change taking place throughout much of the South during the 1970s. Many established traditions were broken during the subsequent turmoil of change.

This is the story of one of the most infamous deeds in Alabama criminal history.

Acknowledgments

The purpose of this book is to recount as factually as is possible the events surrounding the bombing of Loy Campbell on First Monday, December 1972. Admittedly, it is a tiny slice of Alabama history, albeit a powerful and colorful slice. It is hard to imagine a case of litigation that brought more notable Alabamians together at one time than did the case of Hugh Otis Bynum.

The research for this book consisted of the use of newspaper accounts, court and police records, trial transcripts, and oral interviews with many who were involved in the case. To those who so graciously agreed to contribute their recollections to this project, I am extremely grateful. In some cases, information is based on the author's personal experience and observations.

Sadly, detective George Tubbs passed away before he could be interviewed for this project. His contribution would have been significant and is sorely missed.

There are many others who assisted with this project and to whom I am grateful. First, thanks to my wife, Kathy, the best editor and critic a writer could have. Thanks also to Bill Buckner of WKEA Radio, Scottsboro, for his audio reproduction skills, and to Leroy and Irene Gist for their photographic reproduction skills. Thanks to Jackson County Circuit Court Clerk Leonard Griggs and his assistant, Carrie Bolte, for helping to locate court records, and to Scottsboro Police Chief Keith Smith and Inspector Clarence Bolte and Jackson County Sheriff's Deputy Paul Mount for their assistance in locating police records. Thanks to Alex Newton of Birmingham for his assistance in locating trial transcripts. Thanks to Carmen Wann for helping me find the "lost" newspaper articles, and to Dee Singleton of the Gadsden Public Library for her assistance.

My thanks and gratitude to Rickey and Jo Davis of Pisgah and to David and Juanita Tombrello, Dr. Ron Dykes, Brenda Lusk, and M. J. Hess, all of Scottsboro, for their encouragement and words of advice. Thanks to Malcolm MacDonald of The University of Alabama Press and Dr. Harvey Jackson of Jacksonville State University for their editorial comments and encouragement. A special thanks to Tallulah Bush of Scottsboro for the inspiration for the book's title.

Also a special word of thanks to my friends Gini Boyd, Sal Franco-Ruiz, Sherry Helmstetter, Pearl Hunter, Jan Johns, Dr. Harry Kinnane, Lorrie McGaha, Karen Pate, Rick Robins, Robbie Robinson, Regina Smith, and Lucy Schwartz. In their hearts they know why they are so special.

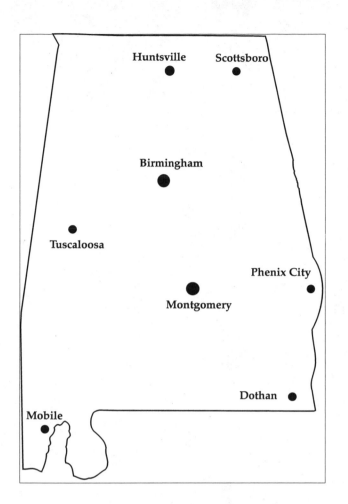

Part One   The Cauldron

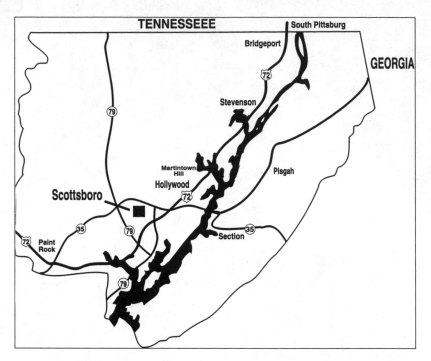

Jackson County, Alabama

I   *First Monday*

On the first Monday of each month, the square around the courthouse in Scottsboro, Alabama, takes on the look of a festive and colorful country fair as traders and bargain hunters gather for the traditional First Monday Trade Day. At the turn of the century, court was held on the first Monday of the month as the circuit judge made his scheduled visit to the county seat. Many residents of Jackson County had cases to be heard or were to be called as witnesses or just came to town that day to gawk and catch up on the latest gossip, and the tradition of First Monday Trade Day began.

Although First Monday would evolve into a large, open-air flea market, in the beginning it was an opportunity for farmers to trade cattle, mules, dogs, and other livestock for needed equipment or cash. As the tradition grew, much of the daily routine for the country folk paused for that one day when the family would load up the wagon and make the trip to Scottsboro. Later the wagons were replaced by pickup trucks and family cars.

There are the legends of those who became modestly wealthy by perfecting the art of bartering at First Monday. One story has it that an enterprising fellow started in the morning trading a pocketknife and wound up at the end of the day with a fine pair of plow mules. To this day, knife traders and whittlers can be found loitering about the courthouse on any given day of the week. They spend hours perfecting the art of shaving a cedar stick into paper thin strips that fall to the ground in springlike coils. Piles of the sweet-scented cedar shavings often litter the sidewalks around the courthouse and mark the spots where knife trading and tale swapping have occurred.

For the most part, First Monday was one of the few opportunities for many families to get away from the daily chores of country life in the rugged mountains and hollows of northeast Alabama. Throughout its history, First Monday has been as much a social event as an opportunity to find a bargain. Country and gospel music filled the air as fiddlers and self-taught musicians performed on the corners of the square or under the protection of the gazebo that sits by the main entrance to the courthouse.

There were preachers who took advantage of the roaming audiences to thump their Bibles and spread the gospel of fire and brimstone. At election time, politicians also took advantage of the available crowds. Often a wagon or flatbed truck carrying a piano player or band would announce the vote stumper, who would try to harangue the crowd into believing he was the best candidate.

There was a multitude of farm tools and implements to haggle over. Plow points, furrowers, wagon trees and wagon wheels, bucksaws, one-man and two-man crosscut saws, double- and single-bit axes, wedges, mauls, cooper and shingle froes, every conceivable carpenter's tool, and every accoutrement of farming were available to the shrewd barterers. Work and pleasure horses, mules, goats, sheep, piglets, and shoats were also for trade. All breeds of hunting dogs could be found. Rabbit, coon, and fox hounds, bird dogs of all sorts, baying dogs, treeing dogs, and the occasional feist that someone would pass off as an excellent squirrel dog. Men in blue-bibbed overalls openly carried long guns, shotguns, and pistols as they searched for a potential buyer or someone with whom they might haggle out a trade. Poultry included geese and odd-looking guinea fowls and chickens of all types—fryers, layers, and the strutting game chickens the men bought to enter in the cockfights that were held secretly for both amusement and gambling. Vendors displayed used shoes, clothes, coats, shawls, and beautiful handmade quilts. Visitors saw huge metal milk cans and butter churns and handcrafted slat-bottomed chairs made from hickory or oak—anything and everything that could make the job easier or the task lighter could be found at First Monday. Today many of these items are valuable collectibles or antiques, but for much of the history of First Monday, these were items of necessity. No trip to First Monday would be complete without buying boiled or parched peanuts sold by vendors who cooked their foodstuffs as the customer watched.

One day each month the courthouse square in Scottsboro was transformed into a cacophonous blend of sights, sounds, and colors. On First Monday, the country life came to town. But not everyone cherished the tradition of First Monday. The retailers and businessmen whose shops lined the avenues surrounding the courthouse resented Trade Day. The friction of First Monday and the business community grew out of a simple fact. With the

Tourists and bargain hunters continue to flock to Scottsboro's
First Monday Trade Day. On the first Monday of December 1972,
many of those gathered on the square thought the explosion they
heard was a sonic boom.
(Photo by Byron Woodfin)

exception of the few eateries around the courthouse (such as
Payne's Drug Store, where the thirsty could get a cold soda or
a hamburger and milk shake), few retail businesses profited from
First Monday. In fact, business was slowed on that day each
month as the crowds descended on the square in Scottsboro to
find a bargain. The swarm of First Monday visitors would take
up all available parking, making it difficult for customers to do
business with the retail shops.

Over the years the business community made several attempts
to have an outright ban placed on First Monday. Every few years,
the frustration would reach the point where businesses would
form a delegation and make appeals to the county commission-
ers or the city council to stop the tradition or at least move
it somewhere else. "Just get it off the square," would be their
battle cry.

But stopping the tradition, an important seam in the fabric
of Jackson County history, would prove to be impossible. Every
effort by the business community to stop First Monday would
be ignored by those who supplemented their livelihood by trading and selling their wares. Many of the businesses themselves
finally moved from the square and relocated in the shopping cen-

ters and malls that sprang up along the major highway that connected Scottsboro with Huntsville and Chattanooga.

In the latter part of the 1970s, the health department began cracking down on the display and selling of livestock, fighting chickens, and dogs at First Monday, and in the 1980s, the sale of guns, once a major attraction, would also be banned. Eventually, Trade Day would lose its country fair appearance. More and more it became a tourist attraction and less of an opportunity to swap or find a bargain. Though it is still called First Monday, the crowds are now greatest on Sunday, and often by noon on Monday the peddlers have packed their things away and headed home. First Monday has less appeal for the locals, and fewer of those living in and around Scottsboro now make the monthly trek to find a bargain.

But in 1972, First Monday was as popular as ever. On the first Monday of December of that year peddlers, traders, and bargain hunters had filled up the sidewalks along the four sides of the Jackson County Courthouse. The town was decorated for Christmas, and on the previous Friday the Downtown Merchants Association had held the largest Christmas parade in the town's history. A pretty high school senior, Linda Gamble from Pisgah, Miss Jackson County Junior Miss, had ridden the winning parade float, sponsored by the Jaycees.

On that First Monday, Jackson County Probate Judge Robert I. Gentry stood on the steps of the courthouse and surveyed the crowd. Unlike the business community, Gentry generally enjoyed First Monday. The judge had a passion for antique furniture and in his spare time he would often make the round of the courthouse square on First Monday in search of furniture that could be bought, refinished, and resold for a profit. Gentry noted the weather was unusually warm for the time of year. Although winters in northeast Alabama rarely are severe and generally are short-lived, the weather this First Monday was exceptionally pleasant and no doubt was the main reason for such a large turnout of vendors and bargain hunters.[1]

On that same morning, Hugh Otis Bynum, Jr., began the day as he had begun every other day for nearly twenty years. Bynum was the wealthiest landowner in town. The great-grandson of Robert Scott, the man who founded Scottsboro, Bynum had inherited much of his wealth and land from his father. Known as an eccentric, he lived alone in a rambling, two-story wooden frame house that had once been the family home. It was rumored that he slept on a mattress thrown on the floor of the nearly empty house. Over the years he had developed a ritualistic routine that revolved around the care of his prized Angus cattle.[2]

Each day and each week the routine was the same: breakfast of oatmeal at the Variety Bake Shop on the courthouse square, lunch consisting of mashed potatoes and asparagus at Tom's Restaurant, also on the square, and dinner of eggs over-easy with sausage, also eaten at Tom's. On Sunday, he always took his meals at the Liberty Restaurant, located on the outskirts of town. Each day was filled with as many as a dozen trips to various cattle farms he owned or rented in and around Scottsboro.[3]

On that First Monday in 1972, Bynum left his home at 7:30 and drove his luxury car the few blocks to the square. After breakfast at Fred Casteel's Variety Bake Shop, he drove to a cattle farm he owned at Tupelo Pike, some five miles outside of town. At about nine o'clock, after making sure the cattle were all right, Hugh Otis Bynum headed back to the square and Tom's Restaurant.[4]

In another part of town, Scottsboro attorney Loy Campbell hurried to get his six-year-old daughter Ramona ready for school. Recently divorced, Campbell lived with his only child in a modest home on Hamlin Street less than a hundred yards from Caldwell Elementary School, where the girl was in the first grade. Campbell was a protective father, and it was his routine to get Ramona ready and drive her the short distance to the school entrance before heading into Scottsboro to the law office he shared with his brother, H. R. "Bunk" Campbell.[5]

On Monday, 4 December 1972, Campbell had overslept and now he hurried to get the young girl off to school before classes began.[6] He and Bunk and a younger brother, John Paul, a schoolteacher, had spent the weekend in Birmingham to attend the Alabama-Auburn football game. The three Campbell boys were graduates of the University of Alabama and avid Crimson Tide fans. Few college football rivalries match the intensity of the rivalry between Alabama and Auburn. Auburn had defeated Alabama 17–16 in a thrilling come-from-behind fourth-quarter scoring frenzy, and Loy was ready for the ribbing he would take from his friends downtown. He especially dreaded the good-natured teasing he would get from Judge Gentry, an Auburn graduate.[7]

The Campbell brothers had not returned to Scottsboro until

late Sunday, and by the time he had picked up Ramona from the friend's house where she had spent the weekend and gotten to his own home, it was close to 5 P.M. Tired from the trip to Birmingham, he simply had overslept that Monday morning. Though it had rained during the night, the weather had cleared somewhat, and he felt it would be all right this morning to let Ramona walk the short distance to the school. Loy walked the little girl a block to a corner crossing and watched as she entered the safety of the school. He then returned to his home and turned to the task of getting ready for work.[8]

At a few minutes before 9:00 A.M. that first Monday of December 1972, Loy Campbell walked from his house to the 1971 Pontiac sedan parked in the driveway, got in the driver's seat, and put the key in the ignition.

2   *Currents of Change*

Scottsboro, Alabama, is a southern hamlet snuggled close to the banks of the Tennessee River. Flanked by the long bony ridge of Sand Mountain to the east and the Cumberland Mountain to the west, the town lies in a valley in the northeast corner of the state. Tennessee and Georgia can be reached in a few minutes' driving time.

For most of its history, Scottsboro has been a quiet agricultural town linked to the rest of the South by the Tennessee River and the railroad that runs from Chattanooga to Huntsville. Cotton was, for most of this century, the area's main crop. Reflecting the influence of cotton, most of the early manufacturing jobs were in textiles, and the textile industry remains an important contributor to the local economy. As cattle farming grew in the area, cotton slowly gave way to row crops, such as corn and soybeans, and the "land of cotton" became more and more a thing of the past. Today, farmers in Jackson County grow little cotton and the once bustling cotton gins are now idle.

Not until the late 1960s and early 1970s did Scottsboro begin

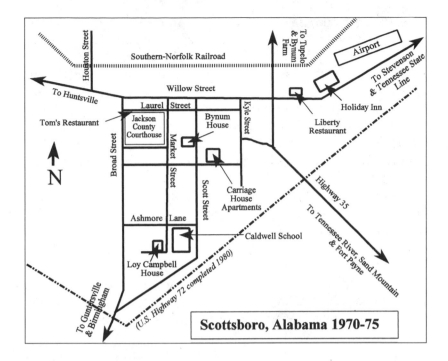

Scottsboro, Alabama 1970-75

to see a boom in major manufacturing jobs. Taking advantage of low wages and cheap river transportation, several northern companies built factories in and around Scottsboro. Revere Copper and Brass built a large aluminum smelting plant on the outskirts of town, creating hundreds of jobs and bringing an influx of Northerners who moved to Scottsboro, many from the Baltimore area. Goodyear Tire and Rubber opened a metal spinning plant, creating more manufacturing jobs, and the Tennessee Valley Authority launched its ambitious project of constructing a multimillion-dollar nuclear power plant at Bellefonte, a stone's throw from Scottsboro. The construction of the nuclear plant created hundreds of temporary jobs for local workers and brought another influx of outsiders to the area. But there has always been a scarcity of well-paying jobs in the county. Even with the relocation of the northern industries, many Jackson County citizens are forced to seek work in Chattanooga or Huntsville, and many have had to leave the area in search of a reliable income.

Scottsboro was named after an enterprising lawyer, Robert Thomas Scott. If it had not been for Scott's hard-driving ambition, the town might never have come into existence. Scott's father had immigrated to the United States from Scotland and had originally settled in North Carolina. The Scott clan moved to Alabama in 1817 in search of new opportunity in the lands being opened up to settlers in the West. Robert Thomas Scott, seeking better opportunities, moved his family in 1834 to Jackson County from neighboring Madison County. The ambitious Scott bought a large farm at Bellefonte, which was then the county seat. His holdings included a hotel named Belle Tavern that was the scene of many of the big social events of the time.[1]

Robert Thomas Scott was a man of varied talents. During his lifetime, he served nearly twenty years in the Alabama Legislature, and he made one unsuccessful bid for a seat in the U.S. Congress in 1836. He also published a small newspaper, *The Bellefonte Courier*, which he used to espouse his overriding political belief that holders of public office were overpaid and taxpayers were underserved. As a young man, Scott studied law at Franklin, Tennessee, and in addition to his business ventures, he practiced law during much of his life.

Between 1850 and 1853, Scott moved his family to what was then called Sage Town. He went about buying up large tracts of land and built a large house on Backbone Ridge. He called the house "White Cottage." In 1856, the Memphis-Charleston Railroad began regular stops at what the railroad had begun calling "Scott's Station." Reflecting the Scottish influence on the area, Scott's Station became Scottsborough, and that name in turn was shortened to Scottsboro.

Robert T. Scott died in 1863, shortly after Federal troops sacked and burned his beloved White Cottage following one of the few Civil War skirmishes that took place in the area. According to one story, the Federal troops, after sacking the house, forced Scott to pull a wagon loaded with booty. The exertion proved too taxing for the old man and he died a few days later. According to the stipulations of his will, Scott's heirs donated land for the construction of a courthouse on the condition that Scottsboro be named the county seat.[2]

Scottsboro became like so many county seats found in the South. The courthouse, built in the center of town, was the hub of all business, private and not-so-private. The town radiated from this site, and as it grew, it was crisscrossed with the streets and tree-lined boulevards that now bear the names of the first settlers and the families that propagated themselves and contributed to the town's growth. This area of the country was rugged but beautiful, and the availability of land drew many settlers. Family and religion became the threads that held the fabric of the new communities together. For many of the new settlers, the importance of family ties outweighed everything else—even, in some cases, their firm belief in God.

Like their European forefathers, the first settlers in north Alabama were solidly entrenched Protestants; Jews and Catholics were a rarity. Although there were many Protestant sects in the area, the Baptists eventually became the predominant religious group. Not only is this area a part of the Heart of Dixie, it is also a solid link in the Bible Belt. Throughout its history, northeast Alabama has been molded by religion. Even politics has, at times, been controlled by the churches. Many a local politician's career was ruined by rumors that he had been partaking of whiskey or had not been regular in his church attendance. It was not uncommon for preachers to influence the outcome of an election from the pulpit. Like much of Alabama, Scottsboro and Jackson County remained dry after the repeal of Prohibition.

But dry laws and the preaching of abstinence did not always prevail. To satisfy the thirst of those who went against the teachings of the church and in defiance of the law, bootleggers and moonshiners flourished in the hills and hollows surrounding Scottsboro. Like religion, bootlegging became a fact of life and in many ways was as accepted as religion. Most communities had at least one active bootlegger, who would sell illegally transported beer and white lightning or moonshine whiskey that was cooked up in stills hidden out in the hardwood forests. In some cases these bootleggers, far from being community outcasts, became woven into the social fabric of the town. If they ran a clean operation, free from rowdiness, they could almost become respectable citizens. Sometimes the bootleggers and still runners were seen as romantic heroes. With a dearth of economic opportunities, bootlegging and moonshining were alternative and understandable ways of making a living. This tolerance was extended to the rowdies, ruffians, and felons who made up a social subculture that mixed, at times, with Scottsboro's high life.

In the latter part of the 1960s and on into the 1970s, the sale of marijuana, cocaine, and other drugs began to compete (or in some cases were combined) with the activity of the bootleggers.

In 1984, Scottsboro legalized the sale of alcohol. A few bootleggers remain, but they are not as common as they once were. Moonshiners and still runners are today virtually extinct. The discovery of a still is now a newsworthy event.

Unlike its south Alabama counterparts, Scottsboro was not a product of the plantation era that spawned a social strata above and apart from the working class. Like much of the South, many of the towns in south Alabama were built around founding families, landed gentry who controlled much of the power that guided the direction of the town. The power, the wealth, and the ownership of the land reached back generations to the time of the founding of the nation. As time passed, these families grew into a class unto themselves, separated from others by their conception of style and grace and their traditions—and their wealth and subsequent privileges. The social earthquake of the Civil War did little to change this pattern. In the second half of this century, during the turbulent fight for integration and civil rights, this gentried class became a bulwark against change.

But Scottsboro was much different. There was no lineal tradition reaching back to the birth of the nation. The town was barely in existence during the Civil War. It was founded by people who sought an opportunity they had not found elsewhere. There was no local history, land, or wealth to inherit or to pass on. Family fortunes, successes, and failures had to be built on the bedrock belief in God, family, and hard work. No landed gentry controlled the town's destiny. Families that came to guide the direction of the town rose from the ranks of those who seized and made good the opportunities available to them.

As in much of the South, there evolved in Scottsboro a spirit of stubbornness, fierce independence, and self-reliance. A neighbor's business, including connubial and criminal transgressions, might be a subject of speculation, but meddling was not tolerated. This doctrine of personal nonintervention permeated and shaped the character of the entire region.

An upper class of sorts eventually did emerge, but this upper crust was thin. Many of the new well-to-do families had made their fortunes through the hard toil it takes to pull oneself to the pinnacle of economic security. Many of them remembered whence they had come. The commingling of the working class and this upper crust both in terms of social interaction and marriage was more accepted in Scottsboro than elsewhere. The professionals—doctors and lawyers and educators—rounded out the class of citizens that determined the town's direction.

In spite of this uniqueness, the quaint little town isolated in the foothills of the Appalachians would have remained anonymous had it not been for an event that tainted the town forever after as the epitome of racial bigotry in this country. In March 1931, nine young black men were charged with the rape of two white women aboard a train headed for Huntsville. For most of the country and much of the world, the name *Scottsboro* became synonymous with racial injustice.[3] The "Scottsboro Boys," as they became known, were arrested in the small town of Paint Rock on the border of Jackson and Madison counties and brought back to Scottsboro to stand trial. As word of the arrest spread, an angry mob formed outside the jail. Fearing the nine men might be lynched, authorities moved them to Gadsden until a trial could be held.[4]

On 9 April 1931, less than two weeks after their arrest and with the Alabama National Guard standing sentry around the courthouse in Scottsboro, eight of the young men were declared guilty and sentenced to death. A mistrial was declared for the ninth, Roy Wright, who was only twelve years old at the time. The convictions were overturned, however, and a second trial was ordered, to be held at Decatur in the northwest part of the state. During the second trial, one of the women, Ruby Bates, recanted the story she had told in Scottsboro. The second woman, Victoria Price, steadfastly maintained she had been brutally raped by the men.[5]

The case drew international attention to the Alabama town. Riots broke out in Harlem in reaction to the case. Violent protests took place in far-off cities like Dresden and Moscow as social activists demanded the men be freed. With the start of the second trial at Decatur, the young men's defense was taken up by the International Labor Defense League, a workers' group based in the North and firmly grounded in a belief in communism. A New York lawyer, Samuel S. Liebowitz, traveled to Alabama to serve as defense counsel. Later, another northern-based organization, the fledgling National Association for the Advancement of Colored People, joined the defense. In all, appeals and more trials lasted the next six years. On 24 July 1937, the last trial was held in Decatur. Four of the men were set free while the other five received sentences ranging from the death penalty to seventy-five years in prison.[6] None of them was executed.

So it was that Scottsboro was burned into the American psyche as a symbol of backwoods intolerance and racial injustice. The poet Allen Ginsberg evoked the Scottsboro Boys in his sprawling poem "America," which chastises the nation for its inequities. Radical black leaders such as Malcolm X also raised the specter of these young men in their fiery rhetoric.

For over sixty years, the tiny town of Scottsboro has carried with it the stigma of the Scottsboro Boys case, and for more than sixty years the town has been in a perpetual state of denial and blame seeking. The town continues to chafe whenever the incident is rehashed by writers or reporters. Local historians and defenders of the town are quick to point out that the boys were truly guilty of the crime, as eight separate trials proved. Others defend the town by saying Scottsboro was a victim of fate. "It wasn't our niggers and it wasn't our whores" is a frequent observation. It could have happened anywhere, the defenders murmur; it just happened to be Scottsboro. Had the incident happened a few miles farther north, it would have been Tennessee's problem. A few miles farther west and it would have been Huntsville's problem. When there is no one else to blame, the defenders castigate the media. The whole incident was blown out of proportion, they argue.

When other arguments fail, they are quick to fix blame on the Communists, the northern radicals, the outside agitators who were responsible for the perpetuation of the case. Once the case had been decided in Scottsboro, the defenders reason, there was no need for the meddling of outsiders in the dispensation of judgment as determined by the good (and white) citizens. It would be the same argument later used to justify the bloody and deadly violence when such groups as the Freedom Riders converged on the South during the divisive civil rights battle.

The irony of the Scottsboro Boys case is that Scottsboro and Jackson County had experienced very little racial trouble—though not for a lack of racism. As in much of the South, racism in Scottsboro and Jackson County was deeply rooted and at times overt. Sand Mountain in particular was a stronghold of white purity, and many blacks did not venture into that part of the county for fear of their lives. There had not been much racial violence in the Scottsboro area simply because there were not many blacks living in that part of the state. The U.S. Census figures for 1970 show the population of Scottsboro as 9,324. Of that number, 429 (or less than five percent) were black.[7]

During the 1960s, while much of Alabama and the South were embroiled in racial violence brought on by the struggle for the civil rights of blacks, Scottsboro quietly went about the business of integration. While the state's governor, George C. Wallace, stood in a doorway at the University of Alabama to bar black students from entering, Scottsboro and the rest of Jackson County peacefully merged the all-black schools with the all-white schools. In 1967, the integration of public schools in Scottsboro, Alabama, went as quietly and as uneventfully as could be hoped.

Despite the peaceful merging of the schools, however, the status quo of segregation continued. Although the shared experience of education brought the two communities closer together, the social barriers between blacks and whites remained. Black athletes might shine as stars during a Friday night high school football game, but on Saturday, they retreated to their own social activities within their community, which was separated from the rest of Scottsboro by the railroad tracks that geographically divided the town. The merging of the schools did little to improve the economic opportunities available to blacks. Black teachers being the exception, few black professionals live in the town. Today, there is not a single black attorney in Scottsboro or the whole of Jackson County. Many blacks still must leave the area in order to seek career opportunities elsewhere.

The integration of the schools coincided with the influx of outsiders who were brought to the area by the northern companies setting up factories in Scottsboro. It was a time of great transition for the town. The flood of newcomers brought with it a new social conscience and new values that created an atmosphere of change in the social order of the town. The town began to view itself in more urban terms. Once isolated, Scottsboro began to look beyond itself. The completion of a four-lane highway more securely linked the town to Huntsville, its urban neighbor to the west. Scottsboro slowly began to lose much of its once-sleepy agrarian appearance, and with a surge of new houses being built, took on the trappings of suburbia. Perhaps celebrating its new found urbanness, the town purchased several hundred acres of land on the shores of Guntersville Lake and developed a sprawling recreation complex that included a well-manicured golf course, a civic center, and a public swimming pool.

The early 1970s were the greatest period of economic growth for the town. In response to this economic growth, shopping centers sprang up on the town's fringes. Many of the family-owned country general stores soon met their demise as huge supermarkets opened in Scottsboro. Fast-food restaurants sprang up and competed with the established eateries like the Liberty Restaurant and Tom's Restaurant on the courthouse square. The availability of the new retail outlets drew shoppers from the out-lying areas of Sand Mountain and Cumberland Mountain, help-ing fuel the economic boom.

But for some of the established residents, the onslaught of progress had little meaning. One man in particular, Hugh Otis Bynum, seemed oblivious to the transition thrust upon the town. The eccentric landowner continued his ritualistic daily routine, ignoring the currents of change swirling about him.

3   *The Enigma*

Hugh Otis Bynum, Sr., was a shrewd mule trader. "H. O.," as he was known in Scottsboro, was the grandson of the town's founder, Robert T. Scott. He inherited much of Scott's land-holdings and much of Scott's ambition for wealth.

For most of his life, H. O. ran a mule-trading business just off the courthouse square in Scottsboro. The business eventually grew to occupy a block-long barn and provided Bynum and his family a sizable income.[1] For the farmers and sharecroppers in the county, a good pair of mules was a necessity and one of their most valued possessions. Even after the advent of the automobile and power-driven tractors, the mule remained the favored animal of labor. Many a Ford and quite a few tractors owed their rescue to a pair of dependable mules that pulled them from where they had become stuck in the thick Alabama red clay mud. Dealing in mules was a lucrative and dependable business.

But as technology improved, the increasingly powerful tractors and pickup trucks pushed the mule from its long-held place of importance in agriculture. H. O. Bynum changed with the times also, turning the mule barn into the Bynum Tractor Company. But it was the accumulation of land that eventually provided him his wealth. "Buy land. They're not making any more of it" was the advice he gave and the creed he followed.[2] Buy land he did— hundreds of acres in and around Scottsboro. It was the most dependable investment he could make. Land purchased for ten dollars an acre later sold for as much as ten thousand dollars an acre.[3]

Like many of the families in north Alabama, the Bynums were hit hard by the Great Depression. Even with his business dealings and land holdings, H. O. had less than five dollars in his checking account when the banks were closed in 1933. Hard work and the desire to own land became even more a matter of survival. H. O. passed on the value of hard work to his three children, Hugh Otis, Jr., Jessie Sue, and Lucy Scott. Hugh Otis helped his father with the mule business; the girls worked with their mother milking cows and making butter and cheese.[4]

H. O. Bynum had the reputation of being ruthless and unfeeling in his business dealings. Although he performed acts of charity, as when he donated the land for the construction of a county hospital, there were people who told stories of how he would confiscate the belongings of families that were indebted to him and found themselves overdue on their payments to him. According to some reports, Bynum would show up at the debtor's farm and take everything of value, including work horses, milk cows, chickens, and eggs, and in some cases would raid fruit cellars and confiscate dried fruit and canned vegetables, leaving the families with very little on which to survive. Though perfectly legal, the unsympathetic acts left bitterness and deep resentment in their wake.

The younger Hugh Otis's childhood centered around his father's business. Working with his father at the mule barn or helping around the family farms and attending Jackson County High School, where he played football, Hugh Otis spent his youth just like many other young men growing up during the Great Depression in Scottsboro. When Hugh Otis was nineteen, he attended Auburn University for one year. He returned to Scottsboro to help his father in the family business.[5]

His two younger sisters, highly intelligent, followed in their mother's footsteps and became teachers. Jessie Sue went on to earn a master's degree, and Lucy earned a doctorate. Neither woman ever married. It is said their father would never let them have friends or date suitors, saying that all the young men wanted was to get at the Bynum money.[6]

Until World War II, Hugh Otis's life remained relatively uneventful. When war did break out following the bombing of Pearl Harbor, Hugh Otis volunteered for service but was turned down because of poor eyesight. (He wore thick eyeglasses all of his life.) A couple of years later he was drafted and was assigned to a U.S. Army combat engineer outfit headed for action in the South Pacific and Asia. In the spring of 1946, at age 32, Hugh Otis was discharged with the rank of sergeant. He returned to Scottsboro and became a partner in the family's growing tractor business.[7]

In the late 1940s, Hugh Otis married a Birmingham widow who had a son from the previous marriage. Little is known about his wife, and the marriage lasted only a few months. She disappeared from Scottsboro following the breakup. Bob Gentry, always on the lookout for antiques to buy and sell, once asked Hugh Otis if there were any furniture in the old family house that he might be interested in selling. "That woman got it all. There's nothing left up there," Hugh Otis told Gentry. It was one of the few times Hugh Otis ever mentioned his wife.[8]

Hugh Otis's life changed after his mother's death. It is said that he was deeply devoted to his mother, and he remained devoted to his sisters all of his life. Not one to show emotion easily, Hugh Otis was noticeably stricken when his mother, Lora, died on 12 October 1950 after a lengthy illness.[9] Lora Allen Bynum was a gentle and well-educated woman who spent most of her life as a schoolteacher, first at the Old Baptist Institute and then later at the Jackson County High School in Scottsboro. She was well loved by her students. In announcing her death, the local newspaper wrote, "She was a woman of high intellect and culture and her home was always one of hospitality." [10]

In the months following his mother's death, Hugh Otis was involved in a string of violent attacks on others that landed him in jail on three occasions. In December 1950, just weeks after his mother's death, he was charged with assault with intent to commit murder. On 20 March 1951, he was again charged with assault with intent to commit murder, and the same charge was made against him a third time in March 1952. Each time the case was dismissed before coming to trial.[11] Many people suspected that Bynum money was used to placate the victims and to keep Hugh Otis from being prosecuted.

At least one of the assaults was particularly violent. At gunpoint, Bynum marched a man by the name of Vaughn Parker away from a cockfight near a popular gambling spot known as Saltpeter Cave. He then proceeded to cut the man with a knife so badly that it took surgeons hours to patch the man up. The doctors were said to have quit counting after three hundred stitches.[12]

Another story describes an eight-year-old black boy who was sitting on a porch one day with his puppy. Hugh Otis told the boy to put the puppy down, and, while the boy watched, Hugh Otis shot the little dog. The shotgun blast severed the dog's head from its body.[13] On another occasion, he shot a young white high school student, Ray Webb, as the boy was walking across a pasture owned by Bynum. No charges were filed in that case. Nor was Hugh Otis charged when he attacked a local attorney, Harold Foster, as the lawyer was walking past the tractor company. With a pistol in hand, Bynum lit out after the attorney, who escaped to the bathroom in a nearby service station. Foster, a big man, finally escaped by squeezing his huge frame through a tiny window that led to an alley outside, much to the amusement and amazement of the town. In a similar attack, Hugh Otis held Fred Bucheit, the publisher of the local newspaper, on the floor of a barber shop and threatened to cut the newspaperman's throat. Bynum apparently thought the publisher had slandered his cattle in an article published in the newspaper. Bucheit was saved when bystanders pulled the angry Bynum off of him.[14]

The outbursts of violence are part of the enigma of Hugh Otis Bynum. It will always remain a mystery as to why he should become so prone to violence while his sisters remained quiet, unobtrusive, educated, and genteel southern women. But it became no secret around Scottsboro that you didn't want to cross Hugh Otis. Even today, the man evokes a dichotomy of answers from those who knew him. Some describe him as one of the most generous men they have known. "Would do anything for you if he liked you" is a common statement about Hugh Otis Bynum. Others describe him as mean, vindictive, and ruthless—a man who easily held grudges and a man to be feared.

For many of those who knew the man, however, there was no mystery about Hugh Otis Bynum. For them, he was a product of his heritage. Allowed to get by with his many acts of meanness and violence, he was spoiled by his father and to some extent by the whole town. Because of his family, because of his position in the town, his many transgressions were dismissed with impunity. Simply put, he felt he could do as he pleased because of who he was.

In the summer of 1952, there was an intermission in the string of Hugh Otis's violent acts. That was the year the illness set in that nearly killed him. In July 1952, Hugh Otis was admitted to a Veteran's Administration hospital in Nashville, Tennessee, where he was a patient for six months. He began to lose weight, dropping from a hefty two hundred pounds to ninety, and his skin mysteriously began to harden. He was sent home, but shortly had to return for another four-month stay in the hospital.[15] Finally, his father was told to come fetch him. The son was going to die, the doctors said. Later, experts at a Birmingham clinic were able to diagnose the illness as scleroderma, a chronic and debilitating disease that causes a shrinking and hardening of the skin and, in some cases, a hardening of the internal organs.[16]

Hugh Otis's face and the muscles of his throat began to shrink and harden. His once-large hands became shriveled. The disease affected his esophagus, making it difficult for him to speak. Thereafter, he could only speak above a whisper, making it difficult at times for others to understand him without looking directly at him and watching his lips as he talked. His face took on an unemotional and stony look, and his mouth was turned down in a perpetual frown. Although the disease remained with him for the rest of his life, he fought off death for close to five years after the affliction first set in. By then the routine of his life was rigidly set. His diet remained the same for the rest of his life—oatmeal for breakfast, lunch of mashed potatoes and asparagus, and for dinner, eggs over-easy and sausage.[17]

During his recovery the prized Black Angus cattle became his most valued possessions. Raising the cattle and caring for them

Hugh Otis Bynum's House on Scott Street
(Photo by Leroy Gist)

became a therapy and a reason to live, and they too, like his peculiar diet, became a cornerstone of his daily existence. He occupied himself most of the day with frequent trips to check on the cattle, which he kept on farms scattered around Scottsboro. He was always dressed in khaki shirt and pants, a wide-brimmed white Stetson hat and the heavy black work shoes that most country folks simply call brogans.

During the mid-1950s, Hugh Otis's father and sisters moved from the family home on Scott Street to a new home on a ridge overlooking town. Hugh Otis refused to move with them, remaining alone in the two-story, multiroom, wooden house in the residential part of town. The neighborhood children delighted in sneaking up to the old house to peer in the windows to catch a glimpse of the strange man. The times he caught them, he tried to shoot them with an air rifle. It was almost like a game—almost.[18]

But the quiet appearance of Hugh Otis's life was an illusion. During all those years, he continued to hang out with the seedier characters in Jackson County. He loved to gamble and spent many nights in marathon poker games with his number one "running buddy," Billy Ray McCrary, a well-known felon. Why one of the richest men in Scottsboro, whose highly educated sisters were a part of the cultured fabric of town, would choose to spend so much of his time with known bootleggers, thieves, and ruffians will remain one of the great mysteries surrounding Hugh Otis Bynum.

On 11 April 1964, Hugh Otis's father died and all the land and all the wealth the old man had accumulated was now under the control of Hugh Otis and his two sisters.[19] Things remained pretty much quiet with Hugh Otis until September 1970, when two black teenagers crossed paths with the vindictive man.

4   *"Not So Damn Good"*

Late in the afternoon on 24 September 1970, Hugh Otis Bynum arrived at his cattle farm on Oak Street on the north side of Scottsboro. As he stepped from his car, the sound of gunshots told him there were unwanted guests in the pasture. He pulled a twelve-gauge shotgun out of the car and went looking for the intruders.[1]

Two black teenagers, Willie Lee McCamey and Claxton Green, Jr., had gone to the town's water reservoir near the Bynum farm in hopes of bagging a few doves.[2] The hunting season had just opened and the boys knew the water reservoir was a good place to hunt for the fast-flying birds. After the hunt, the two boys came out to the public chert road near the reservoir and headed back to town. That's when Bynum spotted them. He yelled at the pair to stop and the two boys turned to face him. As they turned, Bynum leveled down on the boys. The first shotgun blast brought the eighteen-year-old McCamey down. Green turned to run and a second shot from the shotgun felled him as he tried to escape.[3] Seriously wounded, the two young men had to be hospitalized. McCamey had been shot in the face, and the sixteen-year-old Green had wounds in his arm and shoulder.[4]

There was a time when the shooting of two black youths by

a wealthy white landowner would have gone virtually unnoticed and, more than likely, unpunished. At best money might have changed hands and the incident might have been forgotten. But the racial climate of the South and of Scottsboro had improved. Because of an increased awareness of civil rights, violence against blacks could be ignored no longer. An arrest warrant was issued for Bynum, who was charged with assault with intent to commit murder.

Nothing could have infuriated Bynum more than to be arrested for shooting the black teenagers. The Bynum family ruled Scottsboro, he reasoned, and it was beyond thinking that he would be locked up for shooting two black youths unfortunate enough to be caught trespassing on his property. Just protecting my cattle, he would protest.[5]

It was the task of the town's chief of police, Barney Harding, to arrest the wealthy landowner. Bynum was taken to city hall, booked, and then, as was customary, was taken to the courthouse on the square to be locked in the county jail. His stay in jail was short-lived, however. Bail was set quickly, and he was released on two $1,500 bonds.[6]

That night, in reaction to the shooting of the two black teenagers, the frustration and tension of the small but vocal black community erupted into violence aimed at Hugh Otis Bynum, Jr. As word of the shooting spread, anger and resentment built among the blacks who lived in the section of Scottsboro known as "The Hill"—that part of town across the railroad tracks to which most of the black population of Scottsboro was relegated.

Bynum was a good target for the anger of the blacks, who felt they had been neglected by the leaders of Scottsboro for far too long. It was an accepted fact that Bynum was a racist, and his many acts of violence toward blacks were legendary.[7] Even though he had been arrested and jailed for shooting the two boys, the blacks doubted that the wealthy, white landowner would ever be tried and convicted for the shooting. It was time for the long-simmering frustration, resentment, and anger of the black community to boil over.

Shortly after midnight on the morning of Friday, 25 September 1970, the first fire was set and spread quickly through the wooden structure of the abandoned house on Mountain Street where Bynum's unmarried sisters Lucy and Jessie had once lived. While firefighters were trying to extinguish the blaze at the

Mountain Street house, someone torched a barn belonging to Bynum and shot several of his prize Angus cattle. A third fire broke out at about 7:30 that Friday morning in another Bynum barn, which only recently had been filled with three hundred bales of hay. Firefighters were delayed in reaching the barn on West Maple Street when their trucks had to stop for a passing freight train. When the firefighters finally arrived, the barn was totally ablaze, and the two fire trucks soon ran out of water before the fire could be extinguished. The trucks went for more water and again were delayed by a passing train. By the time the trucks finally made it back, the barn had been totally destroyed.[8]

State Fire Marshall Erbie Liles was called in from Montgomery to investigate the cause of the fires, but there was little doubt in anyone's mind that they had been set deliberately and were a direct response to the shooting of the two black youths.

The town's reaction to the sudden racial violence was one of fear. The scenes of violent racial clashes in cities like Birmingham and Selma were etched on the minds of the white citizens. The Scottsboro police were called out in full force, armed with military carbines and batons and wearing riot helmets. It was the only time the officers had cause for such equipment.

Bynum estimated the fires and the loss of cattle had cost him over $90,000. Even for a wealthy man, that was a big loss, and he resented it.[9]

Over the ensuing weeks, Bynum demanded an arrest be made. He pressured his onetime friend, Jackson County Sheriff Bob Collins, to charge someone with setting the fires, but even though Collins and his men helped with the investigation into the cause of the fires, they could do little toward making an arrest.[10] The setting of the fires had been an act of spontaneous and vindictive violence and it can be hard to find a suspect in such crimes. Anyone in the close-knit black community who knew anything about the fires would not be talking. The chance of making an arrest in the case was remote. Still, Bynum pressured Collins to arrest someone. It was bad enough that he was being charged with the attempted murder of the two black youths; now his barns had been burned, his cattle shot, and no one would pay for it.

Collins had known Bynum for years, had known him even before he was elected sheriff. Bynum frequently dropped by his office for long talks about farming or politics. Both men were cattle farmers and both owned farms near Tupelo, just outside of Scottsboro. The two men could often be seen together at Tom's Restaurant, drinking coffee and talking. As a symbol of their friendship, Bynum had given Collins's daughter a diamond necklace as a gift when she graduated from high school. Collins was one of a close circle that Bynum claimed as friends.[11]

Shortly after the shooting of McCamey and Green and the burning of the barns, however, the friendship soured. Bynum's visits to the sheriff's office became less frequent, and when he did come by to see Collins it was to inquire if an arrest were to be made in the arson case. The visits finally ceased altogether, and when the two men chanced to meet, Bynum did not speak to Collins. If the sheriff happened into Tom's or the Liberty Restaurant and Bynum was there, Bynum got up and left without saying a word to Collins. Bynum came to hate Collins and made it known.[12]

But Bob Collins was not the only man who incurred the hatred of Hugh Otis Bynum. Another was John T. Reid, the mayor of Scottsboro. Reid had been mayor since 1956 and had worked hard to change the image of the town in order to put the stigma of the Scottsboro Boys behind. He dubbed Scottsboro "The Friendly City" and worked to recruit new industry to the area and to project a progressive image for the town. He was well liked by the citizens in general and he had little trouble being reelected, serving as mayor for twenty years.[13]

Reid knew Bynum all too well. At the time Bynum's barns were burned, the two men had only recently had trouble when one of Bynum's cows wandered onto city property and inexplicably wound up dead. Bynum demanded that the city pay for the cow, but the town refused, claiming that the death of the cow had not been the town's fault. Bynum blamed Reid for the town's refusal to reimburse him for the loss.[14]

Nor was Bynum pleased when the town, under the leadership of Reid, had condemned some of the Bynum property to build what Hugh Otis called "a nigger park."[15] Reid, made sensitive by the racial violence that was taking place in other parts of Alabama and the South, worked to make sure similar outbursts of unrest did not occur in Scottsboro by seeing to it that at least some of the demands for improvement to the black community were met.

When the violence directed at Hugh Otis Bynum erupted,

Left: Sheriff W. R. "Bob" Collins. *Right*: Mayor John T. Reid.
(Photos by Leroy Gist)

Reid met with some of the town's black leaders in an effort to restore calm to the area. This meeting was another strike against the mayor, in Bynum's mind. He resented the way Reid was running the town his family had founded.[16] All of Scottsboro, he reasoned, should be indebted to the Bynum family.

The burning of the Bynum barns was not the first time Bynum property had been put to the torch. During the summer of 1969, a year before the shooting of McCamey and Green, two men, Paul Warren Bates and Ollie Price, Jr., had been arrested and charged with attempting to burn a house belonging to Bynum's sisters. Both men had lengthy criminal records, and the men had been seen near the house just before the fire broke out. But some people suspected that Bynum himself had hired the pair to torch the vacant house belonging to his sisters in an effort to collect an insurance settlement.[17]

County Judge John Haislip appointed Loy Campbell to defend Bates and Price. Campbell, a former state legislator, had practiced law in Scottsboro for close to twenty years. The easygoing and likeable lawyer shared his practice with his brother, H. R. "Bunk" Campbell. Over the years, Loy Campbell had earned the reputation of being an effective lawyer, and he had served as an assistant district attorney. For many years, he represented the county government in all its legal matters. One of his clients over the years had been Hugh Otis Bynum. Campbell had known Bynum for most of the twenty years he had been in Scottsboro and had handled most of Bynum's legal matters involving business transactions, including mortgages. He had even prepared Bynum's will.[18]

Now Campbell had the duty of defending Bates and Price against the charges filed by his former client. The trial of the two accused arsonists was delayed several times, once because the Bynum sisters were vacationing in Europe. Not until April 1971 did Bates and Price face a Jackson County jury.

A few weeks after the shooting of McCamey and Green, a county grand jury indicted Bynum on the formal charge of assault with intent to commit murder, and the case was set to be tried in April 1971, the same month Bates and Price were to stand trial.

This was not the first time Bynum had had a run-in with the law, but this charge was serious. If convicted of attempted murder, he could serve time in jail. At that time, his lawyer was a Scottsboro attorney named Morgan Weeks. In addition, Bynum turned to the services of Roderick Beddow, Jr., and James M. Fullan, Jr., members of the expensive and prestigious Birmingham law firm of Beddow, Embry, and Beddow, to defend him against the assault charges.[19]

Shortly before the trial of Bates and Price on the arson charge, Campbell met with Bynum to discuss the case. Campbell told Bynum that the men had said they had been hired to burn the house, and he told him it would not do Bynum or his clients any good for this claim to come out in court. Apparently, Bynum agreed with Campbell because there was no mention of it during the trial of the two men on the arson charge. Later that same day, Campbell and Bynum went to the house to survey the damage.[20]

Although the case against Bates and Price was mostly circumstantial, it was a strong one. On that Tuesday, 19 August 1969, the two men had been drinking and had been seen at the remote house by two teenagers parked nearby. After dousing the house with gasoline and setting the fire, Bates and Price retreated to a hamburger stand a mile or so away to watch for the smoke from the burning house. When no smoke appeared, the two men drove their pickup truck back to the house. In the meantime, the two teenagers had notified the police, who were waiting for the men when they returned. The police found a gasoline can in the back of the truck, and the two men, both from Huntsville, could not explain what they were doing in such a remote area of Scottsboro. For the prosecution, it seemed to be an open-and-shut case.[21]

On Wednesday, 7 April 1971, Bates and Price were tried for burglary and the attempted arson of the Bynum home. The only hope for Campbell to win an acquittal was to explain somehow why these two men from Huntsville should have been near the house. In his closing statement to the jury, Campbell said the men had been victims of circumstances. The two men had been drinking that day and had to urinate. Unfamiliar with Scottsboro, the men were unable to find a restroom, so they had gone to the remote location in order to relieve themselves, Campbell said. The explanation was apparently enough to plant the seeds of doubt in the jury's mind. After a short deliberation, the jury vote to acquit the two men.[22]

Campbell, being the shrewd attorney that he was, did not put Bates and Price on the stand in their own defense. Once the men were on the stand, their long history of previous crimes, including several convictions for burglary and a charge of attempted murder against one of them, could be brought out. The checkered past of the two men might have been enough to convince the jury the two were indeed responsible for attempting to set fire to the Bynum house. In not calling the two men to the stand, Campbell correctly reasoned that sometimes the best defense is to keep quiet.

The failure of the jury to convict the two men did not set well with Bynum and from that time on he would not have any business dealings with Loy Campbell.[23]

A little over two weeks after the Bates-Price trial, Bynum was back in court. This time, he was the one on trial.

Loy Campbell knew Bynum's defense lawyer, Roderick Beddow, Jr. In fact, the two attorneys had worked together only recently on another criminal case. Beddow, not knowing the people of Jackson County, turned to Campbell for help in picking a jury that would be sympathetic to Bynum. There was no denying that Bynum had shot the two young men, and his attorneys made every effort to seat a jury that would believe he had been justified in protecting his property. At least one of the candidates Campbell recommended, Jimmy Cordell from the tiny Sand Mountain community of Flat Rock, was chosen for the jury.[24]

On Monday, 26 April 1971, an all-white jury sat in the large courtroom in the Jackson County Courthouse to hear the evidence against Hugh Otis Bynum, Jr. The case was being prosecuted by J. T. "Jay" Black of Fort Payne and Scottsboro attorney Allen Lee, who had been appointed assistant district attorney. Black, a cousin to Associate Justice Hugo L. Black of the U.S. Supreme Court, had first been elected district attorney in 1954. His jurisdiction included the three counties of DeKalb, Jackson, and Cherokee.

The trial lasted two days and the jury was faced with the choice of believing the word of the two black youths or that of the wealthy—and white—landowner. The specter of racism hung like a cloud over the trial.

The first witness to testify was Willie Lee McCamey, who described how he and Green had been hunting and had come out on the road near the town's water reservoir. He said Bynum was waiting for them on the road and hollered at them, asking them what they had been doing in his pasture. McCamey said he told Bynum they had not been in the pasture. McCamey said that all this time, Bynum had a shotgun pointed at them while they held unloaded guns.[25]

Claxton Green, Jr., then took the stand and recounted how Bynum had shot them. Green repeated the story told by McCamey, again emphasizing that their guns were not loaded. He told of Bynum shooting Willie Lee in the face. Green said he turned to run and that as he fled he had been shot from behind.[26]

On Tuesday, the second day of the trial, Bynum took the stand and told a decidedly different story of the events of 24 September 1970. According to Bynum, he saw McCamey and Green in his pasture near a spring where his cattle were watering. He said he had seen the boys shooting at the cattle and at a nearby barn. Bynum said he went back to his car to get his gun and when he returned the boys had come out onto the road.[27]

Bynum said he hollered at the boys and asked them what they had been shooting. As the boys turned to face him, Green told him he was out of shells and that his gun was breached. Bynum testified, however, that McCamey had his gun pointed at him, and it was at this time that he slung his shotgun to his hip and shot McCamey.[28] He said Green started to run after the shooting of McCamey and that when the boy broke for cover, he shot the gun from the boy's hand. The picture Bynum attempted to paint for the jury was that of a man protecting his property and threatened by a nineteen-year-old black man with a gun. In an apparent effort to portray the two youths as ruffians looking for trouble, the defense called three witnesses who testified to the boys' characters.

Jay Black, in his closing argument to the jury, blasted Bynum. At one point, Black called Bynum a coward.[29] The harsh words were something to which Hugh Otis Bynum was not accustomed.

On Tuesday afternoon, the jury returned what can be interpreted as a compromise verdict. Bynum was acquitted of the more serious charge of assault with intent to commit murder but was found guilty of the lesser charge of assault. He was fined $500.[30]

There was no question that Bynum had shot the two boys, but the jury may have felt that in some way the boys deserved it. The jury also may have felt that Bynum could have gotten by with just running the boys off or calling the sheriff; perhaps he really need not have shot the boys. Nevertheless, the jurors had not been convinced the wealthy landowner had meant to kill the two boys.

Shortly after the trial, Loy Campbell chanced to meet Bynum as he was leaving the courthouse. "Looks like you came out pretty good," Campbell remembers saying to Bynum.

"Not so damn good," the resentful landowner said. Then he walked away.[31]

By some strange kind of reasoning, Campbell had now transgressed against Bynum, as had Jay Black, the prosecutor who had won his conviction, and Sheriff Collins, who had failed to make an arrest for the barn burnings, and Mayor Reid, who was running the town the Bynum family had built.

In Scottsboro, Alabama, a cauldron of twisted anger had begun to simmer.

5   *Threads of Skin*

The explosion that ripped through Loy Campbell's car on 4 December 1972 rocked all of Scottsboro.

Probate Judge Bob Gentry, standing on the courthouse steps over a mile away from Campbell's home, heard the sound of the explosion reverberate through the valley and listened as the rumble slowly rose to the hills and mountains around Scottsboro. He thought one of the town's factories had exploded. Many of those gathered on the square for First Monday Trade Day thought the explosion was a sonic boom from a passing jet.[1]

The explosion rattled the quiet upper-middle-class neighborhood where Campbell lived. The explosion broke the windows of a nearby house and shook Caldwell Elementary School, where Campbell's daughter, Ramona, had just started class.[2] Thick, black smoke filled the air, and parts from the demolished car and pieces of metal rained down on the well-kept lawns around the Campbell home. Many of the neighbors, unsure of what had happened, at first thought the school had been bombed.

Rescuers who arrived at the Campbell home found a horrific sight. The front end of the car was totally demolished, making it almost unrecognizable. Campbell was barely conscious. His legs had been shredded by the explosion and were entangled in the car's debris. A fire truck arrived on the scene and an ambulance was summoned, and the injured man was rushed to the hospital, where doctors had been alerted to expect him.

Word of the blast and what had happened to Campbell now began to sweep through the town. The explosion that had broken the Monday morning stillness had not been a sonic boom but a bomb intended to take the popular lawyer's life. Local radio stations interrupted their programs with bulletins on the bombing. Few expected, given the seriousness of his injuries, that Campbell would live.

The town's initial shock over the bombing slowly turned to bewilderment. Why would anyone want to take the lawyer's life? Campbell had not been involved in any controversies of which the town was aware. The amiable attorney did not have any enemies, as far as anyone knew. For the people of Scottsboro, the reason for the brutal attack was a troubling mystery.

The smell of dynamite hung heavy in the air as law enforcement officials converged on the scene. Scottsboro Police Chief Barney Harding and Sheriff Bob Collins surveyed the wreckage. There was little doubt that a bomb had been involved. This was no freak accident that had caused the car's gas tank to explode. As in most bombing cases, local law enforcement officials would have to call in the federal authorities.

Campbell was semiconscious when they wheeled him into the emergency room of Jackson County Hospital. For a rural hospital, it was remarkably well equipped and well staffed. The hospital had been in operation less than twenty years and had been built on land donated by H. O. Bynum, Sr., in memory of his wife, Lora. Campbell was moaning and was obviously in excruciating pain when doctors first saw him in the emergency room. Both of his legs had been blown off below the knees and what was left of them was held on by threads of skin. There were metal fragments, pieces of wiring, and pieces of the automobile's upholstery imbedded in his thighs and what remained of his legs. There were lacerations to his abdomen and face, and his face appeared to have been burned. The doctors went to work in an effort to save the man's life. They decided immediately that what remained of Campbell's legs would have to be amputated. He was taken to the hospital's operating suite and was given blood and anesthesia in preparation for the operation. The lawyer's life would never be the same.[3]

Loy Campbell was born the oldest of three sons to John H. and Dot Campbell on 26 November 1927. His father and mother were schoolteachers, as had been his great-grandparents on both sides of the family. Several aunts and uncles had also been schoolteachers.[4] In north Alabama during the Great Depression, money for the operation of schools was scarce. In many cases, a community was able to raise enough cash to operate the local school for only a portion of the school year. So it was that Campbell's parents found themselves moving from one community to another and from one teaching job to another. At the time of Loy's birth, his father was teaching at Langston, a small community on the banks of the Tennessee River in the southernmost part of Jackson County. His mother was bedridden at her parents' home in the tiny Sand Mountain community of Fyffe in DeKalb County. It was there that Loy was born.

Two years after Loy's birth, a second son was born to the Campbells. Christened H. R., the infant was given an unusual nickname when his parents first showed him to the young Loy. Asked what he thought of the new baby, Loy gave his one-word reply. "Bunk," he said, and the name stuck. A third son, John Paul, was born some fifteen years after Loy.

During his childhood, Loy's parents continued their itinerant teaching careers. Loy recalls that in one of those years the family moved five times to various communities on Sand Mountain. The transient way of life continued until 1939, when his father was elected tax assessor for DeKalb County. Three years later, the family moved to the bustling textile town of Fort Payne, the county seat, nestled in a valley between Sand Mountain and Lookout Mountain. Loy remained here until leaving for college.

Politics has always been an integral part of the close-knit Campbell family. Loy recalls that whenever there were guests or visitors to their home, politics was the topic of conversation. His father was a staunch "yellow dog" Democrat. (In the South, the term *yellow-dog Democrat* refers to the creed, "I'd vote for a yellow dog before I'd vote for a Republican.") However, at the time his parents married, his mother was a Republican. Loy remembers how his parents reached a compromise. His father was a Primitive Baptist while his mother was a Missionary Baptist. The two agreed that Mr. Campbell would convert to the Missionary Baptist faith if Mrs. Campbell would become a Democrat. It was a compromise that served them well. However, Loy jokingly says of the compromise, "I think she made a better Democrat than he made a Baptist." The passion for politics was instilled in the three Campbell sons at an early age and remains an important part of their lives.

In 1946, Loy graduated from DeKalb County High School in Fort Payne. He had proven himself to be an able scholar and had earned a scholarship to Vanderbilt University in Tennessee, where he was to major in political science. But he was an avid fan of the "Crimson Tide" and so he forsook the scholarship to attend the University of Alabama. Beyond his love for 'Bama football, another factor helped him make his school choice. He had decided that a degree in political science would be useful only in a teaching position. Though teaching was as ingrained as politics in the family's history, he decided he did not want to teach and chose instead a career in law. He earned an undergraduate degree in business and commerce at Alabama and then spent two years in the university's School of Law.

Bunk had also decided on a law career and a year after Loy arrived at the west Alabama college town of Tuscaloosa, Bunk joined him at the university. It was a good time for the two brothers, marred only by a bizarre malady that afflicted both of the young men and required them to undergo lung surgery. Doctors diagnosed the disease as a rare form of emphysema. Bunk recovered well from the surgery, but the usually robust Loy had a difficult time during his recovery. An infection and a bad blood transfusion caused his temperature to skyrocket. The doctors feared he might die. He eventually overcame the illness, but his recovery was taxing.

In January 1952 Loy graduated from the University of Alabama School of Law and decided to set up practice in Scottsboro. He thought there was more opportunity available to a young lawyer in Scottsboro than in Fort Payne, where a fresh crop of young lawyers had set up practices. Bunk graduated a year after Loy, and after spending two years in the military, he joined Loy in Scottsboro, and the brothers set out to build a law practice by handling any and all legal cases that came their way. Times were lean for the two brothers but improved greatly when, in the mid-1950s, the state passed a law requiring drivers to have some form of automobile insurance. Until then, representing people involved in or injured in auto accidents in civil cases was fruitless, because in most cases there was no money available to be recovered for damages. The law requiring auto insurance provided victims and lawyers with a source of monetary restitution. It was a boon for many struggling lawyers in Alabama.

In 1954, Loy Campbell was appointed city attorney for Scottsboro, a position he held for one year. That same year, he was appointed county solicitor, the equivalent of a part-time assistant district attorney. He held this position for several years, abandoning it only after it began to interfere with his growing law practice. In 1962, Campbell stepped from the sidelines of politics and entered the race for Alabama House of Representatives. His opponent was Joe Money. The contest was a close one, but after the primary election Campbell emerged as the victor with 4,230 of the votes cast to Money's 3,579 votes.[5] For most of its history, Jackson County had been a one-party county, with the Democrats firmly in control. Campbell faced no Republican opposition. His victory in the primary virtually assured him a seat in the state house.

A federal court ordered reapportionment of the state house seats, however, forcing Campbell into another election. On 28 August 1962, Campbell faced J. D. Sargent in the special called election. After the first tally of the votes, Campbell held a slim, thirteen-vote lead. Sargent, however, filed a contest of the election when it was discovered that the results of one of the voting booths had been mistakenly recorded in reverse. A correction of the error would have given Sargent a slim, nine-vote victory.[6]

The election was turned over to a three-member subcommittee of the Alabama Democratic party to decide. In late September 1962, the subcommittee ruled that indeed there had been an error in recording the results of the voting box in question and that it should be corrected. After an investigation of the election, however, the subcommittee ruled that because of the many irregularities in two voting precincts the results of those precincts should be tossed out. The subcommittee prefaced its ruling by saying, "The evidence from all the witnesses pertaining [to the two precincts] is the most flagrant violation of election laws ever witnessed by any member of this subcommittee." Among the irregularities, the subcommittee cited the fact that one of the voting precincts had been closed at 11:00 A.M. on election day after only thirteen people had voted. The subcommittee also determined that the election officials in that precinct were loyal supporters of Sargent. The elimination of the results of the two precincts gave Campbell a comfortable lead over his opponent and he was declared the winner.[7]

In January 1963, Campbell took his seat in the Alabama House of Representatives, in the same year that a feisty judge from Barbour County by the name of George Corley Wallace was sworn in for his first term as governor of Alabama. It was a tumultuous time to serve in the Alabama house. The desegregation battle was at its height in the state. When he is asked to recall what it was like to serve in the legislature at that time, Loy Campbell answers, "Segregation. Segregation. Segregation. That's all we heard."[8]

Campbell was not a great fan of Wallace, but he had great respect for the man's political acumen. "The power of Wallace during that term of the legislature was awesome," says Campbell. "He was so popular in Alabama that he could do virtually anything he wanted in the legislature."

Campbell considered himself a moderate when it came to the racial question. He disagreed with many of Wallace's policies. It also became clear to Campbell early in that legislative term that Wallace was capitalizing on the racial issue in order to further his ambition to become president. More than thirty years later, Campbell's assessment of Wallace is less than flattering. "He set this state back at least a generation," Campbell says.

At the end of his four-year term in the legislature, Campbell returned to his law practice in Scottsboro. He had no desire to return to Montgomery and was determined not to seek reelection. The four-year stint in the legislature had hurt him financially. He once told his friend, Bob Gentry, "When I went to Montgomery, I had a pretty good business. When I came back, I didn't have much of anything left." In the years to come, people speculated that Campbell would seek a seat in the state senate. However, he says he never again had any intention of running for any political office.[9]

To say that 1972 was not a good year for Loy Campbell is an understatement. The year began with a life-threatening bout with diverticulitis that kept him in the hospital for weeks. In April, his father, John H. Campbell, died. Then on 4 December with only days remaining in the year, he walked to the car parked in his driveway and put the key in the ignition.

As federal agents arrived on the scene of the bombing, a crowd of curious onlookers had gathered. Special agent Donald Barrett took charge of the scene and immediately launched a careful and intensive search of the area for physical evidence. Barrett had served the U.S. Treasury Department's Bureau of Alcohol, Tobacco, and Firearms for over ten years. He was stationed in Huntsville, and most of north Alabama was in his assigned territory. Over the years, one of his main tasks had been to locate and destroy the many moonshine stills hidden in the mountains and hollows of northeast Alabama.[10] He was what was known in the old days as a "revenue agent" or a "revenuer."

On the morning of Monday, 4 December 1972, he was at the Huntsville Police Department when the call came about an explosion in Scottsboro. Barrett, along with two other BATF agents, arrived at Campbell's house less than an hour after the explosion. One of the first things Barrett noticed was the strong smell of nitroglycerin, the main ingredient of dynamite. It was a smell that was very familiar to him, as he had used dynamite on many occasions to destroy the stills he had helped discover.

When they first viewed the automobile, the agents were amazed that anyone could have survived the explosion. The entire front end of the car had disintegrated and parts of the car were discovered more than a block away and on the roof and playground of Caldwell School. A piece of the left front fender had landed 150 yards from the car, and pieces of the same fender and part of the car's hood were found behind the Campbell home, having been blown over the house by the force of the blast.[11]

The explosion also had caused extensive damage to Campbell's house. It had blown out a picture window at the front of the house and blown a door to a storage area in the carport off its hinges. Inside the house, the blast had cracked an entrance door and much of the sheetrock. Pictures, knocked off the walls, lay scattered on the floor of the living room and kitchen. A kitchen cabinet door hung by a single hinge.[12]

Barrett ordered that photographs be taken of the scene, both outside and inside the house. Later, agents took aerial photographs of the blast site. Each piece of the car debris was carefully marked, and investigators noted meticulously where the parts were found.[13] Later that day, after having what remained of the car moved a few feet, Barrett and BATF agent Larry Luckey found, embedded in the driveway concrete, what appeared to be the remains of an electric blasting cap used to detonate dynamite. The agents also found a piece of a blasting cap "leg" wire on top of what was left of the car's engine. The leg wires are used to conduct the electric charge that triggers the dynamite blast.[14] The agents carefully labeled the blasting cap fragment and the piece of leg wire, sealed them, and sent them to the BATF laboratory in Atlanta for testing. Barrett also had a portion of the car's protective fire wall removed and sent to Atlanta for tests.[15] Though there was little question in Barrett's mind that dynamite had been used, the laboratory tests proving it would be important in a trial—if there ever was a trial.

In the hospital's emergency room, Loy Campbell clung to life. That morning, Bunk Campbell had been eating breakfast at

Above: Loy Campbell's Pontiac viewed from the driver's side. Investigators determined the dynamite bomb was placed on the car's frame just in front of the driver's seat. Caldwell Elementary School, where Campbell's daughter was a student, can be seen in the background. *Below:* View of Campbell's car in relation to his house.
(Photos Courtesy Alabama Attorney General's Office)

Charles' Cafe just off the square in Scottsboro with his close friend Norman Farrior when he learned that his brother's car had exploded and that Loy had been seriously injured and taken to the hospital. Bunk took Loy's startled six-year-old daughter Ramona out of Caldwell School and sent her to stay with relatives in Fayette County, Alabama. (She was told only that her father had been hurt, and it was some time before she learned the truth about the bombing.) He then went to be with his brother. Their mother, Dot, soon joined Bunk for the vigil. Later that day, the younger Campbell brother, John Paul, joined them at the hospital.

Farrior, a Scottsboro insurance agent, went to his office before heading to the hospital to check on Campbell's condition. After staying at the hospital for about an hour, he returned to the courthouse square, where he saw a knot of men standing on the corner by Payne's Drugstore. Farrior recognized some of the men. Among them were Hugh Otis Bynum, Jr., and Billy Ray McCrary. Farrior noticed the two men were talking together and standing apart from the other men.[16] On that Monday, however, Farrior gave little thought to seeing the two men. At that time, he was wondering who would want to kill Loy Campbell, and he was worried that Campbell might not live.

6   *No More Races*

In the days following the bombing of Loy Campbell, police investigators turned to the task of trying to uncover a motive for the attempt on the lawyer's life and compiling a list of possible suspects in the case. A team of investigators pored over records at Campbell's law office to see if a former client had any reason to kill him. The investigators questioned Campbell's brother Bunk at length but he could not provide them with a reason or a suspect for the bombing.

On the day after the bombing, Campbell's condition at the hospital had stabilized enough to allow BATF agent Don Barrett and other investigators to question him. Much of the questioning focused on former clients of Campbell's law practice. The investigators were especially interested in any divorce cases he might have handled. Perhaps, they reasoned, an angry spouse, feeling that he had been given a raw deal in a divorce settlement, had decided to get even with Campbell. However, Campbell could think of no one with whom he had any unpleasant dealings.[1]

The investigators questioned him at length about his own divorce from Ramona's mother, Betty. The Campbells' marriage had been short and stormy and had ended two years before the bombing. Loy Campbell had won custody of the couple's only child. Perhaps Betty Campbell, angry over losing the custody battle, had hired someone to bomb her former husband. But he was adamant that his former wife could not have had anything to do with an attempt on his life. Betty would not do something like this, Campbell told the investigators.[2]

What about Dr. Gus Prosch, whom Betty Campbell had married following the divorce? The medical doctor had met Mrs. Campbell while he worked at a hospital near Bridgeport, some twenty-five miles north of Scottsboro. Loy Campbell could think of no reason why Prosch would want him killed.[3] What about Billy Ray McCrary? the investigators asked. McCrary had just been released from federal prison and had been seen in town. Although Campbell had done some legal work for McCrary, and although McCrary had been charged and sentenced during Campbell's tenure as county solicitor, as far as Campbell could remember, their relationship had always been good. Despite McCrary's unsavory reputation, it was hard for Campbell to imagine that McCrary would try to kill him.[4] In all, the questioning of Campbell did not produce any leads. He could not provide the investigators with a reason for the bombing or think of anyone who might have had enough hatred for him to try to kill him.

There was now a cadre of investigators in Scottsboro. The FBI had joined the case, and Alabama Attorney General Bill Baxley had sent a task force headed by the state's chief investigator, Jack Shows. Accompanying Shows was Jamie Moore, the former Birmingham police chief, and Donald G. Valeska II, one of Baxley's assistant prosecutors. Shows and his men lent only minimum support to the investigation, choosing to stay out of the way of the federal investigators. It was Baxley's policy to enter an investigation only when invited by local authorities. He was not one to charge in where he was not wanted.[5]

Besides, Baxley was already deep into the investigation of an earlier bombing. In 1963, a bomb blast had ripped through the Sixteenth Street Baptist Church in Birmingham, killing four young black girls as they prepared for Sunday school. The murder of the four young girls had affected Baxley deeply, and he had vowed to solve the nearly ten-year-old case when he first took office as attorney general. During the investigation into the church bombing, problems had developed when the FBI would not cooperate with Baxley. He did not need any further conflict with the feds over the Scottsboro bombing.[6]

On the Wednesday following the Campbell bombing, Gov. George C. Wallace put up a $1,000 reward for information that led to a solution of the case. Over the next year, private citizens put up their own reward money, and the cash reward offered grew to more than $20,000.[7] On that same Wednesday, BATF agent Barrett questioned the well-known local criminal, Billy Ray McCrary. Barrett knew McCrary well. Only two years earlier, McCrary had been arrested for operating a whiskey still, and Barrett had tried to get McCrary to implicate some other people in the illegal liquor venture.[8] McCrary might not have had anything to do with the Campbell bombing, but there was a good chance he would know who did.

Billy Ray McCrary is one of the most felonious characters ever to come out of Jackson County. The habitual criminal had a lengthy arrest record for crimes ranging from assault to writing bad checks to bootlegging and whiskey making.[9] He was an integral part of the criminal underworld in Jackson County. If there was an illegal dollar to be made, it was a safe bet that McCrary had a part in it.

One of the first times McCrary ran afoul of the law came in 1954, when, just short of his twentieth birthday, he was charged with attempted murder. Five years later, he was again charged with attempted murder after he cut a man's ear off in a brawl. In all, by the time he was forty years old, Billy Ray had been arrested a total of forty-seven times for various crimes. He would spend much of his life in county jails, state prison, or the federal penitentiary.[10]

At one time or another, Billy Ray McCrary was involved in

thefts, whiskey making, bootlegging, and dope dealing. Mc-Crary's nefarious reputation was so well known that he became the focus of at least one political campaign. In 1962, Clair T. Dean, a candidate for sheriff, campaigned on the promise to rid Jackson County of the likes of Billy Ray McCrary. Dean won the election by a hundred-vote margin over a young Alabama highway patrolman by the name of Bob Collins.[11] Dean made good on his campaign promise, although McCrary denied that Dean was responsible for his being convicted in 1965 of dealing in stolen goods.[12]

Despite his lengthy record of crime, Billy Ray McCrary was known as a likable criminal.[13] He was known as much for being a con man as he was for being a criminal. A smooth talker with the gift of gab, he could and often did charm himself out of trouble, and he often charmed other people out of their money. He was known, too, for his intelligence. It was often said that if McCrary had devoted his energies to legitimate business instead of a life of crime, he could have been a real success story.[14] Instead, it was through his street smarts that he made his mark on Jackson County history.

In 1970, McCrary was charged with operating a moonshine operation along with Robert Reed, the mayor of McCrary's hometown of Hollywood. After McCrary's arrest, BATF Agent Barrett asked McCrary to help him find the stills of another known moonshiner, John T. Dolberry. But McCrary could not help Barrett, claiming he didn't know where Dolberry's stills could be found. McCrary knew better than anyone how the system worked; more than likely, Barrett couldn't offer McCrary any help with his current legal problems, so he conveniently had a lapse of memory.[15]

McCrary turned to Loy Campbell and asked the attorney to help defend him against the moonshining charge. Campbell told McCrary that he had not had experience in selecting a jury in federal court and told him to contact an attorney in Huntsville. McCrary eventually pled guilty to the distilling charge, and on 29 September 1970, United States District Court Judge Clarence Allgood, calling Billy Ray "a menace to society," gave him the maximum sentence: five years in the federal penitentiary. The honorable mayor of Hollywood, Robert Reed, had testified against McCrary and was rewarded with three years of probation instead of prison time.[16]

Shortly after going to the federal prison in Texarkana, Arkansas, McCrary wrote a letter to Judge Allgood in which he claimed that he had been set up as the fall guy in the case and that it was unfair for him to be sent to prison while his partner in crime, Mayor Reed, only got probation. McCrary also accused the former sheriff of Jackson County, Fred Emmett Holder, of being in the bootlegging and still business, as well as Ed Pepper, a member of the state's Public Service Commission in Montgomery. The authorities largely ignored McCrary's letter, and McCrary later admitted that most of the content of the letter, a desperate effort to win a sentencing bargain, was the product of his imagination.[17]

After serving a year of his five-year sentence, McCrary succeeded in getting the sentence reduced to three years. He was first transferred to the federal prison at Springfield, Missouri, then to the federal prison in Atlanta, where he worked in the prison's cotton mill for sixty dollars a month. He was released from the prison in Atlanta on 15 November 1972 and after fooling around in Atlanta for the day arrived at his father's house in Hollywood on 16 November, just two weeks before the bomb ripped through Loy Campbell's car.

On the Wednesday following the First Monday bombing, Don Barrett called McCrary by telephone at his father's home, and McCrary agreed to come to the Scottsboro courthouse to meet with Barrett.[18] McCrary had been through interrogations in the past and was not easily intimidated by Barrett's questioning. He denied having any knowledge of the bombing and told the investigator there had never been any trouble between himself and Loy Campbell.[19] Barrett, though wary of McCrary, had little choice but to take him at his word.

That Friday, Robert Morgan, a Scottsboro police investigator, along with one of the federal investigators, questioned McCrary's wife, Lilah. She had been married to McCrary for fifteen years and had had six children by him. Her husband's habitual life of crime made her experienced in dealing with the police. For the most part, she knew that her best strategy, to avoid incurring McCrary's wrath or endangering him with arrest, was to avoid cooperating with the police. She professed to know nothing about the bombing of Loy Campbell and simply chose not to answer most of Morgan's questions.[20]

While investigators were questioning the many possible suspects, Barrett and other BATF agents continued the task of gathering additional physical evidence from the scene of the bombing. Within a few days of the blast, Barrett had learned that the only place where dynamite and military style blasting caps were available in the Scottsboro area was at the State Highway Department's local supply station, located at what was once a convict camp on the outskirts of Scottsboro.[21] Barrett visited the supply station and questioned many of the workers there, including the supervising clerk, Wendell Britt, and a young man by the name of Charles Xavier Hale.[22]

Charles Hale had worked at the highway department for less than two months when Barrett made his visit. Hale was in his early twenties and was generally considered a dependable worker. Much of the time, he handled the dynamite that the highway department used on its construction jobs.[23] A clean-cut, good-looking young man, Hale was described as quiet and polite and a loner. He was always loyal to his mother and when he was away from her, never failed to call at least twice a week. He had had many brushes with the law. In 1969, when he was twenty-two years old, he and two others had broken into a Scottsboro laundromat and robbed the coin machines.[24] The break-in had earned him a stay in the state prison.

Hale loved to frequent the local poolrooms and was considered to be good with a cue stick.[25] He also was known to be involved in small-time drug trafficking, usually involving marijuana or pills.[26] He was often seen with Billy Ray McCrary, and while hanging out at the pool halls could be seen talking with Hugh Otis Bynum, who frequently stopped by the pool halls. But Hale was a chameleon of a man. The clean-cut, quiet, and polite appearance, it turned out, masked a man who was a cold-blooded killer.[27]

Barrett's visit to the highway department did not produce any leads. He did, however, pick up several of the M6 blasting caps kept there, as well as some sticks of dynamite.[28]

On the Friday following the bomb blast, a part-time janitor at the Caldwell School, across the street and down the block from Loy Campbell's home, made what turned out to be a significant discovery. By that Friday, workers had removed most of the debris from the Campbell car. Jimmy Dewayne Evett was cleaning up along the sidewalk outside the Caldwell School when he found the car's air filter assembly hidden in some bushes. Evett

Billy Ray McCrary
(Courtesy *The Jackson County Advertiser*)

Charles Xavier Hale
(Courtesy Scottsboro Police Department)

took the air filter to the school's principal, William G. Dean, who in turn called the Scottsboro police.[29] When BATF Agent Don Barrett saw the air filter assembly at the Scottsboro police station, he instantly knew one thing: if this was in fact the breather assembly from the Campbell car, it definitely had not been in any explosion. Barrett sent the air filter assembly, along with the blasting caps and dynamite samples from the highway department, to the BATF laboratories in Atlanta for fingerprinting and chemical analysis.[30]

On the day Jimmy Evett discovered the air filter, Loy Campbell was transferred from the hospital in Scottsboro to Baptist Montclair Hospital in Birmingham. Campbell had been blind in one eye since birth, and the doctors feared that he would lose the sight in his good eye as a result of the bomb blast. The physicians in Scottsboro summoned Dr. Lamar Campbell, an ophthalmologist from Birmingham (no relation), to examine the lawyer. Dr. Campbell recommended that the patient be taken to the Birmingham hospital, where he remained for just over a month.[31] On 16 January 1973, doctors released Campbell from the Birmingham hospital, and he returned to Jackson County to stay with his brother, Bunk. Campbell was reunited with his daughter, but the reunion was short-lived. After a two-and-a-half-week stay at home, Campbell entered the Spain Rehabilitation Center in Birmingham to begin the long, arduous, and painful road to recovery.[32]

Loy Campbell had always been a man of strong character. This trait served him well following the loss of his legs. Campbell refused to be psychologically devastated by the loss and viewed his recovery as a new challenge in his life. "With the exception of the initial shock, I never got depressed about my situation," Campbell said. "Life was a challenge for me."[33]

Upon entering the Spain Clinic, Campbell was assigned to Dr. George Traugh, who was to oversee the lawyer's physical rehabilitation. Dr. Traugh recognized Campbell's fighting spirit. "He began to challenge me in every way," Campbell said of the doctor. At that time it was generally accepted that middle-aged patients who have lost their legs should not be fitted with prostheses. Learning to walk with artificial legs is a physically demanding chore, and older patients do not always have the strength and stamina necessary to accomplish the feat. Dr. Traugh felt that Campbell, who was in his mid-forties at the time, was an exception. At the doctor's urging, technicians fitted Campbell with the prostheses.[34]

The hours of therapy were torturous work for the lawyer. Oftentimes he was drenched with perspiration following the sessions, which sometimes went on for hours. He prevailed, however, and as Dr. Traugh had predicted, Campbell, with the aid of crutches, learned to walk using the artificial legs. He was to use the artificial legs for a total of eight years, until the use of his arms and upper body muscles became too taxing for him. "Psychologically, learning to walk again was very good for me," Campbell says of his recovery. "I think I was very fortunate to have the mental state that permitted me to accomplish that."[35] For years following the bombing, Campbell was plagued by phantom pain. "You actually feel pain in the feet," Campbell describes the sensation, "and I can tell what part of the foot it is, whether it's the big toe or the arch. It's a stinging, shooting pain. It's disconcerting, because you feel you can reach down, rub it, and stop it."[36]

On 16 April 1973, Campbell returned home to his brother's house to begin rebuilding his life. On 2 May, the local newspaper heralded his return to his law practice. Ironically, in the same edition of that newspaper and next to the article detailing Campbell's return to work was an article describing Governor George C. Wallace's first speech to the state legislature since he had lost the use of his legs after bullets fired by a would-be assassin paralyzed him.[37] In spite of their past political differences, Wallace and Campbell now shared a common bond. Upon his admission to Spain, Campbell was given the room that had been occupied by Wallace during the wounded governor's stay at the rehabilitation center. Wallace sent cards and flowers to Campbell during his stay at Spain and continually inquired about the lawyer's progress. Campbell's feelings toward the stricken governor in turn softened. "Naturally, I could identify with his situation and had a lot of sympathy for him."[38]

Campbell's return to work was the final phase of his recovery, both physically and mentally. During this phase, he set for himself the course of recovery that would shape the rest of his life. "I sat down one day and had a long talk with myself. I just decided I wasn't going to get eaten up with bitterness. Most of the time, it is a promise I have been able to live up to. I believe that attitude saved my life."[39]

Campbell, like his brothers, is a man of robust humor and that, too, served him during his recovery. Not long after returning to Scottsboro from the rehabilitation center, Campbell was bothered by a burr inside one of the artificial legs. The burr chafed him and he asked Probate Judge Bob Gentry to take the leg to Gentry's woodshop and smooth down the burr. Asked what had become of the leg, Campbell said with a straight face, "Oh, Judge Gentry has taken it to the shop to trim the toenails."[40]

The investigators continued to question Campbell about any possible motive or anyone he thought might be a suspect. He still could not conceive any reason why someone would want him killed, and the investigation into the bombing dragged on without any significant leads.

On Friday, 15 December 1972, while Campbell was recovering in the Birmingham hospital, Billy Ray McCrary's father, Grover, died.[41] Grover McCrary had spent most of his life as a hardworking farmer and had reared four sons and four daughters. He was sixty-four years old when he died. On Sunday, 17 December 1972, his widow, Annie Ruth, and his children gathered for the funeral. On the day of the funeral, Billy Ray gave his younger brother Virgil two hundred-dollar bills. When Virgil asked where Billy Ray, fresh out of prison and having no job, had gotten the money, Billy Ray replied that it had come from Hugh Otis Bynum.[42]

Virgil did not find it unusual that Billy Ray should get money from Bynum. It was common knowledge that Billy Ray and the rich old landowner were close friends and had been so for years. One of the first people to visit Billy Ray when he was released from prison in 1972, Virgil recalls, was Hugh Otis Bynum. Whenever Billy Ray found himself strapped for cash, he often would turn to his benefactor for a loan.[43]

Bynum loved to gamble, and he often traveled around the county with McCrary and staked him in marathon poker and dice games. But McCrary had a penchant for losing. It was said that McCrary could lose as much as $10,000 of Bynum's money at a whack. Some people suspected that the crafty McCrary purposely lost the money and later slipped back to the game and split the winnings with the other gamblers, his accomplices in the scheme. No one knows whether Bynum suspected Billy Ray was intentionally losing his money, but if he did suspect it, it did not keep him from keeping close ties with Jackson County's perpetual bad boy. On almost any given day, the two of them could be seen riding around in Bynum's black-over-white Buick Electra, or standing on the courthouse square talking, or drinking coffee at Tom's Restaurant.[44]

Bynum was also a frequent visitor at McCrary's trailer in Hollywood, where McCrary ran his bootlegging business. Bynum spent many hours hanging out at McCrary's with many of the county's known criminals and ruffians, men like C. W. "Bighead" Johnson, one of McCrary's childhood chums, and the violence-prone Brent Gant from Sand Mountain, and the ever-polite and clean-cut Charles X. Hale from Scottsboro.[45] In the case of McCrary, however, as with many of Bynum's so-called friends, there was always a hint of fiduciary fellowship. What friends Bynum had were more often than not bought and paid for with Bynum money.

Not long after he returned to his law practice, Loy Campbell had his first chance encounter with Hugh Otis Bynum since the bombing. Campbell and his brother Bunk were eating lunch at the Liberty Restaurant when Bynum spotted them. Bynum ambled over to where the Campbells sat. "You won't be running no more races," he mumbled and walked out of the restaurant. Campbell took the ambiguous remark to mean he would no longer be involved in politics.[46]

However, Bynum's words troubled the attorney for months.

7   *What's Going On Up There?*

After months of frustration, dead ends, and disappointment, the investigation into the bombing of Loy Campbell took a dramatic turn during the autumn of 1974. On Saturday, 14 September 1974, Circuit Court Judge John B. Tally pulled his 1973 Oldsmobile into a Scottsboro service station. The judge asked the station attendant, Johnny Bell, to fill the car's tank with gasoline and to check the oil. While under the car's hood, Bell found what he thought at first was a misplaced soda bottle. He lifted the six-inch-long plastic bottle and found there were wires attached to the bottle's cap. Bell traced the wires to the car's headlights and realized that what he had found was a bomb intended for the judge.[1] Bell called the Scottsboro police to the scene, and the police summoned a bomb disposal squad from the U.S. Army Depot at Fort McClellan in Anniston to remove the device. The judge said his son Bill had seen the device on the car some three weeks earlier, but had mistaken it for part of the car's windshield washer unit.[2]

Judge John Tally had served on the bench since 1968 and, like all judges, had received several threats on his life. "I'm sure there's always somebody who is dissatisfied," the judge told reporters at the time. "There are always two sides in any court case."[3]

The federal Bureau of Alcohol, Tobacco, and Firearms dispatched Agent W. K. Blankenship to Scottsboro to handle the federal investigation into the attempt on Tally's life. Blankenship sent the plastic bottle to the BATF laboratory in Atlanta, where agents determined that the explosive device, complete with a dynamite detonating cap, had been wired to explode when the judge switched the car's headlights to high beam. Tally said he had driven the car many times at night while the device was on the car and had switched his headlights to high beam during that time. Only Providence—or the faulty wiring of the device—had spared the judge's life.[4]

As word of the attempt on Tally's life spread, people speculated that the bomb discovered in Tally's car was connected with the bombing of Loy Campbell. The authorities had made no arrests in the Campbell case, and many people felt the Scottsboro bomber had grown bold enough to attempt another assassination.[5] A sense of fear and foreboding began to spread through the small town.

The discovery of the bomb in Judge Tally's car was significant because it caused Alabama's attorney general, Bill Baxley, to focus his attention on the Campbell bombing case and because it brought a veteran investigator by the name of John East to Scottsboro. Baxley had been told the investigation into the bombing of Loy Campbell had stagnated, and he was being urged by a friend of Bunk Campbell to help solve the case. Upon hearing of the attempt on Judge Tally's life, Baxley told his chief investigator, Jack Shows, to send someone to Scottsboro. Shows sent East to Scottsboro with orders to "snoop around. Find out what's going on up there."[6]

East had been with the attorney general's office for just two months when he came to Scottsboro in September 1974. For the previous five years, he had been the chief investigator for the Phenix City, Alabama, district attorney's office and had gained a reputation as a thorough and innovative investigator who got results. Working with Phenix City District Attorney Bill Benton, East helped devise a method to streamline how cases were presented to grand juries and to speed up an otherwise cumbersome and confusing process. He also developed a system of presenting background information on witnesses and evidence so that the prosecutor could prepare better for a trial.[7]

East had come to law enforcement in a roundabout way. After serving in the navy during World War II, he had returned to his home in Phenix City and made his living as a bricklayer. In his spare time, he became a reserve deputy for the county sheriff and then became a full-time deputy. As his interest in law enforcement grew, he attended college at night and studied law on his own. He became an investigator with the sheriff, then went to work for the district attorney. During his five years as investigator in Phenix City, he averaged putting together 150 cases a year for Bill Benton. Many of those cases were resolved without a trial, but as many as thirty of the cases on which East worked each year were presented before juries.[8]

East was in his fifties when he went to work for Bill Baxley, but he had the physique of a bricklayer and the appearance of a much younger man. Blessed with a silky smooth and melodious south Alabama accent, East had the ability to win the confidence of the very people he was investigating, enabling him to pry information from them that might not be forthcoming as a result of more conventional and sometimes tougher approaches. He called himself "a trial technician" and "a choreographer of evidence" and prided himself on putting together a case so that a prosecutor could best win a conviction.

What East found in Scottsboro was an investigation that was going nowhere. Each agency involved—the BATF, the FBI, the Scottsboro police, the Jackson County Sheriff's Department, and the attorney general's office—though cooperating with the other agencies, was in essence conducting a separate investigation. East urged Sheriff Bob Collins to hold a meeting in order to focus the investigation and to put it back on track. It was at this time that East met George Tubbs, an investigator with the Sheriff's Department, and Keith Smith, a Scottsboro city investigator.

Tubbs, a tough and dedicated detective, had spent much of his time since the bombing of Loy Campbell trying to break the case. He had questioned scores of suspects, and had sought information about the bombing from each of the county criminals with whom he came in contact. A native of Jackson County, Tubbs knew the backgrounds of most of these criminals and that knowledge added to his savvy as a detective. Tubbs, like East, had come to law enforcement in an indirect way: Tubbs had been a carpenter before joining the sheriff's department.

Tubbs and Smith had just returned from Orlando, Florida, where they had questioned Linda Darlene Sullivan, the girlfriend of Charles Xavier Hale. Sullivan was in her early twenties when she took up with Hale in February 1974. Raised on Sand Mountain near the communities of Rosalie and Henagar, she had lived

John East
(Photo by Byron Woodfin)

Detective George Tubbs
(Courtesy George Tubbs Family)

a hard life. An attractive woman, she was in her second marriage, and her husband, Tom Sullivan, was serving time in the state penitentiary. She herself had suffered personal problems and had spent some time in a Georgia mental hospital.[9] Her relationship with the smooth-talking Charles Hale involved her in a string of robberies and eventually landed her in federal prison.

Tubbs and Smith went to Orlando to question Sullivan about several crimes in the Jackson County area for which Hale was a suspect. They particularly wanted to know about the armed robbery of two fishermen on 7 April 1974, at Mink Creek, a popular fishing spot on Guntersville Lake just outside of Scottsboro.[10] Following the robbery of the fishermen, Hale and Sullivan had fled Alabama to Florida, where they had assumed false names and worked at odd jobs. But bad luck set in for Linda Darlene Sullivan on 23 August 1974, when the pair robbed a bank in Mims, Florida. Trying to escape the robbery, the couple wrecked the getaway car. Hale was able to flee from the scene on foot, and the young mother of two hid in a ditch as the police converged on the getaway car. As she lay in the ditch, she heard her name and Hale's name being broadcast over the police radios as being wanted for the bank robbery.[11] Sullivan was able to slip away from the scene and made her way to Fort Oglethorpe, Georgia, where she stayed with friends. Her freedom was short-lived, however. Federal agents arrested her in Georgia, returned her to Florida, and took her to the Orlando city jail. Authorities identified the fingerprints on a pistol used in the robbery as those of Charles X. Hale, and he became the subject of an FBI manhunt.[12]

Though in serious trouble and left to her own defenses, Sullivan was calm and confident as Tubbs and Smith questioned her about the robberies. She made the decision to cooperate with Tubbs and described how Hale and an accomplice had robbed the fishermen while she waited in the getaway car. She also provided some chilling details for the two investigators.[13] After leaving the scene of the robbery, Hale became worried that the fishermen would identify them. Sullivan said Hale then returned to the scene in order to kill the men. Fortunately, the fishermen had left before the would-be killer returned and the two men were spared. As it turned out, Hale had been right to worry about the fishermen; he was wanted in connection with the robbery.[14]

At the end of the questioning, Keith Smith recalls casually asking Sullivan, "Is there anything else Charles has been involved in that we need to know about?"[15] George Tubbs caught the look in her eyes: the way she blinked, the experienced investigator knew there was more that Linda Darlene Sullivan could tell them.[16]

It was then that the young woman broke completely. The lying in order to cover for her lover was over. She could no longer run from the truth. Hale had killed a man while in Florida, she told the two detectives.[17] Pressed for details, Sullivan told how Hale had met a man in a Florida bar. The two men knew each other from Scottsboro. At that time, Hale was using the alias of "Kenneth Smith," but the barroom acquaintance insisted on calling him "Charles." Sullivan said Hale grew increasingly nervous, fearing that someone might overhear the man and realize his true identity.[18]

Hale told the man that he had some stolen televisions hidden in the woods outside of town. The man agreed to go with Hale and Sullivan to the place where the televisions were supposedly hidden. Hale drove to a deserted wooded area outside of town, and while Darlene waited in the car, Hale and the man walked into the woods. A few minutes passed, then Darlene heard four or five shots, and Charles walked back to the car alone. There had not been any stolen televisions. The story was part of a plot to get rid of the man who insisted on calling Hale by his real name. Later, Hale told Sullivan how he had shot the man in the back of the head.[19]

Hearing the details of the murder related by Sullivan, Smith and Tubbs stopped the questioning and told an Orlando detective what they had learned. A check of unsolved murders in the area revealed that there had been a recent murder that matched the details Sullivan had supplied. A team of Florida detectives quickly took over and whisked Sullivan away. She later agreed to testify against Hale, who now was wanted for murder and bank robbery, as well as several crimes in Alabama.[20]

This was not George Tubbs's first encounter with Linda Darlene Sullivan. In April 1974, Darlene had been arrested on theft charges. While in the Jackson County Jail, she had been befriended by Delbert Beavers, the courthouse janitor. Beavers, who lived on Sand Mountain, had known Darlene as a child and he routinely visited her in the jail. During one of the visits, Darlene confided in Beavers she had information about the bombing of Loy Campbell. Beavers passed the information on to Tubbs, and the investigator met with Darlene.[21]

It had been the break Tubbs had hoped eventually would come. He had learned long ago the importance of informers in solving such cases. However, before Tubbs could get the information he wanted, he needed to bargain with Darlene. She had told him enough to pique his interest but had said she would not tell him the whole story until after she was released from jail. Tubbs had agreed to help her to get her bonds reduced and she, in turn, had agreed to tell him everything she knew about the bombing. Once out of jail, however, she had disappeared, and Tubbs had not seen her again until his visit to the Orlando city jail.[22]

When Tubbs and Smith returned to Scottsboro from Florida, they invited John East to join them while audio tapes of the Sullivan questioning were transcribed. "This is something you might be interested in," Tubbs told the investigator. Listening to the tape recordings, East could tell that Sullivan had some knowledge of the Campbell bombing. Sullivan had been evasive when Tubbs and Smith had asked about the bombing. As Smith described it, she had "talked around it" when pressed about the bombing. Still, she had revealed enough to convince East that Sullivan knew more than she was telling. He called Attorney General Baxley in Montgomery and told him what he had learned.

"Drop everything else," Baxley ordered his investigator, "and concentrate on the Campbell case." The young state prosecutor obtained the clearance necessary for East to go to Florida to talk to Sullivan.[23] Joined by BATF Agent Don Barrett and detectives Tubbs and Smith, East went to Orlando, and on 24 September 1974, met Linda Darlene Sullivan for the first time.[24]

8   *A Woman Scorned*

The story of Linda Darlene Sullivan is like that of thousands of women born into the poverty of southern Appalachia. Poorly educated, they have little opportunity for success beyond the most menial and tedious of jobs, found mostly in textile factories or poultry processing plants. The luckier ones find jobs as waitresses or barhops or retail sales clerks. More often than not, these women are thrust into situations over which they have little control and in which they have few choices. The dreams of economic security and family stability are often elusive. They are reared with the assimilated belief that women are dependent upon men, and that their destiny and happiness are fused with wedlock. But this dependence often flounders on the rocks of a broken marriage, leaving the woman to her own resources.

For many of these women, adolescent marriage is a common avenue of escape from broken homes that spawn a lack of security and a lack of a viable future. But instead of finding the escape they desire, they are quickly saddled with the burdens of marriage and youthful motherhood and find they have only swapped one entrapment for another. Always optimistic and hopeful, they soon find themselves repeating the mistake in second and even third marriages. Sometimes they resign themselves to their fate and find happiness through compromise. A few are lucky and return to education, true independence, and self-fulfillment. Many more end up separated from their husbands or divorced and are left to fend for themselves.

Such is the case of Linda Darlene Sullivan. With her second husband away in prison, she was forced to provide for her two small children by herself. Like many in her plight, she became a survivalist. Survival became the sole motivation for all her actions. Tall and thin, with straight dark hair and prominent cheekbones, she was an attractive woman. As part of her instinct for survival, she learned to use her beauty and the desires of men to her advantage.

This burden of self-dependence, however, bred a yearning for security and escape, resulting in a certain vulnerability. It was then that she met the alluring Charles Xavier Hale. In many ways he provided her with the financial and emotional security she needed. Just as important, however, he provided the titillating excitement and escape she had sought so desperately. He was tinged with the danger of an outlaw and she was drawn to him. Before meeting Hale she had not had any trouble with the law. However, her relationship with Hale thrust her into a subterranean world of deceit, drugs, robbery, and murder.[1]

When John East met Sullivan for the first time, she had been housed in the Orlando, Florida, city jail for nearly two weeks. She had now resigned herself to the fact that she was in serious trouble. Ready to purge her conscience, she now was willing to talk. A guilty conscience was not, however, her only motivation for talking to the agents. The old saying "hell hath no fury like a woman scorned"[2] had never been more true than in the case of Linda Darlene Sullivan. Hale had made no attempt to contact her since the botched bank robbery a month earlier, and now she felt that her lover had abandoned her.

"He used me like a rag and threw it in the corner," she later told East. She admitted that for the last seven months she had been under the spell of the outwardly polite young man from Scottsboro.[3] "If he were to have told me to kill you," she told East, "I would have done it."

Don Barrett had devoted more than a year and a half to the investigation of the bombing of Loy Campbell. Having more knowledge of the details of the case than the other investigators, Barrett conducted the interview of Sullivan. Under his skillful and direct questioning, the story of Charles Hale's involvement in the bombing began to unfold.[4]

Sullivan told the agents how she had met Hale through some friends in Scottsboro. She distinctly remembered the date, 7 February 1974, because it was her youngest son's birthday. The relationship quickly blossomed, and Hale soon moved in with Sullivan and her two children in the government-subsidized apartment in the small town of Pisgah on Sand Mountain. She was working at a textile mill located within walking distance of the apartment, and he was working a third-shift job at a textile mill in Scottsboro.

When she first met Hale, Sullivan knew he was involved in drug use and drug dealing and that he recently had been released from Draper Penitentiary. She told the agents that judging from things he had said, she suspected he was involved in more serious crimes. Sometime around 1 March 1974, after the couple had been living together for about a month, the love-smitten Hale had confessed his part in the bombing of Loy Campbell.

"We was sitting, talking, and he finally told me he had fallen in love with me," she told Barrett matter of factly. " 'But before you make up your mind whether you're going to stay with me or not,' " she recalled his saying, " 'there's some things you got to know about me. You can decide from that whether you want me to stay or whether you want me to leave. I want you to know it all so that there won't be nothing between us or say I'd been hiding from you.

" 'I was the one who blew up Campbell,' " she said Hale had told her.

Sullivan then told the agents what Hale had told her had happened the night before the bombing. Hale had gotten the dynamite and detonating caps for the bomb while he was employed at the State Highway Department in Scottsboro. He had gone to the Campbell home late that night, crawled under the car parked in the driveway, and wired the bomb to the automobile's ignition. Hale told her he had almost been caught when a police patrol car made an unexpected visit to the neighborhood.

Sullivan told the agents that it had been Billy Ray McCrary who had hired Hale for the job and that it had been Hugh Otis Bynum who had wanted the man killed. Hale had told Sullivan that he had been paid by Hugh Otis Bynum after a news article about the bombing appeared in *The Huntsville Times*. For the first time, the name of Hugh Otis Bynum was linked to the bombing. Donald Barrett had long suspected that McCrary might have been involved in the attack but the mention of the prominent landowner presented a new twist, with new questions and new problems.

Sullivan said Hale liked to boast to her about the bombing. "He laughed about it a lot," she said, "about doing it. And he bragged about the alibi he had for that night and bragged about getting away with it and them not being able to prove it." Sullivan told the agents that Hale never disclosed his alibi. But Sullivan said Hale was surprised and concerned that Loy Campbell had not been killed. "He said for some reason, the man just wouldn't die," Sullivan said.

Was Bynum angry because Campbell didn't die? Barrett asked.

"He wasn't really mad. Seeing him suffer like that—suffering was enough. Hugh Otis told Charles this," said Sullivan.

Hale told her that Bynum continued to send him money after he was sent back to prison in 1973 for a parole violation. "Hugh Otis would give him money any time he wanted it and he would be a very rich man and never worry for anything as long as he got rid of the others," Sullivan said she had been told.

Others! Who were the others Hale was talking about? Barrett and East wanted to know.

Sullivan said that Hale had told her there were four people that Bynum wanted dead before he himself died. She said Hale was to receive a different amount of money for each person killed. "One was Loy Campbell," she told Barrett. "One was the sheriff of Jackson County, and the other was Jay Black, the district attorney. The fourth person's name was never mentioned."

Had she ever questioned Charles about the fourth person? the investigators asked.

"I didn't want to know any more than what I had already found out," she bluntly told them.

John East pondered the implication of what he had heard. If what Sullivan said was true, the attack on Loy Campbell had not been an isolated incident but was a part of a larger scheme to assassinate several people. All these months, the scope of the investigation into the bombing attack had been too narrow. With Sullivan's statement, the investigation would have to take a different course, and the investigators would have to pursue the truth concerning the prominent landowner, Hugh Otis Bynum.

Sullivan then told the agents about the day she and Hale had gone to Tom's Restaurant on the courthouse square in Scottsboro to meet with Bynum. She said that Hale was flat broke when he went into the restaurant, but that when he returned to the car where she waited, he had given her three fifty-dollar bills. He said he had gotten the money from Hugh Otis Bynum. She distinctly remembered that the bills had been folded in a peculiar way. Each of the three bills had been folded once lengthwise, then folded again in half. If Linda Sullivan could be believed, she could be used as a witness to show that Charles Hale indeed had been hired by Hugh Otis Bynum and that he had gotten money directly from the wealthy landowner.

For Don Barrett, parts of Sullivan's story rang true. Both McCrary and Hale had been suspects early on in the investigation and lawmen had questioned both of them more than once and had taken their fingerprints. Barrett knew that Hale had worked at the State Highway Department and might have had access to the dynamite, as Sullivan had said. However, Hale and McCrary had continued to deny any involvement in the bombing and there was no other evidence that had linked them to the attempt on Campbell's life.

Sullivan then told the agents about the night she had gone with Hale to search for dynamite he had hidden. She said Hale had hunted for the dynamite in a hedgerow behind the Carriage House Apartments in Scottsboro but that he had returned empty-handed, saying it had been too dark to find the stash. Pressed by Barrett, Sullivan gave him directions to the apartment complex and then drew him a map detailing how Hale had hunted for the dynamite.

Later that same night, over Sullivan's protests, Hale had robbed the two fishermen at Mink Creek. Sullivan had remained in the car during the robbery. As luck would have it, a Scottsboro police car had pulled up beside the parked car and, after checking her identification, the police learned she was wanted for possession of stolen goods. She was taken to the county jail, where she remained for almost a month. The police impounded Hale's car and, fearing capture, Hale left town.[5]

It was while she was a prisoner in the county jail that Sullivan had confided in Delbert Beavers her knowledge of the Campbell bombing and had been questioned by George Tubbs. Now she freely admitted to the agents that she had been less than truthful with the county investigator. "I've lied to Tubbs like crazy," she told Barrett, "to work around and get out of jail."

She freely admitted also that she had resorted to her feminine wit and charm to win her freedom. While in jail, Darlene cultivated a relationship with a jail trusty from Bridgeport. He quickly became infatuated with her. She used this infatuation to get out of jail and back to Charles Hale. "Well, I kind of talked to him and had him convinced I would go live with him and marry him," she said of the trusty, "to get out of jail." When the man was released from jail, he returned with bonds signed for Sullivan's release. Around 1 May 1974, Sullivan went to Bridgeport to live with the man. But unknown to her new boyfriend, Sullivan sent word to Hale's younger sister where she could be found, and on 7 May, Charles Xavier Hale walked back into her life.

Sullivan remembers the date because 7 May 1974, was an election day. She was hanging around a Bridgeport poolroom when Hale walked in. After a brief reunion, Hale, now without a car and traveling on foot, headed out to South Pittsburg, Tennessee, some three miles north of Bridgeport, where he told Darlene he would wait for her at a fish market. An hour later, Darlene turned her back on her family, her Alabama roots, and her two children, and in a desperate act of love and devotion she walked through wheat fields and cow pastures and waded creeks to meet her paramour at the fish market. The two lovers then walked to the nearby interstate highway and hitchhiked to Florida. Their relationship came to a screeching halt when, after robbing the bank in Florida, their getaway car landed in a ditch.

Sullivan's catharsis was now complete. Although it was motivated by spite toward her wayward lover, her confession was as much that of a woman seizing the opportunity to set a new course for herself. "I'm tired of lying and I'm tired of all this," she had told the agents, and John East sensed she was sincere. The fact she had not tried to cut a deal with the agents bolstered her credibility. She had not asked for any leniency in the prosecution of the criminal charges pending against her.

On Wednesday, 25 September 1974, the day after the jailhouse interview of Sullivan, Barrett, Tubbs, and Smith returned to

Scottsboro. John East remained in Orlando to take part in the administration of a polygraph test to Sullivan. The results of the lie detector test, while inadmissible in court, showed that Sullivan was telling the truth. East was convinced she would be a good witness, and he took a plane to Montgomery to report to Bill Baxley.[6]

Baxley knew that although the woman might be telling the truth, there would have to be more evidence linking Hugh Otis Bynum, Charles Hale, and Billy Ray McCrary to the bombing before investigators could make an arrest. Hale very well could be the man who, under the cover of darkness, had wired the bomb to Loy Campbell's car. But it would take more than the testimony of Hale's former girlfriend to prove that the wealthy and eccentric landowner in Scottsboro had paid to have Campbell killed. More significantly, Sullivan had never given an explanation as to why Bynum would want Campbell or the other men killed. No motive for the attack had been uncovered.

Baxley ordered East back to Scottsboro. On Friday, 27 September, agents uncovered the first physical evidence proving Sullivan's story. Armed with the map she had drawn, Don Barrett, George Tubbs, John East, Scottsboro Chief of Police Ed Cotten, and a Scottsboro detective named Raymond Bell went behind the Carriage House Apartments where Sullivan had said Charles Hale had searched for the hidden dynamite. A search along the hedgerow behind the apartments produced a paper sack containing five sticks of dynamite, wired with a military style blasting cap.[7]

The dynamite obviously had been hidden for some time, and the damp north Alabama climate had taken its toll. The paper sack and the dynamite were badly rotted, and the ground around where the investigators found the explosives reeked of the nitroglycerin that had seeped out. Barrett, an expert in explosives, felt certain that the dynamite and blasting cap were of the same type used in the attempt on Loy Campbell's life. Results of tests conducted at the BATF laboratory in Atlanta confirmed his conclusions.[8]

Barrett knew something else. The only place in Scottsboro that one could find this type of dynamite and military style blasting caps was the State Highway Department depot on the outskirts of town. A check of the employment records kept at the department showed Charles Hale had gone to work there on 25

September 1972, and the records showed he had worked on several job sites where dynamite had been used. A check with the clerk revealed also that the department had been lax in keeping records of the dynamite used. The workers, including Charles Hale, could easily pilfer dynamite and blasting caps for their own use.[9]

Over the next few weeks, John East, who had set up headquarters in the courthouse, took on the job of gathering information that could be used to confirm further what Sullivan had told them. A month after the interview in Orlando, Sullivan pled guilty to her part in the bank robbery and was sentenced to serve time at the federal prison in Lexington, Kentucky. Not long after she arrived at prison, East made the trip to Kentucky to again interview Sullivan in hopes of garnering more details about the bombing. He was especially interested to find out whether Sullivan knew why Campbell and the other men had been targeted for murder.[10]

When East interviewed her in the Kentucky prison, Linda Darlene Sullivan had undergone a transformation. She was now calm and relaxed and seemed ready to take the advice Don Barrett had given her in Florida. Barrett had urged the young woman to take this opportunity to turn her life around. "It was as though the world had been lifted from her shoulders," East said of the meeting in the Kentucky prison.[11]

East again went over the details of Sullivan's statement. Sullivan repeated how Hale had gotten the dynamite, how he had planted the bomb on the car, the meeting with Hugh Otis Bynum at Tom's Restaurant, and the failed search for the dynamite behind the Carriage House Apartments. Her story had not changed. However, she was unable to tell East why Bynum wanted the men killed.[12]

Even though the investigators had the physical evidence of the rotted dynamite to substantiate Sullivan's statement, there still was not enough evidence to justify an arrest. The investigators would have to find some additional evidence, or someone else would have to talk. As he talked to the townspeople in Scottsboro, East began to learn more about the man people knew as Hugh Otis. East heard the stories of the violent bursts of anger and the tales of Bynum's mean-spirited threats and attacks on others. But townspeople continually told East something else. There was no way that Bynum would be arrested. There was no way that Bynum would have paid someone to kill Loy Campbell or anyone else, because if he had wanted it done, he would have done it himself, the townspeople said.[13]

During the course of the investigation of the bombing of Loy Campbell, the name of Hugh Otis Bynum had surfaced, but investigators had never seriously considered him a suspect. Insisting there had never been any problems between Bynum and himself, Campbell had inadvertently steered the investigators away from the culprit.[14] About the time that Barrett and East were in Florida questioning Linda Darlene Sullivan, a friend of Hugh Otis Bynum named Ernest "Ern" Morris paid a visit to Campbell's law office. During their conversation, Morris made what was for Campbell a revealing statement. Apparently, Morris had served as a peacemaker between Bynum and Harold Foster, the attorney whom Bynum had once tried to kill.

"You know I've got Hugh Otis and Harold Foster back together," Campbell remembers Morris as saying. "I'm going to try to get you and Hugh Otis back together."[15]

Campbell was stung by what Morris had said. The statement revealed to Campbell that, unknown to him, there indeed had been a problem with Hugh Otis Bynum. "Suddenly everything fell into place and became clear to me," Campbell recalls. "Until then, I just couldn't believe Hugh Otis was mad at me." For some unknown reason, it had been Bynum who had wanted Campbell killed.[16]

During the first days of October 1974, agent Don Barrett summoned Bynum to the courthouse to be questioned and fingerprinted. Bynum denied any involvement in the bombing. Offered a polygraph test, Bynum refused, telling Barrett the machine might tell the truth, but the men operating the machine might not.[17] Interestingly, Barrett had a tough time getting the old man's fingerprints. Bynum's scleroderma had left his hands shriveled, and the hardening of the skin around the fingers forced Barrett to try several times to get a usable set of prints. It was doubtful that Bynum ever would have left much trace of his fingerprints on anything he touched.[18]

Although Bynum denied any connection to the bombing, he did make a telling admission. He told Barrett he didn't like Loy Campbell, that he disliked the mayor of Scottsboro, John T. Reid, and that he didn't have any use for Sheriff Bob Collins, the man who had failed to make an arrest when his barns were burned and his cattle shot.[19] But there was little hard evidence against Hugh Otis Bynum or Billy Ray McCrary, and now there was little for the investigators to do but wait and hope that something would break. Perhaps Charles Hale would be captured or someone else would feel compelled to talk. Most assuredly, given enough time, Billy Ray McCrary would slip up and fall into their hands. The break they were hoping for came in November 1974.

Not long after Don Barrett had returned to Scottsboro from Florida in September 1974, he paid a visit to the habitual felon, McCrary. Investigators had suspected all along that McCrary knew more about the First Monday bombing than he was saying. But in spite of repeated questioning by Barrett, the veteran criminal steadfastly had maintained that he had had nothing to do with the attack on Loy Campbell. McCrary's name had come up in the Sullivan statement, however, and Barrett wanted to question him once again. McCrary again denied any involvement in the bombing, and Barrett came away frustrated.[20]

McCrary recently had divorced his wife Lilah and married his young girlfriend, Joyce Turner. He also had taken over operation of a small gas station at Martintown Hill, some five miles north of Scottsboro on the main highway leading into Tennessee. Though Billy Ray sold gasoline and cigarettes and soft drinks at the station, the place of business served mainly as a cover for his bootlegging of illegal beer and whiskey.[21] There were also rumors that the station served as a brothel.

McCrary had taken over operation of the station after the previous owner, seventy-three-year-old Jess Ward, had been killed by sheriff's deputies when they tried to arrest him on a bootlegging charge. The old man had refused to be taken in by the deputies and threatened them with a shotgun. In the ensuing struggle, the deputies shot Ward to death.[22] McCrary had leased the station from Ward's daughter, and it served as the perfect place for McCrary's bootlegging business.

But the bootlegging came to an end on 26 November 1974, when agents with the state's alcoholic beverage control board swooped down on the station and arrested McCrary and his longtime friend and confederate, C. W. "Bighead" Johnson. The state charged both men with violating Alabama's prohibition law. In addition, McCrary faced charges of violating his parole from federal prison.[23] If convicted, he faced a very lengthy prison sentence.

Now that he was in jail, the investigators knew that McCrary was in a vulnerable position. They decided to take him to Montgomery for further questioning about the bombing. On 4 December 1974, two years to the day since the bomb had ripped through Loy Campbell's Pontiac, investigators drove McCrary to Montgomery to meet with the state's chief prosecutor. The tough, young, and ambitious Bill Baxley was eager to meet Billy Ray McCrary.[24]

9   *First One to the Table*

William J. "Bill" Baxley II was born into one of the founding families of Dothan, Alabama, a border town tucked away in the southeast corner of the state near Florida and Georgia. His grandfather and namesake, William Joseph Baxley, had served as mayor of the town, and his father, Keener Baxley, had a long career as an attorney and served as circuit court judge for the two-county area around Dothan. Over time, the Baxley family became one of the most influential families in Alabama politics.[1]

Baxley graduated from law school at the University of Alabama in 1964 and, after a short stint in the U.S. Army Reserve, went to work as a legal assistant for the Alabama Supreme Court. In January of 1966, he returned to Dothan and opened a private law practice. Six months later, the office of district attorney became vacant. Baxley had always wanted to be a prosecutor and he sought the appointment to fill the vacancy. After receiving unanimous support from the local bar association, Baxley was appointed by Gov. George Wallace to fill out the remaining year of the term. At age 24, Bill Baxley had become the youngest district attorney in the state and was quite possibly the youngest in the nation. He soon gained a reputation as an aggressive and effective prosecutor.[2]

The new district attorney faced one of the busiest caseloads in the state. At that time, the Twentieth Judicial Circuit encompassed the south Alabama counties of Houston and Henry. The two-county area bordered Florida to the south and Georgia to the east, and as transients moved in and out of the three-state area, the crime rate rose. Many of the cases Baxley argued were tried before his father. There are legendary stories of shouting matches between the two men as father and son clashed over differing interpretations of the law. It was during these years that Bill Baxley honed the skills that served him so well as the state's chief prosecutor.[3]

His reputation had grown to the point that MacDonald Gallion, then the attorney general of Alabama, began calling on Baxley to argue cases in his place. Baxley was sent all over Alabama in service to Gallion, and on one occasion investigated the charges of corruption lodged against the district attorney of Huntsville, in north Alabama. In 1970, Gallion sought reelection, and the young Baxley made the decision to oppose his sometime boss.[4]

In addition to his skills as a prosecutor, Baxley had honed his political skills. Promising to be an active, prosecuting attorney general, Baxley pulled off one of the greatest upsets in the history of Alabama politics when he defeated Gallion. In January 1971, at age 28, he became the youngest man to serve as the state's attorney general.

As attorney general, Baxley held true to his promise to be a hands-on prosecutor. He often chose to argue criminal cases himself and several times won convictions in cases in which other prosecutors had failed. He also aggressively pursued enforcement of the state's environmental laws and, in several cases, represented the state in civil suits brought against industrial violators.[5] In 1974, he became the only attorney general in the state's history to run unopposed for reelection.

When Baxley first took office as attorney general, he made a pledge to solve the 1963 bombing of a Birmingham church, a bombing that had killed four young black girls. It was a pledge that would take him years to fulfill. In 1977, after six years of dogged investigation, he was able to do what federal authorities had failed to do. A leader in the local Ku Klux Klan, Robert "Dynamite Bob" Chambliss, went to prison for his part in the bombing that ripped through the Sixteenth Street Baptist Church.[6]

Bill Baxley represented a new breed of politician in Alabama. A man of definite principles, his liberal viewpoints often clashed with the state's established political machinery. He openly disagreed with the segregationists. Though his beliefs earned him many admirers, they also earned him many enemies. The controversy that surrounded Baxley eventually thwarted his ambition to become governor of the state.

A handsome man, he was among the state's most eligible bachelors, and tales of his drinking and womanizing plagued his political career. Of moderate height and build, he had a boyish face with brown eyes and thick, dark brown hair. His deep, loud voice had a clear south Alabama accent that in a courtroom resonated like that of a fire-and-brimstone preacher.

Baxley often said, "As a prosecutor, you can't pretend to be a Sunday school teacher and deal with criminals."[7] During his career, he had dealt with numerous unsavory characters, many of them worse than Billy Ray McCrary. In December 1974, when Baxley met McCrary in Montgomery, the attorney general was not even pretending to be a Sunday school teacher.

John East had informed Baxley about McCrary's history and his suspected involvement in the bombing of Loy Campbell. East also told Baxley that McCrary was no petty criminal and that he was a smooth talker who rarely could be believed. The attorney general knew from the outset that even if McCrary talked, it would be difficult to make a jury believe him.[8]

Baxley's meeting with McCrary was curt and to the point. This was serious business, and Baxley wanted McCrary to know it. He told McCrary that he had taken over prosecution of the case from Jackson County District Attorney Tommy Armstrong and that within the day he would have a judge issue a warrant charging McCrary and Charles X. Hale with the bombing that had nearly killed Loy Campbell. The charge would be exploding a bomb near an occupied dwelling. If convicted, McCrary would face a life sentence.[9]

"Billy Ray, you've had brushes with the law and brushes with the court," Baxley remembers saying, "but we didn't bring you to Montgomery to waste our time. This time, we're going to clobber you."[10] Baxley's tough attitude worked. McCrary said that he had information about the bombing but that he wanted to cut a deal before he talked. John East recalls McCrary smiling and telling Baxley, "The first one to the table gets the sugar."

The veteran criminal was clearly a man of opportunity. McCrary knew it was just a matter of time before the truth of his involvement in the bombing would come out. Charles Hale could be captured any day and might make his own deal with the authorities. McCrary knew his freedom hinged on being the first to exchange what he knew for immunity from prosecution in the case.[11]

Baxley had been here before. Making deals with criminals in order to establish a case was the one part of his job as prosecutor he had always despised. "It just makes you want to wash your hands after dealing with that kind of slime," he was known to say. Often, however, there was little choice but to make such deals. Something had to be done in Scottsboro or these bombings and attempts on people's lives might continue. The attempted bombing of Judge Tally was fresh in Baxley's mind. His decision to make a deal with Billy Ray was born out of a real concern that someone else might wind up like Loy Campbell or be killed. The miasma of fear had spread beyond Scottsboro.[12]

Baxley knew that without McCrary's help, he might never bring the case to trial. His investigators had tried everything they legally could do to break someone. Reluctantly, Baxley entered into a devil's pact with McCrary. In exchange for McCrary's testimony, the state would drop its bootlegging charge against him and would grant him immunity from prosecution for any involvement he might have had in the bombing.[13]

With the assurance of immunity, McCrary laid it all out for Baxley and his team of investigators. The story he told bordered on craziness. McCrary told Baxley that after he had gotten out of the federal penitentiary in November 1972, one of the first people to visit him had been Hugh Otis Bynum. He told Baxley that the eccentric landowner had wanted four men killed and wanted McCrary to find someone to do the job. The four men Bynum had marked for death were Loy Campbell, the mayor of Scottsboro, John T. Reid, the sheriff, Bob Collins, and the former district attorney of Jackson County, Jay Black.[14] McCrary said he had recruited Charles Hale to carry out the killings and that it had been Hale who had wired the bomb to Loy Campbell's car.

But what was the motive? Baxley wanted to know. Why did Bynum want these men killed?[15] McCrary said that Bynum blamed the four men for the loss of his barns and cattle during the racial violence that had broken out after Bynum had shot the two black youths for being in his pasture. He repeatedly told McCrary that the four men had cost him $92,000 in damages resulting from the barn burnings.[16]

McCrary said that Bynum later added a Scottsboro car salesman named Sam Holland to the list of men he wanted dead.[17]

What did Holland have to do with all this? Baxley wanted to know.

Holland had nothing to do with the barn burnings, McCrary told him. It was just another one of Bynum's crazy ideas, he said. Subsequently, Bynum had told McCrary that he suspected Holland and the sheriff of stealing some of his cattle, and that was why he wanted the car salesman killed.[18] McCrary described one occasion when Bynum had given Charles Hale a rifle and scope with orders to go up to Sheriff Collins's cattle farm at Tupelo. McCrary said Bynum told Hale to shoot the sheriff when he came to the farm to feed his cattle.[19]

Bill Baxley was not convinced that what McCrary was telling him was the truth. As badly as he wanted to make an arrest, it could be an enormous blunder to act solely on the word of a character like Billy Ray McCrary. There would have to be some other proof to substantiate what he was saying. Ever the tough prosecutor, Baxley told McCrary that investigators were going to check out every aspect of his story and that if they found that he was lying, all deals were off.[20]

It was then that McCrary made the bold proposal for them to return him to Scottsboro. Wired with a tape recorder, he would meet with Hugh Otis Bynum with the aim of getting Bynum to talk once again about killing the four men.[21] Baxley carefully pondered McCrary's proposal and agreed to have him taken back to Scottsboro, but not on his own. An undercover agent would accompany him. It would be the agent who would be wired with the tape recorder, and he would pose as a killer for hire. It would be McCrary's job to introduce the agent to Bynum in hopes that Bynum would want to deal with the bogus hitman.[22] Baxley reminded McCrary of one thing: If they found out that he had lied, he would be going to prison for a long time.

On the morning of 6 December 1974, agents put Billy Ray McCrary in a car, and, with undercover agent Harold Wilson in another car, they made the four-hour drive north to Scottsboro to meet with Hugh Otis Bynum.

10   *"It's About Four, Isn't It, Hugh?"*

Harold Wilson had been with the Alabama State Troopers for eleven years. Most recently he had worked as an undercover narcotics agent with the Alabama Bureau of Investigation. Because of his experience posing as a drug dealer, he was the man tapped to act as the killer for hire who would accompany Billy Ray McCrary to meet with Hugh Otis Bynum. Standing six feet one inch tall and weighing 225 pounds, Wilson was built like a football player and looked the part of a hitman.[1]

On Friday, 6 December 1974, after being introduced to McCrary and briefed on the background of the case, Wilson headed out for Scottsboro. His traveling companion was Lt. Brady Taylor, the Alabama Department of Public Safety's electronic surveillance expert. In a separate car, McCrary was escorted by Jackson County deputies Paul Mount and Troy Ferguson.[2]

The two cars pulled into Scottsboro in the early afternoon and headed immediately to the Holiday Inn, where Sheriff Bob Collins had set up headquarters in one of the guest rooms. Waiting with Collins at the motel were investigators John East, Don Barrett, and George Tubbs. Agents from the ABI were also present. Chief among them was Marvin Bryant, a veteran agent who made Scottsboro his home. It was to be Bryant's job to monitor the radio transmission of any conversation that might take place between Hugh Otis Bynum and the undercover agent.[3]

Once at the Holiday Inn, Lieutenant Taylor fitted Wilson with a hidden radio transmitter. The investigators equipped Bryant's car with a receiver and a tape recorder in order to document the conversation. The agents checked out the equipment and searched Billy Ray to ensure he had no money on him in the event that money changed hands during the meeting with Bynum. The two men were now ready for their hoped-for meeting with the millionaire landowner. They awaited the arrival of Attorney General Baxley.[4]

Baxley had made the decision to fly to Scottsboro and personally oversee the undercover operation. He was suspicious of McCrary and was not thoroughly convinced that the man was telling the truth. Hugh Otis Bynum might have been the man who masterminded and paid for the bombing of Loy Campbell, but it would take more than the testimony of a habitual felon ever to justify an arrest, let alone take Bynum to trial. "I had to hear it with my own ears," Baxley later said.[5]

Baxley's plane landed in Scottsboro in the late afternoon on that Friday and, along with Maj. E. Jennings Dixon, head of the Alabama Department of Public Safety, Baxley went directly to the Holiday Inn, located just over a mile from the center of town. Baxley recalls that it was a bitterly cold evening and the winter chill added to his anxiousness. Baxley knew he was taking a terrible gamble. If Bynum failed to incriminate himself, or if McCrary was lying, there might never be an another opportunity to bring someone to trial for the Campbell bombing. Baxley arrived at the motel in time to review the details of the undercover operation.[6]

Scottsboro had been decorated for Christmas and the merchants' association was set for the annual holiday parade scheduled for the next day. The Scottsboro Lions Club had chosen high school senior Darlene McGee as parade queen. Santa Claus had arrived in town by way of helicopter and was set to lead the parade. The town was in a festive mood.

At about 4:30 on that Friday evening, Wilson and McCrary drove from the Holiday Inn to Tom's Restaurant on the courthouse square, where McCrary felt certain Bynum could be found. It was part of Bynum's daily ritual to eat his evening meal at Tom's.[7] The two men entered the restaurant and sat together at a booth away from the other customers. Wilson ordered coffee and McCrary ordered himself a soft drink. A short time later, Bynum entered the cafe and spotted McCrary. Bynum went directly to the table where the two men waited and sat down with them.

By way of an introduction of the "hitman," McCrary said, "Hugh, this is a man here I have been hunting to do the job you want done."

"You've had trouble finding him before," Bynum replied.

A few minutes passed, then McCrary suggested they go outside to the car. While Bynum lagged behind in the restaurant to pay the bill, McCrary got into the car and sat in the driver's seat, while Wilson sat in the back seat on the passenger's side. In a few minutes, Bynum left the cafe and at McCrary's suggestion got into the car and sat in the front seat next to McCrary. Just a few parked cars away, Marvin Bryant and another agent sat in their car ready to monitor what was about to be said.

"Now, this man here," Billy Ray began, "is the man I have been trying to contact for a long time. I want him to stay here until you get the goddam work you wanted done and let him get on his way. Now I don't know how you want to handle this or how you want to take care of all this damn thing."

Bynum remained silent. He sat in the car listening.

Wilson later admitted that he was not posing as a preacher and that he freely sprinkled his conversation with Bynum and McCrary with profanities. "Like I said, if the price is right, I will blow his shit away," the agent said.

Bynum still had yet to say anything.

McCrary, the experienced con man, continued to try to draw the old man out. "That damn old sheriff. Tell him how he travels, Hugh. Goddam, then, I will show him the place." Then McCrary, weaving a tale of woe and explaining away how he had gotten out of jail, said, "See, Tally didn't set me a bond. That man in Fort Payne set me one. John Tally wouldn't set me one."

"What? The hell you say," were the first words Bynum had spoken since getting in the car.

The conversation continued as the three men remained in the car parked outside of Tom's Restaurant.

"Tally didn't give me probation, the other fellow did. Tally wouldn't set bond. Now, explain to him [Wilson] how all this shit goes on here. Now, I have told him how damn things are around here. It wouldn't be too hard, would it, to get the job done?" McCrary asked.

"Why hell, I could have done it myself before this news got on him, any time myself, damn near," answered Bynum.

"Well, I can do the fucking job, and be gone, if you want the fucking job done. That is the way I am," Wilson told the two men.

Then McCrary, perhaps trying to explain to the counterfeit hitman why Bynum was hesitant, said, "Like Hugh knows, we got beat for some money the other day. Didn't we, Hugh? With a deal with a guy, we put up some goddam money and the guy, well, I got put in jail, see."

"That's right," replied Bynum. Then he said to McCrary, "Tell him to leave a card where you can get in touch with him in a day or two."

But McCrary, playing the part of the desperate convict afraid of what the authorities had planned for him, pressed on, saying, "I am going to have to do it, Hugh, for now, they are liable to bust me, see, and if this [killing the sheriff] comes down, I won't get busted."

"Well, I haven't got the money right now, and if I borrowed it, they would go right there," Hugh Otis told him.

At this point, McCrary suggested that the men go for a ride and he backed the car away from Tom's Restaurant and headed in the direction of the Holiday Inn, where, unbeknown to Bynum, Alabama's attorney general and a room full of police awaited the results of the undercover operation.

On the way to the motel, McCrary continued to test the old man. "Well, just tell him, Hugh, what all you got that you really want done. Just what needs doing now," he said.

Bynum repeated that he had no money and added, "I could get all the money I wanted, but there would be some son of a bitch that wanted to know what I used that money for."

"Talking about money, how much are you talking about?" asked McCrary.

"I am talking about any sizeable amount," Bynum said, continuing to insist that he could not get any money.

Then McCrary turned to the undercover agent in the back seat and asked, "How much would you start? How much would you do the job for?"

Wilson asked, "How many are we going to get? How many do you want?"

McCrary answered, "Well, its about four—about four. It's about four, isn't it, Hugh?"

Although barely audible to those listening in on the conversation, Hugh Otis Bynum muttered the one-word reply that would prove to be part of the most damaging evidence against him. "Yeah," was his answer to Billy Ray's question about killing four people.

Then the undercover agent made his proposition while the three of them sat in the dark in the parked car behind the Holiday Inn. Wilson said he would kill the sheriff for $5,000 or that he would kill all four of the men they wanted killed for $2,000 each. He said he would take $500 down on the job, and after the job was done would return for the rest of the money. "My friend, if you want a goddam bargain," said the agent, "that's a bargain, and the only reason I am doing that is because I know you," referring to McCrary.

Bynum, however, continued to insist that he did not have any money. "I have just spent until I have spent out," he told the agent. "If I was to borrow that money, why, them son-of-a-bitches would ask me, 'What in the hell did you do with that money?' "

"They would know you had the sheriff killed," Wilson said.

"They would know it because everybody knows I don't like the son of a bitch," Bynum said.

Wilson, saying he had "places to go," pressured the men to make up their minds. Once again, however, Bynum said he could not get any money to have the job done. Then Billy Ray turned to the old man and said, "Tell him how much that bastard [the sheriff] cost you."

Answered Bynum, "$92,000."

"Just tell him, by God, how, just tell him how they done you, Hugh," McCrary urged.

"I shot two damn niggers that was in my cattle. They put me in jail. I have lost a house and two barns and had to sell my cattle at commercial price, and they were registered cattle. All in all, it cost me about $92,000," Bynum told the agent.

The quick-thinking Wilson then said, "Goddam. If he cost you that much, he ain't worth $2,000 more?"

At that, Bynum laughed and said, "It ain't a question of worth, it's a question of getting the money. I can get any amount of money, but, if uh, if I was to get it—you had that poor sheriff killed—they would say old Hugh had the old sheriff killed." Bynum laughed again. Those listening to the taped conversation described Bynum's laugh as "a blood-curdling cackle."[8]

Wilson suggested to the men that they make a down payment as a commitment for the job. "I am either going to have to have partial payment and do it and then come back—," Wilson said. But Bynum interrupted him and said, "If I was to say I would pay you, I would pay every dime of it."

Again Wilson pressured the men to make a decision. "We will do it if you want to do it. If you don't want to do it, say so, because I have places to go."

Then McCrary said, "Well, you definitely want it done, don't you, Hugh?"

Bynum replied, "Yeah. I wouldn't give a damn if it was done a month ago."

McCrary then wanted to know when Wilson would be able to do the job.

"I could do it this goddam weekend and he won't know what the fuck hit him," Wilson said.

"Well, what do you think, Hugh, with that small amount?" asked McCrary.

"That's a reasonable price, but I ain't got much money, and if I borrowed it and something happened to the sheriff, then boom, they would be on my ass."

McCrary suggested to Bynum that he could come up with $300 of the down payment if Bynum pitched in $200. But Bynum remained noncommittal. "I might. I might not," Bynum said.

Feigning frustration, Wilson ordered them to return to Tom's. "He don't want the job done," he said to McCrary.

McCrary suggested to Bynum that he borrow the money from Tom Sisk, the owner of Tom's Restaurant and Bynum's longtime friend.

"I just don't know, Billy," said Bynum.

On the way back to the courthouse square the trio made small talk. At one point, Wilson told McCrary he would not be spending the night in Scottsboro, saying, "This place is too dead." At that the three men again laughed.

Just before they reached the courthouse square and Tom's Restaurant, McCrary asked Bynum, "Hugh, do you think he should come back?"

"I don't know, Billy," he said. After a moment's thought, he said, "Drive around the block."

But a nervous McCrary said he did not want to keep driving around and risk drawing the attention of the police, so he parked the car around the corner from Tom's. Bynum told the agent to remain in the car while he and McCrary went into the cafe. "Let him sit here and I will see what I can do," Bynum said.

"Are you fixing to get some money?" asked McCrary.

"Come on," was the reply.

Wilson, nervous about letting the men out of his sight, protested at being left in the car by himself. "Hell, I ain't going to be sitting here and let no goddam fucking heat come up and catch my ass in this fucking car," he told the two men. "I wasn't born yesterday. The next thing you would know, I would have to do this son of a bitch for nothing."

Bynum laughed at the thought of the hitman having to kill the sheriff for free.

The two men continued on to the cafe, followed by the undercover agent. Before entering the restaurant, Bynum turned to Wilson and told him to wait outside. But Wilson ignored the old man's order and followed Bynum and McCrary into the cafe and watched as the two men walked to the rear of the restaurant and disappeared into the bathroom. In less than a minute, McCrary returned and whispered to the agent, "He's put the bread on me."

Wilson and McCrary left Tom's Restaurant and drove directly to the Holiday Inn, where the anxious Baxley awaited them. Once McCrary was in the motel room, agents once again searched him. Using a pair of pliers, Sheriff Bob Collins pulled from McCrary's shirt pocket two hundred-dollar bills, intended as a down payment for the killing of the sheriff. Each of the two bills was folded in the same way—folded in half lengthwise, and then folded again in half.[9] Linda Darlene Sullivan had described the bills Charles Hale said he had gotten from Bynum as being folded the same way.

Baxley began to go over what the undercover agent and Hugh Otis Bynum had said during their meeting. There had not been the clear-cut confession that Baxley had hoped there would be, but Bynum had said enough to tie him to a conspiracy to kill Sheriff Collins and others. When McCrary had suggested that they wanted four men killed, Bynum had agreed by saying "Yeah." Also, Bynum had boasted that he could have had the sheriff killed himself before the "news had gotten out on him." Then Bynum had told the agent that he wouldn't have cared if the sheriff had been killed a month ago.

Perhaps even more incriminating was what was never spoken. Bynum never had said that he wanted no part in the plan to kill the sheriff or the others and never had made a comment that would distance him from a plot to have someone killed. Then there were the two hundred-dollar bills that Bynum had tucked in McCrary's shirt pocket.[10]

Baxley was troubled by the fact that Loy Campbell's name had never been mentioned in the conversation. But there was something discussed that night that convinced Baxley that what Billy Ray McCrary had told him in Montgomery was the truth. McCrary had talked about the burning of Bynum's house and barns following the shooting of the two black youths. McCrary said that Hugh Otis estimated his losses to be $92,000, the exact figure Bynum had used when discussing with the undercover agent what the sheriff and the others supposedly had done to him.[11]

Baxley gave the order to arrest Hugh Otis Bynum. He planned to charge Bynum with exploding a bomb outside of an occupied dwelling, a charge that under Alabama law carried a life sentence upon conviction.

After leaving Tom's Restaurant, Hugh Otis Bynum drove to his sister's house for a visit. At about 7 P.M., agents spotted his Buick Electra 225 heading out of Scottsboro in the direction of Hollywood to the north. A few minutes later, Bynum pulled his car into Billy Ray McCrary's gas station at Martintown Hill. As he stepped from the car, BATF agents Don Barrett and W. K. Blankenship and Jackson County sheriff's detective George Tubbs pulled up in their cars, stepped out, and greeted Bynum with an arrest warrant. Bynum, however, tried to sit back down in his car, forcing Barrett to pull the man from the car and place him under arrest. The lawmen searched the car and discovered a pistol hidden within reach of the old man.[12]

A few moments later, Sheriff Bob Collins arrived on the scene. Bynum had nothing to say to the sheriff, and Collins ordered him taken to the county jail, located on the second floor of the courthouse, where Bill Baxley was waiting.[13] It was Baxley's first opportunity to meet with the man who was now accused of paying Charles Hale to plant the bomb in Loy Campbell's car and conspiring to have four men killed. Baxley was somewhat startled when he saw Bynum. "He looked like a harmless old man," Baxley later recalled of their first meeting.[14]

During the booking procedure, Baxley told his investigator, John East, to read Bynum his rights and to see if the prisoner wanted to make a statement. East said Bynum did not want to talk. Bynum placed a call to his Scottsboro attorney, Morgan Weeks, and told the lawyer of his arrest.[15] The wealthy land-

owner, the great-grandson of the man who had founded Scottsboro, was then led to a jail cell and locked away. It was 6 December 1974, two years and two days since five sticks of dynamite
had blown away the front end of a 1971 Pontiac and taken Loy
Campbell's legs.

During the ride to the airport, Baxley reviewed the events of
the night. He thought it was a good arrest and, even though it
would take a lot of hard work, he was confident that his team
could put a good case together.

Waiting for the plane to be readied to take him back to
Montgomery, Baxley turned up the collar of his overcoat against
the north Alabama winter cold. He suddenly realized that, while
hurrying to get ready for the plane flight to Scottsboro, he had
picked up his father's overcoat by mistake. Keener Baxley had
died the previous year. Reflecting on his father, Baxley realized
that this date, 6 December, was his father's birthday. "Daddy
would have been proud of that moment," Baxley recalls thinking
to himself.

The tough law-and-order judge from Dothan would have been
pleased that his son had broken such a tough case.[16]

II   *Terrorize Scottsboro*

Word of the arrest of Hugh Otis Bynum spread quickly through
Scottsboro. There were those who had suspected all along that
Bynum and Billy Ray McCrary might have been involved in the
bombing, and there were those who firmly believed there was
no way Bynum could have done such a thing. Differing opinions
of the arrest divided the town, and more than twenty years later,
the guilt or innocence of Hugh Otis Bynum is still a divisive
subject in Scottsboro.

Following Bynum's arrest, his attorney in Scottsboro, Morgan
Weeks, contacted Birmingham lawyer Roderick Beddow, Jr., who
had defended Bynum in April 1971 when he stood trial for shooting the two black teenagers. On the Saturday following the ar-

rest, Jim Fullan, one of Beddow's partners, made the two-hour drive from Birmingham to Scottsboro and met with Weeks and with Hugh Otis Bynum in the jail.

The first task of the lawyers was to have bail set for Bynum so that they could make arrangements for his release.[1] In most arrests, if a judge has issued an arrest warrant, bail is set at the time the warrant is issued. In the case of Hugh Otis Bynum, the warrant had been issued by Jackson County Circuit Court Clerk Charles William Wann. In Alabama a circuit court clerk has the power to issue a warrant after office hours but does not have the authority to set bail amounts. Weeks and Fullan needed to find a local judge who had the power to set a date for a hearing so that bail could be set.

Finding a judge on this Saturday proved to be a challenge. Both County Court Judge John Haislip and Circuit Court Judge John B. Tally were out of town and would not be back in Scottsboro until the following week.[2] Fullan and Weeks sought out the probate judge of the county, R. I. "Bob" Gentry. They learned that Gentry was at an antique auction in Arab, a small town some thirty-five miles south of Scottsboro. The two lawyers drove to Arab, where they found Gentry at the auction.[3]

In Alabama, the office of probate judge is an administrative position and does not require any previous training in the law. A probate judge's duties include the issuing of driver's licenses, fishing and hunting licenses, the filing of wills, deeds, and land transactions, and occasionally performing a wedding. The only time a probate judge comes close to being anything like a court-room judge is when he is called on to preside over an insanity hearing. Gentry was a graduate of Auburn University's School of Veterinary Medicine. He was an animal doctor, not a lawyer.[4]

When Bynum's attorneys first approached him, Gentry was reluctant to sign the writ of habeas corpus, the legal document needed to set a hearing for the posting of bail. Gentry had known Hugh Otis Bynum for more than twenty years, ever since he had moved to Scottsboro from the Long Island community near Bridgeport. But he also knew and was a friend of Loy Campbell. In fact, Judge Bob Gentry was a friend of almost everyone in Jackson County, and the last thing he wanted was to be caught up in a legal nightmare.[5]

Fullan and Weeks assured Gentry that he would be simply setting in motion the legal proceedings to get Bynum out of jail.

"All you will be doing," the lawyers told him, "will be getting the ball rolling to get an old man out of jail." That would be the extent of his legal involvement in the case, the attorneys told him. Reluctantly, he signed the writ and set a hearing in the matter for the following Tuesday. Gentry believed that Judge Tally or Judge Haislip would be back in town by then and that one of them would preside over the hearing.[6]

Although Hugh Otis Bynum was now locked in the Jackson County Jail, the investigation into the bombing of Loy Campbell was far from over. It was now the job of John East and the other investigators to substantiate everything Billy Ray McCrary and Linda Darlene Sullivan had told them. It was also John East's job to put the facts of the case together in such a way as to be best presented to a jury.[7]

Over the next several weeks, investigators questioned dozens of people about their knowledge of the actions of McCrary and Bynum in the days before and after the bombing. The agents found several witnesses who had seen the two men together several times in the days just before the First Monday bombing. Witnesses had also seen the two men together frequently during the months following the bombing.[8]

Baxley and his investigators were also anxious to talk to Charles Hale about his part in the bombing. The elusive Hale was now wanted by federal authorities for his part in the Mims, Florida, bank robbery. He was wanted in Florida for the murder of the hapless young man who had recognized him, and prosecutors in Alabama had named him as a coconspirator with Hugh Otis Bynum in the bombing of Loy Campbell. Surely the young man's luck would run out and he would be captured, giving Baxley the opportunity to question him.[9]

A few days after Bynum's arrest, authorities issued a warrant that allowed John East, Don Barrett, and the other investigators to search the old man's house on Scott Street. East was struck by the dilapidated appearance of the millionaire's home. The white, rambling two-story house appeared not to have been painted since Bynum's father had moved out of the house in the fifties. The yard and grounds around the house were unkempt and overgrown with weeds and wild honeysuckle vines. "It would have been the perfect place for a Halloween spook house," East recalls.[10]

The investigators found the inside of the house just as spooky as the outside. It appeared that Bynum had not cleaned the interior of the house since the rest of the family had moved to their new home on the ridge overlooking town. True to the whispered rumors, the old man did indeed sleep on a mattress in the corner of one room. There did not appear to be a source of heating, and the house had the aroma of a place that had been shut up for years.[11]

In their search of the house, the investigators failed to turn up any significant pieces of evidence linking the old man to the bombing conspiracy. They did find a .30–06 hunting rifle that they confiscated. But there were some things the investigators found that only added to the mystery surrounding Hugh Otis Bynum.[12]

On one side of the mattress where the wealthy landowner slept, the investigators found a newspaper clipping detailing his 1971 conviction for the shooting of the two black teenagers, and there was a list of the men who had served on the jury. There was also a Bible that lay beside the mattress. East recalls leafing through the Bible and coming across a letter written to Bynum by a woman who apparently had visited him during a stay in Scottsboro. East does not recall the contents of the entire letter, but he does remember that the substance of the letter indicated she was disappointed that Bynum was not the gentleman she had supposed him to be. The tone of the letter indicated that something had happened between the woman and the wealthy recluse that she had found offensive.[13]

In a closet, they found two changes of identical khaki pants and shirts. The rich landowner apparently did not own more than three sets of identical clothes. In another room there was a pile of soiled underwear. As he changed his undershorts, the old man apparently chose to buy new ones instead of washing those he had worn.[14] Then, in one room, the investigators made the most bizarre discovery. In that room, there were hundreds, perhaps a thousand or more of the cardboard tubes found at the center of toilet paper rolls. It appeared that the man had never thrown one of the cardboard tubes away, but for some unknown reason had saved them by tossing them into that one room. "I have never been able to change out a roll of toilet paper without thinking about Hugh Otis Bynum," John East says of that strange discovery.[15]

On Tuesday, 10 December 1974, at 10 A.M., the first hearing

in the case was scheduled to be held, and Probate Judge Bob Gentry, the man schooled in veterinary medicine, was shocked to discover that he was the man who was to preside over the hearing. Gentry is surely one of the most colorful political figures in Jackson County history. A native of Chattanooga, he had moved with his family as a boy to the remote Long Island community, north of Scottsboro. He had attended Auburn University and had returned to Jackson County to set up his veterinary practice before deciding to enter politics and run for the office of probate judge. In 1974, he had been probate judge for close to fifteen years. By the time he left office in 1995, his tenure was the longest of any probate judge in Jackson County history and among the longest in Alabama history.[16]

Gentry always has had a friendly and direct manner. Fond of a good joke, he sprinkles his language with expletives, although he is cautious about what he says in the presence of ladies and preachers. Ultimately, he wielded great political power in the county. He was never shy of a political battle and proved time and time again that in spite of his down-to-earth, country appearance, he was a shrewd politician. In addition to his passion for politics, he loved woodworking, and often could be seen around the courthouse dressed in work clothes and smelling of sawdust. Parts of antique clocks often were spread on his office desk.

On this Tuesday in December 1974, it was not the shrewd politician or the lover of antiques who presided over the courtroom in Jackson County but a man determined to be kept from being drawn into the legal maneuvering and a man determined to do what he felt was right. Gentry said he had been misled by Bynum's attorneys when they had asked him to sign the writ of habeas corpus. As a symbol of his displeasure, he refused to sit at the judge's bench in the courtroom; instead, he stood in front of the bench with his arms crossed.[17]

The courtroom was packed with reporters and a crowd of spectators. Loy Campbell, the man who had lost his legs in the bomb blast, sat with his crutches next to the judge's bench and faced Hugh Otis Bynum, who sat at a table with his attorneys. Roderick Beddow, Jr., one of the most prestigious criminal lawyers in the state, had come to Scottsboro from Birmingham to join his law partner, Jim Fullan, for the proceedings. Bynum was dressed in his usual khaki pants and shirt and showed no emotion as the lawyers fought the legal skirmish. At the state's counsel table sat a silent Attorney General Baxley. Noticeably absent from Baxley's side was Tommy Armstrong, the district attorney in whose jurisdiction the proceeding was being held.[18]

Gentry began the proceeding by saying he had no objection to setting bail for Bynum but that he did not have the legal expertise needed to hear the case. He would need more time to prepare, he told Bynum's attorneys. He repeated that Fullan and Weeks had misinformed him and that they had told him he would not have to preside over the hearing.[19] "If it's my cookie, I'll eat it," Gentry said in his colorful manner. "But I have been put unfairly in a very embarrassing position. I was told wrongly, for even though I don't want to keep any man in jail longer than he should be, I am simply not qualified to sit on such a case."[20]

"What we have told you," lawyer Fullan said in reply, "is that we would have no objection to you or any other judge holding this hearing. The plain and simple truth is that the Alabama Constitution and the Code provide that a man is entitled to bond unless there is good likelihood that he will receive the death penalty. We all know that we don't have the death penalty anymore. We are here today on a writ of habeas corpus, the only thing that stands between a citizen and his government."[21]

Gentry was not swayed by the arguments. "I knew I wasn't qualified to have the hearing and all I am asking for is time to conduct it in a proper manner," he said. "I assumed it would be transferred to a proper court." At that, he ordered that the hearing be delayed for ten days.[22]

After the hearing, Fullan told reporters, "I suspect we'll be before the Court of Appeals in Montgomery before the day is over."[23]

Curiously, in spite of repeated invitations by Fullan to enter into the legal argument, Bill Baxley sat at the counsel table and never spoke a word. He later recalled that he had known Gentry had his mind made up. The outcome of the hearing was precast, and he saw no point in entering into the argument.[24]

Following the hearing with Gentry, Baxley agreed to a second hearing that same day, this time before County Judge John Haislip, who was now back in Scottsboro. However, despite the arguments of Bynum's attorneys, the results of the hearing before Haislip were nearly the same as the hearing held with Judge Gentry. Over the objections of the defense attorneys, Haislip

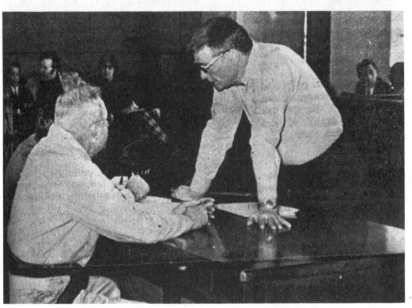

Above: Hugh Otis Bynum, Jr., and his attorney, Roderick Beddow, Jr., on 10 December 1974, during the preliminary hearing. *Below:* Jackson County Probate Judge R. I. Gentry talks with Bynum (*seated*) and his attorney on the same day. (Photos courtesy *The Daily Sentinel*)

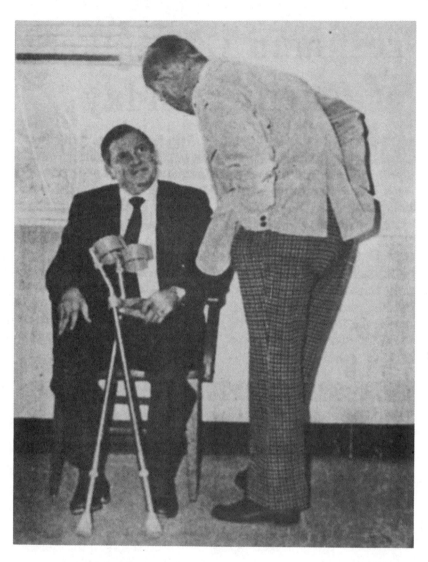

Loy Campbell (*seated*) and Jackson County Sheriff Bob Collins during a break in the preliminary hearings on 10 December 1974. (Courtesy *The Daily Sentinel*)

ruled that the Jackson County court system had jurisdiction over the case and he postponed the hearing. Haislip continued the hearing to the following Tuesday. The judge said he would consider bond for Bynum at that time and that until then Hugh Otis would have to remain in the county jail.[25]

Beddow and Fullan left the Haislip hearing with a resolve to take the case to a higher court. The next day, after filing the necessary papers, the two attorneys found themselves in Montgomery, arguing for the release of Hugh Otis Bynum before the Alabama Court of Criminal Appeals.[26] Beddow vigorously argued that Bynum was being held illegally and he asked the higher court to take jurisdiction and hold a hearing so that Bynum could be set free. However, Baxley argued that the proper jurisdiction was in Jackson County, where the crime had taken place. He also told the court that the crime of which Bynum was accused was so vicious that bond could not be justified.[27] The appeals court justices sided with Baxley and ordered the 17 December hearing before Judge Haislip to be held. They also ruled that Bynum could be kept in jail without bail until the time of that hearing.[28]

While his attorneys fought his legal battle, Bynum remained locked in cell 2 in the Jackson County Jail. He had little to say to the jailers and only grunted when they tried to enter into conversation with him. His loyal friends visited him often. Fred Casteel, owner of the Variety Bake Shop and Bynum's closest friend, made sure he had his breakfast of oatmeal every day, and Tom Sisk, owner of Tom's Restaurant, made sure Bynum had his mashed potatoes and asparagus for lunch and the usual eggs over easy and sausage for dinner. To his friends, he maintained his innocence.[29]

On Tuesday, 17 December, Bynum made his appearance in court before County Judge John Haislip.[30] Once again, the courtroom was packed with reporters and the curious. The jury box was filled with police officers who came to view the proceeding.[31] Billy Ray McCrary was the main witness in the state's effort to block bail for Bynum. He detailed how Bynum had wanted the four men killed and told how he had found Charles Hale to carry out the bombing.[32] Questioned by Jim Fullan, McCrary said he had not been promised anything for his testimony. He said he had not been given immunity for his testimony in the case. A shocked Bill Baxley said nothing as McCrary lied about the lack of immunity.[33] ABI agent Marvin Bryant detailed for the judge how the undercover agent had accompanied McCrary to talk with Bynum. Bryant said he monitored the radio transmission of the conversation between the agent and Bynum.[34]

During a break in the hearing, Baxley got McCrary alone and blasted him for lying about immunity. "What the hell are you doing?" Baxley demanded. "I know you think you are helping us but you are really hurting us. Our deal was that you tell the truth, about everything, or I will send you away for life."[35] Even though McCrary promised that in the future he would stick to the truth, his lie about the immunity heightened Baxley's fear that a jury would never believe the man.

At the end of the day-long hearing, Judge Haislip ordered Bynum to be jailed without bond until a county grand jury could be convened in January. Haislip ruled that there was sufficient evidence to believe Bynum might have been involved in the plot to have Campbell and the other men killed.[36] Bynum's attorneys said the next rung on the legal ladder would be a second appearance before the Alabama Criminal Court of Appeals, and on Friday, 20 December, Bill Baxley and Roderick Beddow locked horns over whether the old man should be released.[37]

While the legal wrangling went on, investigator John East continued to seek evidence that could be used to convince a jury that Billy Ray McCrary and Linda Darlene Sullivan were telling the truth. The day after the hearing before Judge Haislip, East met with McCrary to question him once again. East was especially curious about the statement McCrary had made to the undercover agent, Harold Wilson, while riding with Hugh Otis Bynum, about getting "beat for some money the other day." McCrary had gone on to say, "With a deal with a guy, we put up some goddam money and the guy, well, I got put in jail, see." John East wanted to know what McCrary was talking about.[38]

The perennial con man chuckled as he related to East how he and another man, a salesman from Huntsville, had gypped Bynum out of some money. McCrary had convinced Bynum that the slick-talking salesman was a syndicate hitman. Bynum had given the man the money to kill Sheriff Bob Collins, and later the salesman and McCrary split the cash. McCrary said the incident had taken place two or three weeks before he was picked up on the bootlegging charge.[39]

East was dumbfounded. It was hard to believe that less than a month before he was arrested—and *after* agent Don Barrett had told him he was a suspect in the bombing case—Hugh Otis Bynum had still been plotting to have someone killed and was even willing to put up a sizeable amount of money to have the murder carried out.[40] East wanted to know who the man was and where he could be found. McCrary said that he had only met the man a couple of times and that all he could remember about him was that his name was "Henry." He told East that the man had given him a business card with his name and address. A few days later, McCrary brought the card to East. The man's name was not Henry, as McCrary had recalled; it was John Poarch, and he had a Huntsville address. East immediately set about trying to find him.[41]

East and Baxley agreed that if they could find the salesman and if he could substantiate McCrary's story, it would be an important piece of evidence linking Bynum to a continuing conspiracy to have Loy Campbell and the other men killed. However, over the next few weeks, all efforts to find Poarch failed. On two separate occasions, the investigators sent subpoenas for the man to Huntsville but the documents were returned marked "Undelivered." For the time being, the whereabouts of the salesman who had hoaxed Hugh Otis Bynum remained a mystery.[42]

On Friday, 20 December, Bill Baxley and Roderick Beddow appeared for a second time before the Alabama Criminal Court of Appeals to argue their case. Baxley told the court that Hugh Otis Bynum was a "vicious conspirator" whose release from jail would "terrorize the town of Scottsboro." He was not exaggerating the fear the townspeople felt. Many of the town's elected officials felt they might also be targets of Bynum's unpredictable wrath and some had gone so far as to install elaborate security systems in their homes. Many of them would not start their cars in the morning without first searching for explosives.[43]

But Beddow argued that the prosecution had not presented any evidence that indicated that "Scottsboro would be in terror of this harmless, sixty-year-old man." He called the hearing before Judge Haislip "a sham" concocted by Baxley to hold the old man in violation of his rights. Referring to the state's prime witness, Billy Ray McCrary, Beddow told the court that Baxley had been forced "to reach down into the bowels of the earth" for witnesses to make a case against Bynum.[44]

Once again the appeals court sided with Baxley. In a unanimous ruling, the court ordered Bynum to remain in jail without bail. Beddow again vowed a further appeal in a continued effort to win release of his client.[45] A week later, on 27 December, the attorneys presented the case to the Alabama Supreme Court. Again Baxley emerged as the victor. The high court ruled that Bynum should remain jailed. Sidestepping a potential landmark decision on the argument concerning the denial of bail in cases involving the death penalty (which at that time had been abolished by the U.S. Supreme Court), the court said Beddow should have sought a new hearing before the Court of Criminal Appeals before bringing the case to the higher court.[46]

Nevertheless, Beddow succeeded in winning another hearing with the state supreme court, and on Tuesday, 7 January 1975, the high court once again reviewed the case and once again ruled that Bynum could be held in jail without bond. Baxley had again argued that Bynum's release would terrorize Scottsboro and that if bond were set at all, it "should be set at two billion dollars."[47]

On the first Monday of 1975, 6 January, Billy Ray McCrary's wife Joyce was at home with two children in a house trailer where the couple lived outside of Scottsboro. About 7 P.M., a car pulled up outside the home and someone in it fired a shotgun blast into the trailer. Joyce and the two children were unharmed, but the incident fueled a media frenzy linking the shooting with Mc-Crary's testimony against Hugh Otis Bynum. It turned out, however, that the shooting was a result of more of McCrary's rowdiness. The police learned that the shooting stemmed from a poolroom argument between Billy Ray and another man. Under other circumstances, the media virtually would have ignored the shooting.[48]

During the last week of January, the Bynum case took another turn. Jackson County Circuit Court Judge John B. Tally said he would not preside over the Bynum trial. Tally excused himself from hearing the case, citing the fact that he himself had been the intended target of a bomb. On 30 January, Howell Heflin, chief justice of the state supreme court, appointed Talladega Circuit Court Judge William C. Sullivan to preside over the trial of the wealthy landowner. Sullivan, a graduate of the University of Alabama Law School, had served as a judge since 1958. He had the reputation of being a firm but fair-minded jurist.[49]

On Monday, 3 February 1975, Baxley and Beddow returned for

a third time to the Alabama Supreme Court to argue their case. This time, citing the extraordinary circumstances of the case, the court ruled in Bynum's favor and ordered the bail be set at $100,000 for the old man. Chief Justice Howell Heflin was joined by justices James Faulkner, Richard Jones, and Janie Shores in voting for the setting of bail. Justices Pelham Merrill, James Bloodworth, and Hugh Maddox voted against setting bail for Bynum. Justices Reneau Almon and Eric Embry chose not to take part in the decision. Embry had been a senior partner in Beddow's law firm and had been appointed to his seat on the state's highest court only recently. He did not take part in the Bynum decision because of his past business relationship with the defense attorney.[50]

Later that day, after being locked in the Jackson County Jail for nearly two months, Hugh Otis Bynum was finally released on bail. Two of Bynum's friends, Scottsboro businessmen Eb Cornelison and George Hunter Payne, along with his sister, Jessie Sue, and a cousin, Mark Scott Skelton, signed for Bynum's release, using their land as security for the $100,000 bond.[51]

On Wednesday, 12 February, Judge Sullivan presided over an arraignment hearing for Bynum, formally charged with "willfully exploding a device near an inhabited dwelling." As he had during each of his courtroom appearances, Bynum showed no emotion as he stood before Judge Sullivan. Dressed in his khaki shirt and pants, peering through the thick eyeglasses, and speaking barely above a whisper, Bynum told the judge he was not guilty of the charge.[52]

After hearing the plea, Sullivan set a 24 March date for the trial to be held in Scottsboro. He also set a 26 February date to hear several motions by Bynum's attorneys. At the 26 February hearing, Judge Sullivan agreed to the defense attorneys' motion that Bynum be tried separately from Charles Hale, who was still the subject of an intensive manhunt. The judge also agreed to the defense's request that the tape of the conversation between Bynum and the undercover agent be examined to verify it had not been tampered with or altered.[53]

During the first part of March, investigator John East and Assistant Attorney General Bill McKnight traveled to Talladega to meet with Judge Sullivan concerning the case. Judge Sullivan told the men he had some concerns about the charge brought against Bynum. Sullivan said there were sufficient grounds to argue that Campbell's house had not been an occupied dwelling at the time of the explosion. As incredible as it sounded, one could make the argument that since there was no one in the house when the bomb went off, technically, the house was un-occupied. Had the car been just two feet closer to the garage at the time of the blast, it would be easier to make the charge against Bynum stick. As it now stood, Judge Sullivan said he might be forced to rule in favor of the defense and drop the present charge against Bynum. He told McKnight and East to return to Baxley with the advice that he reconsider his strategy.[54]

On Monday, 10 March, at Baxley's request, Judge Sullivan ordered that a special grand jury be convened in Jackson County to consider a second charge against Bynum. The members of the grand jury agreed that there was enough evidence to warrant a charge of attempted murder against Bynum, and the court ordered Bynum to appear for arraignment on the following Thursday. Just moments before the arraignment hearing, officers formally arrested Bynum for the attempted murder of Loy Campbell. After pleading not guilty to the new charge, Bynum posted an additional $25,000 bond and was released.[55]

All the pretrial maneuvering was over. The stage was set for the two titans of Alabama law, the combative Roderick Beddow, Jr., and the young prosecutor from Dothan, William J. Baxley II, to enter into one of the great legal battles in Alabama history. The legal duel symbolized the clash of values brought about by the change taking place in Scottsboro. In the balance hung the fate of Hugh Otis Bynum, Jr.

Part Two The Trial

12   *The Voir Dire*

Springtime in north Alabama can be one of the prettiest seasons of any place in the world. The dormancy of winter gives way to the awakening of spring with a magnificent display of color. The hillsides are splayed with a vernal green as leaves appear on the oaks, maples, poplars, and other hardwood trees. Wild redbud trees burst forth with a show of pink, and the snow-white flowers of the dogwood trees appear as a bride welcoming the groom of the new season. Wild azaleas and the many varieties of wild-flowers tinge the forest floors with a spectrum of brilliant colors. Bright yellow jonquils burst forth, revealing the places where old homeplaces once stood.

But the beauty of springtime in north Alabama contrasts with violence as nature makes the transition between winter and summer. Violent thunderstorms often rake across the land, and vicious tornados can leave behind them destruction and sometimes death as a springtime calling card. The once-prosperous and thriving town of Paint Rock was virtually wiped out in 1932 when a tornado skipped across Jackson County one morning, leaving thirty-two persons dead in its wake. In all, the killer storm of 1932 left 307 people dead in Alabama. It was one of the great natural disasters in the state's history.[1]

The close of seasons in north Alabama can also be finicky. Spring may begin as early as February or as late as mid-May. Freak snowstorms have been known to mix with dogwood blossoms in April. But in March 1975, springtime had come gently to north Alabama, and during the week before Easter, the mild weather allowed farmers and gardeners to till the land and prepare for the year's crop.

In preparation for the trial of Hugh Otis Bynum, Attorney General Bill Baxley had assembled a team of some of the state's brightest, most talented, and idealistic prosecutors. Baxley's chief assistant was John A. Yung IV. Bespectacled and of small stature, Yung had the appearance of a college professor. The appearance masked a zealous and combative litigator.[2] Yung, a graduate of the University of Alabama School of Law and the Georgetown Law Center, had gone to work for the attorney general's office

John A. Yung IV
(Photo courtesy John A. Yung IV)

in 1971 when Bill Baxley had taken office. A man of rigid principles, Yung came to understand that Baxley was a unique prosecutor. "I didn't realize it at the time," Yung later said, "but there has never been an attorney general in Alabama like Baxley. At that time, he did what was right without regard to politics."[3] At the time of the Bynum trial, Yung had only recently returned to Baxley's staff. He had left in 1972 to join the Peace Corps and had served in Micronesia as a legislative counsel. After two years in the Peace Corps, he returned to work with Baxley.[4]

William M. Bowen, Jr., was a twenty-eight-year-old graduate of the Cumberland School of Law and had been on Baxley's staff since 1973. Bowen had proven his value to Baxley time after time as an exceptionally observant lawyer. Bowen had a talent for taking notes and recording the details of testimony during lengthy trials. The night before delivering his closing arguments in a case, Baxley sat down with Bowen and together they prepared the notes that Baxley used in his final appeal to the jury.[5]

Baxley also asked Donald G. Valeska II to join the team. Valeska and Baxley had been college friends, and Valeska was one of the first attorneys Baxley hired after taking office as attorney general. It had been Valeska who had come to Scottsboro with Jack Shows in the days following the bombing of Loy Campbell.

Attorney General Bill Baxley (*left*) and Don Valeska (*center*) are
accompanied by Baxley's bodyguard, Alabama State Trooper Tom
Moore (*right*), as they leave the Jackson County Courthouse
during a break in the Bynum trial.
(Courtesy *The Jackson County Advertiser*)

Shortly before the arrest of Hugh Otis Bynum, Valeska had left Baxley's office to join the district attorney's office in Mobile County. Because Valeska had been a part of the early investigation into the bombing, Baxley asked him to join the team in Scottsboro.[6]

The four men formed a powerful and talented team of prosecutors, but Hugh Otis Bynum had an equally powerful pair of defense attorneys working to prove his innocence. Roderick Beddow, Jr., of Birmingham had become one of the best defense attorneys in the state. He had a masterful grasp of details that enabled him to chip away at the credibility of witnesses.[7] Beddow was teamed with Al Bowen. A big man, Bowen was an intimidating figure in a courtroom. He had most recently served as a federal prosecutor at the trial of native American activists arrested during the standoff at Wounded Knee, South Dakota. His courtroom skills were superb.[8]

Baxley's case against Bynum was based on the theory that the bombing of Loy Campbell was a single incident in a conspiracy to kill at least four people. According to Baxley, the conspiracy lasted for a period of more than two years. The motive for the attempt on Campbell's life and the plot to kill the others was simple—Bynum wanted revenge for some perceived wrongs committed against him.[9]

But Baxley's case against Bynum was built mainly on the testimony of Billy Ray McCrary, and this fact worried the attorney general. McCrary's criminal reputation was so well known that convincing a jury he was telling the truth would be the greatest challenge of the trial. And the flamboyant McCrary was not helping matters. McCrary had somehow gotten the money to buy himself a flashy red and white Cadillac. He could be seen driving the car around town and around the courthouse square. He was also known to have been bragging and boasting about his part in the case.[10]

The atmosphere in Scottsboro was tense, and emotions surrounding the case were running high. There were many in the town who resented that Hugh Otis Bynum was standing trial while the well-known felon, Billy Ray McCrary, was free to ride around in his big automobile. Reflecting on the case some twenty years later, Baxley and Don Valeska said that they could not recall a case in which they experienced as much hostility as they did in Scottsboro during the Bynum trial. Baxley certainly did not need the added resentment brought on by McCrary's behavior around town.[11] Baxley cautioned McCrary to "keep a low profile," and to "tone down" his behavior, but he later admitted that trying to keep McCrary from doing what he wanted was like trying to tell the wind not to blow. Baxley would have to deal with McCrary's reputation as best he could. He would have to find some way to convince a jury that McCrary, this time, was telling the truth.[12]

Not all the resentment was aimed at Billy Ray McCrary, however. Many townspeople wondered openly why the state's most powerful prosecutor had decided to come to the small town and put a prominent citizen on trial. Some people suspected that Baxley was using the Bynum trial for pure political gain. The resentment over Baxley's involvement, however, went beyond politics. He was viewed as an outsider, just as those who had come to the defense of the Scottsboro Boys had been outsiders, and just as those who had occupied the South following the Civil War had been outsiders. He was a young liberal, just as most of those who had come to the South during the tumultuous civil rights movement had been young and liberal in their beliefs about justice. The resentment people felt toward Bill Baxley was rooted in part in the town's past.

As Baxley was preparing his team for the trial, John East was trying desperately to find the mysterious ring salesman who McCrary had said helped him pull the hoax on Bynum. Baxley had his doubts that the ring salesman even existed. The story seemed so fantastic that Baxley suspected McCrary had fabricated it. However, in the days before the trial began, East managed to make telephone contact with the will-o'-the-wisp salesman, but the man refused to answer any of the investigator's questions and said he would consent to be questioned only in the presence of his attorney. Efforts to get the man to testify seemingly had hit a stone wall.[13]

Anticipating that the defense might try to paint Bynum as a citizen of impeccable character, Baxley ordered East to find witnesses who could testify to Bynum's past acts of violence. All in all, East was able to substantiate, through court records and the testimony of witnesses, more than a half-dozen acts of violence committed by Hugh Otis Bynum.[14] East located William Seabolt Snodgrass, the father of the young black boy whose puppy Bynum had shot. Snodgrass told East he had intended to have a warrant issued for Bynum's arrest but that when Bynum got word of his intent, he showed up with a shotgun at a construction site where Snodgrass worked. Co-workers hid Snodgrass until Bynum left, but the man was so shaken by Bynum's visit that he refused to leave the safety of his house for over a week.[15] East also talked to the widow of Vaughn Parker, the man whom Bynum had cut so badly that it had taken surgeons hours to suture the knife wounds. The woman told East her husband had been in constant pain from the attack until the day he died.[16] East talked to one of the leaders of the black community in Scottsboro, Archie F. Stewart, who told East that Bynum had threatened him. Stewart was not intimidated by Bynum's threats, however, and Bynum backed down when Stewart threatened to use violence in his own defense.[17] East also learned of an instance when Bynum had pulled a gun on one of the town's black preachers and forced him to beg for his life on bended knees.[18]

Curiously, some victims would not talk to East. Harold Foster, the lawyer who had escaped Bynum by crawling through the tiny window in the service station, refused to cooperate with East. No matter how hard the investigator tried, Foster would not agree to testify against the wealthy landowner.[19] Still, East had managed to gather enough evidence and testimony to counter any "character issue" that might be brought up during the trial.

In the week prior to the start of the Bynum trial, federal authorities had brought Linda Darlene Sullivan to Huntsville. On Thursday, 20 March 1975, Sullivan returned to Scottsboro for the first time since fleeing Alabama with Charles X. Hale. Sullivan had been subpoenaed by Jackson County District Attorney Tommy Armstrong to testify against Jerry Brent Gant of Pisgah. Gant was charged with harboring escaped convict Howard Luther Dickerson. The two men had come to know each other while serving time in the state penitentiary.[20] Sullivan's testimony that Gant had told her he knew Dickerson had escaped helped send him back to prison for violating his parole.

On the Saturday before the Bynum trial was to begin, defense attorney Al Bowen traveled to Huntsville to talk with Sullivan. She refused to talk with him, however, and Bowen came away empty-handed. His hopes of discovering what she might say while on the witness stand were stymied by Sullivan's refusal to talk.[21]

On Monday, 24 March 1975, the trial of Hugh Otis Bynum began. It was the week before Easter. It was a rainy, overcast day that threatened to become stormy. In Atlanta, on that same morning, a tornado ripped through the city, killing three people.[22] But Jackson County was spared the violent weather this time.

At 9 A.M. on that Monday in March, a pool of about fifty prospective jurors was seated in the large courtroom in the Jackson County Courthouse. It was the same courtroom that had been the scene of the famous Scottsboro Boys trial more than forty years earlier. Built to seat 170, the courtroom now overflowed with newspaper reporters from all over the state and a crowd of curious spectators who had come to watch what they felt sure was the best show in town. The crowd was so large that the corridors outside the courtroom were clogged with people waiting to get a seat inside. Some of the spectators brought sack lunches to the courtroom so that they would not lose their seats at the noontime break. During breaks in the trial, vendors came into the courtroom and hawked snacks, cold drinks, and parched peanuts.[23]

In one section of the courtroom, a knot of about a half-dozen Bynum supporters viewed the trial. Don Valeska and Bill Bowen dubbed the group "the peanut gallery." The vocal group openly hissed and booed whenever the prosecution scored a legal victory, while cheering and clapping when the defense scored. Throughout the course of the trial, Judge Sullivan repeatedly was forced to demand that order be restored.

In the courtroom only a few feet separate the lawyers' tables from the spectators. During the Bynum trial, it was not uncommon for farmers in starched blue-bib overalls to lean from their seats to advise the attorneys openly and often loudly. "Ask him such and such," Bill Bowen recalls the spectators urging the lawyers as they questioned witnesses. The case may have been one of the last truly populist trials. The people were there for more than the dispensation of justice. They wanted to be a part of it.

For Bill Baxley, jury selection is the most important part of a trial. It was imperative that the court select jurors who would be the most likely to believe Billy Ray McCrary. It was also im-

Above: Hugh Otis Bynum, Jr. (*center*) with his lawyers,
Roderick Beddow, Jr. (*left*) and Al Bowen, at the time of his trial.
(Courtesy *The Jackson County Advertiser*)

Below: Courtroom in the Jackson County Courthouse, site of the
trials of the Scottsboro Boys and Hugh Otis Bynum, Jr.
(Photo by Byron Woodfin)

portant to select jurors who lived outside of Scottsboro and thus were outside the sphere of the influence of the Bynum family. Baxley had hired several local lawyers to aid him in determining which jurors to select. One of those attorneys, Joe Dawson, proved to be the most valuable because of his knowledge of and association with so many of the residents of Jackson County.[24]

During the voir dire examination, Baxley questioned each prospective juror intensely about his feeling toward McCrary and toward Bynum. After more than three hours, the prosecutors and the defense attorneys finished selecting the twelve men who ultimately were to decide Hugh Otis Bynum's fate. The twelve jurors they chose to hear the case were: Wesley Allen of Scottsboro, who worked as an accountant at the Redstone Arsenal in Huntsville; James Bell, a carpenter from Dutton; Archie Douglas Farmer, a factory worker from Pisgah; John H. Graham, a retired TVA worker from Stevenson; Homer Johnson, a farmer from Woodville; Grady Roberts, a farmer from Pisgah; Roy Shaw, a farmer from Fabius; Gaylon E. Stone of Scottsboro, a worker at a local lumber company; J. L. "Buck" Strickland, a merchant from Flat Rock; James Westmoreland, a factory worker from Stevenson; John Wann of Scottsboro; and Allison Wynn of Scottsboro, who worked at a local automobile dealership.[25] At thirty-two years of age, Doug Farmer was the youngest of the jurors. He had only recently become a Church of Christ preacher. During the jurors' first meeting together, they elected Farmer the jury foreman.[26]

Judge Sullivan ordered that the jury be sequestered during the length of the trial at the Holiday Inn in Scottsboro.

At 1:40 P.M. on Monday, 24 March 1975, the all-male, all-white jury took its place to hear the evidence in the case of the State of Alabama versus Hugh Otis Bynum, Jr., for the attempted murder of Loy Campbell.

13   *A Crazy Motive*

Bill Baxley used his opening statements to lay out for the jury his theory of the motive and conspiracy that led to the attempted murder of Loy Campbell. He related to the jury how Bynum had shot the two black teenagers, how his house had been burned by the two arsonists, Bates and Price, and how Loy Campbell had represented the two men and had become a target of the old man's thirst for revenge. Baxley called it "a crazy motive" and promised he would call witnesses to show that Bynum had developed "an obsessive hate" that drove him to want to have Campbell, Bob Collins, John T. Reid, and Jay Black killed.[1]

Baxley also used his opening statement to counter the defense's anticipated attack on the character of his chief witness, Billy Ray McCrary. "If Billy Ray McCrary's word was all we had," Baxley told the jury, "we wouldn't be up here. We're not trying to make a silk purse out of a sow's ear."[2] Baxley told the jury that McCrary was "as guilty in this as anyone else and just as bad as anybody who has ever lived in Jackson County."[3] "Sometimes it's a case of taking half a loaf or no loaf," Baxley said of using McCrary's testimony against Bynum. "If we waited for a whole loaf, sometimes we would have no loaf."[4]

Baxley expected that the defense would try to pin the attack on Charles Hale, who had still managed to elude capture. Baxley told the jury not to focus on Hale, the coconspirator named with Bynum in the indictment. "We are taking this one trial at a time and Hugh Otis Bynum is on trial today," he told the jury.[5]

In response to Baxley's opening statement, Roderick Beddow told the jury that Hugh Otis Bynum was a victim of a frame-up perpetrated by Billy Ray McCrary to save himself. He told the jury he would call witnesses who would testify that it was McCrary who hated the four men and that McCrary had threatened to blow them up. Beddow repeated his assertion that Baxley had to "reach into the bowels of the earth to find witnesses," and he called McCrary a "vermin."[6] "Mr. Bynum says he didn't do it, and he holds no grief or ill will or animosity toward these men and that he is not guilty," Beddow told the jury.[7] Beddow's defense of Bynum was based on his belief that the case was folderol. Beddow believed it was nonsense to think that a man of Bynum's prominence would conspire with the likes of Billy Ray McCrary to have these men killed.

Irene Glass, one of Loy Campbell's neighbors, was the first witness to testify in the trial. A nurse anesthetist, Irene lived only one house away from the Campbell house on Hamlin Street. John East remembers that Mrs. Glass was a compassionate witness who dreaded testifying. Like many witnesses, she found herself a victim of circumstances. Though the motivation to do the right thing ultimately wins out, these witnesses often would rather be somewhere else than in a courtroom. East urged Baxley to handle Mrs. Glass with care and concern.[8]

The nurse recounted the events of that fateful First Monday morning in Scottsboro. "I was standing in the kitchen, and I heard an explosion. And my help, I had help, Minnie Cotten. I thought one of the neighbor's houses across the street had blown up and she ran out the door and came back and said, 'There has been an explosion.' "

"What did you do then?" asked Baxley.

"I grabbed my coat and ran out the door. She and I ran up to Mr. Campbell's house. The smoke was clearing from the car, what was left of it, and I could see Loy in the car; and I thought he was dead."[9]

Glass told Baxley that she and her maid and another neighbor, Dr. Tommy Foster, a dentist, were the first to get to the injured man. "I opened the door, and I tried to get him out, but I could not get him out of the car. His legs were entangled in the debris. And Minnie Cotten and Dr. Tommy were trying to get his legs freed so we could get him out. We were afraid of fire or another explosion. And it seemed forever, but it wasn't, the ambulance arrived. And they put him in the ambulance; and I ran home and called the operating room to ask the operating room supervisor if she would send some doctors to the emergency room, that the ambulance was bringing Loy in and he would need assistance."

Baxley then asked Mrs. Glass to describe Campbell's legs following the explosion.

"Horrible, just barely hanging on by just a little bit of flesh, a little bit of skin." With that memory, the witness broke down and turned to Campbell sitting at the table with the team of prosecutors. "I am sorry, Loy," she said in a voice filled with emotion.[10]

Asked to describe the car, she said, "It's real hard to describe the car, it was torn up so bad. The whole front end and the front seat, all the front part of the car was torn up completely. You cannot describe it. And the back, well, the back was still together; but the front was all torn up."

Bynum's attorneys had no questions for the nurse, and she was excused from the witness stand. John East was so moved by Irene Glass's compassion that after the trial he wrote a tribute to her in what he described as the style of Ernest Hemingway, his favorite author. It was a tribute to the lady who had cradled the injured man's head until help arrived. The day the trial ended, a woman approached East to thank him for the way Baxley had treated Mrs. Glass as she testified. East never learned the woman's name.[11]

The prosecution next called Porter Dawson, who was the fire chief of Scottsboro at the time of the First Monday bombing, to the stand. In response to questioning by John Yung, Dawson testified to hearing the explosion while standing outside his auto parts business located just off the courthouse square. He said he had gotten the call about the explosion and quickly drove the one mile to Hamlin Street where he and Loy Campbell lived as neighbors.

"After you arrived at the scene of the explosion at Loy Campbell's house, what, if anything, did you do?" asked Yung.

"Well, I got out of my car and proceeded to Loy's car. And Mrs. Irene Glass was at the car at that time, and her maid. And I proceeded to help remove Loy from the car."

"Could you describe for the jury the scene as you saw it at that time?"

"Yes, sir. The car, the front part of the car was, of course, blown to bits. The fire wall, the dash, the steering wheel, and all was blown back against Loy and his legs. And the doors were blown open. And Loy, at that time, was slumped toward the outside of the car, with Mrs. Glass supporting him. And of course, I proceeded on the opposite side of the car, the passenger side of the car, to work Loy's legs up out of the debris from the fire wall, the wiring, and installation [*sic*], to get his legs up to where we could remove him from the car." Dawson testified that Campbell's "face had a black-looking texture as if it was burned from powder burns and Loy was just making sort of a gurgling sound." The fire chief also said he smelled the odor of dynamite. Then for John Yung and the jury Dawson described the damage to Campbell's house. He told the jury that the explosion had blown out several window panes, cracked an entrance door, and blown off some of the cabinet doors in the kitchen. Dawson then identified a series of photographs made of the demolished car and the damaged house on the day of the explosion. In the background of one of the photographs, Dawson pointed out his own house located on the opposite side of the street from Loy Campbell's house and at the end of the dead end street.

Then John Yung turned the questioning to the fires that had occurred in September 1970. "Mr. Dawson, were there any fires in or around Scottsboro on the 25th of September, 1970?"

"Yes, sir."

"What first occurred in or around Scottsboro, to your knowledge, on that date?"

"Well, we had three fires. We had one on Mountain Street, one on Oak Street, and one on West Maple."

"What was the extent of the damage done by these three fires?"

"Total loss."

"Do you know who was the owner of the three structures?"

"Yes, sir."

"Who was it?"

"H. O. Bynum."

In his cross-examination of Dawson, Roderick Beddow did not dispute that there had been an explosion on 4 December 1972, and that it had critically injured Loy Campbell, but he did attempt to dampen the fire chief's testimony concerning the fires that followed the shooting of the two black boys in 1970. He knew that the aim of that testimony was to further Baxley's theory about the motive for the bombing.

"Do you know how many fires you had in Scottsboro on the 24th day of December, 1970?" asked Beddow.

"Not without checking the records."

"The 23rd?"

"I would have to check the records, sir."

"26th?"

"I would have to check the records."

"Or the 28th?"

"I would have to check the records."

"Did you check with the probate office to find who, in fact, did own these residences?"

"Mr. Bynum."

"That isn't what I asked you, chief."

"No, sir, I did not."

The prosecution next called agent Donald Barrett of the Bureau of Alcohol, Tobacco and Firearms to the witness stand. Baxley considered Barrett's testimony to be vital to the case. But problems had developed with the federal agent. Barrett had spent two years trying to solve the Scottsboro bombing case, and apparently it had irritated him to know that in the end, state and local authorities had broken the case.[12] Loy Campbell recalled the day, shortly after Hugh Otis Bynum had been arrested, that Barrett stopped him and, in a fit of anger, began cursing George Tubbs, the county investigator who had played a major part in solving the crime. "All he is is a damn carpenter," Campbell remembered Barrett saying; "he's not an investigator." It seemed that Barrett's frustration at not being able to solve the case had boiled over.[13] Baxley needed his testimony, however. The attorney general knew the agent had done a good job in collecting the physical evidence at the bombing scene. It had also been Barrett who had questioned Linda Darlene Sullivan, the woman who had first linked Hugh Otis Bynum to the bombing of Loy Campbell.

Barrett began his testimony by telling how he had been called from Huntsville to the scene of the bombing in Scottsboro. He described for the jury the destruction of Campbell's 1971 Pontiac. "Well, parts of the car were scattered over about a block portion, parts of it on top of the Caldwell Elementary School. . . . The most damage was to the front end, with the charge being placed over the frame by the left front wheel. The front of the car was disintegrated and scattered over a large area, parts of it, and part of the hood and other large pieces thrown over the house into a yard, as far away as a block, nearly." Barrett then described the discovery of a fragment of an M-6 military electric blasting cap underneath the car. He also told the jury that a piece of wire, later identified as a piece of the leg wire leading to the blasting cap, had been found in the area of the car's engine.

The prosecution introduced as evidence the air filter that Jimmy Dewayne Evett had found in the shrubbery near the

Caldwell School several days after the bombing. Barrett testified that tests showed the air filter was from Campbell's car and that it had not been on the car at the time of the explosion.

Over the objections of the defense attorneys, Barrett testified about the interview of Linda Darlene Sullivan and the discovery of the dynamite buried behind the Carriage House Apartments in Scottsboro. He identified a photograph of the five sticks of dynamite and blasting cap, and the prosecution introduced the photograph as evidence. Barrett testified that laboratory tests of the wires and the blasting cap found behind the apartment showed that the blasting caps were identical to those collected at the State Highway Department and that the wires matched those found at the bomb scene. He told the jury that the only place in and around Scottsboro where military style blasting caps could be found was the State Highway Department bunker in Scottsboro. Baxley ended his questioning of Barrett by asking the federal agent to identify the two hundred-dollar bills taken from Billy Ray McCrary the night Hugh Otis Bynum was arrested.

In his cross-examination of Barrett, defense attorney Al Bowen attempted to cloud the agent's testimony as an expert. Referring to the fragment of blasting cap found beneath the car, Bowen asked the agent, "Well, you don't know of your own knowledge, Mr. Barrett, that that's a piece of an M-6 blasting cap, do you?"

"Only by the laboratory report."

"Well, you didn't make a laboratory report?"

"No, sir."

"You're not qualified to, are you?"

"No, sir."

In response to Bowen's questioning, Barrett then testified that over the course of the investigation he had interviewed Billy Ray McCrary at least three times, the first time just three or four days following the bombing. Bowen did not pursue this line of questioning and the court excused Barrett from the witness stand.

The ambulance driver, Joe Morrison, Jr., in response to questioning by John Yung, described what he found when he arrived at the scene of the explosion. "Well, Mr. Campbell was in, I guess you could say he was in shock, sitting in a car. There was, seemed like a gentleman and a lady standing there holding his head up.

Of course, his legs were badly mangled. And of course, black smoke, I mean black particles all over his clothing and stuff."

"Did you assist in removing him from the wreckage?"

"Yes, sir."

"Approximately how long did it take you to get him out of the wreckage?"

"Well, after we once got up under it, I would say it took us a couple of minutes, myself and my attendant, and one of the firemen helped." Morrison said it took no more than three or four minutes to get the injured man to the hospital.

The prosecution next called Dr. Durwood Hodges to the witness stand. In response to questioning by Yung, the doctor told the jury he had been called to the hospital's emergency room to treat Loy Campbell on that Monday morning in December. The doctor described for the jury the surgical procedures that the treatment team had taken to save the man's life. He said that initially, they had amputated Campbell's right leg above the knee. The surgeons, according to the doctor, tried to save the knee joint of the left leg, but he said that later it also had to be amputated because, he said, "it had some, too much damage to it, too much explosive damage, and it had some foreign bodies in it, also."

In an effort to drive home to the jury the seriousness of Campbell's injuries, Yung asked the doctor again if the explosion had blown the man's legs off. This graphic testimony tested the patience of Roderick Beddow. "Now, we are going to object to that, if it please the Court. That's the third time he's been through it with this witness." Judge Sullivan sustained the objection.

Before excusing Dr. Hodges from the witness stand, Judge Sullivan had a question of his own. "Doctor, one question. It's kind of a legal question. Would you describe the wounds that you found on this patient you testified about to be the type that would be greatly dangerous to life and health?"

"Yes. The leg injuries and the abdominal injuries would be dangerous, too."

Dr. Hodges's testimony concluded the first day of the trial, and Judge Sullivan allowed the jury to retire to the Holiday Inn with instructions not to discuss the case among themselves.

Although there had been no testimony in that first day to link Hugh Otis Bynum or Charles Hale to the bombing of Loy

Campbell, the statements of the witnesses had established the basis of the attempted murder charge. Their graphic testimony had established that a bomb had been planted in Loy Campbell's car and that indeed there had been an explosion that day in December 1972. The judge's final question of Dr. Hodges and the doctor's response established that the injuries caused by the explosion had been life-threatening. Bill Baxley was confident there would be no disputing that there had been an attempt on Loy Campbell's life.[14]

On Tuesday, the second day of the trial, however, the first major test of the case against Hugh Otis Bynum was to come. The prosecution was to call the flamboyant and controversial Billy Ray McCrary to the stand.

14   *He Will Bleed to Death*

Billy Ray McCrary was enjoying his role as star witness in the trial of Hugh Otis Bynum. On Tuesday, 25 March 1975, the second day of the trial, McCrary drove his red and white Cadillac to the courthouse for his day in court. Sporting a bright red polyester leisure suit and with his long white hair combed straight back, he looked the part of a flashy country and western music star.[1]

McCrary began his testimony by telling Bill Baxley and the jury that he had known Hugh Otis Bynum since he was a boy. He detailed his release from the federal penitentiary in Atlanta on 15 November 1972. He said he had gone to stay with his father and mother in Hollywood, and that within a week after his release, Bynum had come to see him. He said he remembered Bynum was driving the white 1970 Buick Electra.

"When he first come up, my mother said, 'There is Hugh Otis out there,' and I got up and went to the door and went outside. And by that time, he was outside the car. And he shook hands with me and asked how I was doing and when I got out of prison and he said, 'I got some people I want to get killed.' And I said,

'Who is it?' He said, 'Loy Campbell, Bob Collins, Jay Black, and John T. "Mayor" Reid.' I told him I didn't know nobody. I hadn't been out fooling around. I would look around and see if I could find somebody. He said he had $2,000 each.''

Baxley asked McCrary why Bynum wanted the men killed.

McCrary told the jury, "I said, 'Why do you want these people killed?' He said, 'They cost me $92,000'; and I said, 'How did they cost you $92,000?' And he said, 'I shot some niggers over in my pasture,' and said, 'they, Bob Collins, put me in jail,' and said, 'the niggers burnt my house, my barns, and my hay, and done away with some of my cattle.' "

"He said that cost him $92,000?"

"Yes, sir."

McCrary told the jury he had met with Charles X. Hale and the young man had agreed to kill the four men marked by Hugh Otis. Baxley then asked McCrary to describe how he and Charles Hale had met with Bynum outside Tom's Restaurant on the courthouse square.

"What did you say when you first saw Hugh Otis in Tom's Restaurant with Charles Hale?" Baxley asked.

"I said, 'Hugh Otis, I got you a man here.' And he said, 'Well, here's ole Charles back.' "

"And then you went outside?"

"Right. We come out, the three of us, Hugh Otis Bynum, Charles Hale, and me, come out and got in the car; and he told Charles that he would give $2,000 to kill Loy, Bob Collins, Mayor Reid, and Jay Black. I stayed in the car with them probably fifteen minutes. I got out of the car and Charles stayed in the car with Hugh Otis."

Then McCrary told the court about meeting with Charles Hale the night before the bomb exploded. He said Hale had come to visit him at the home of his ex-wife, Lilah, and had called him outside the house. "He said, 'I am going to blow up Loy Campbell and Bob Collins tonight.' "

"What did you say to him?"

"I told him, 'You have the job; you know what to do.' I told him, 'Don't fool around and blow yourself up.' "

McCrary then described meeting with Hugh Otis Bynum on that First Monday in December 1972, an hour or so after the bomb exploded in Loy Campbell's car. "Hugh Otis Bynum was over in front of Tom's Restaurant. I was standing there talking to John Frank Hurt, Roy Barclay, and George Hunter Payne. Hugh Otis was standing over close to Tom's door. He nodded for me to come over. I walked over there, and he said, 'Well, we got the job done'; and I said, 'He might not die'; and he said, 'Oh, yeah, he will bleed to death.' "

"Who said that?" Baxley asked.

"Hugh Otis Bynum."

McCrary said Bynum had suggested that the two men not be seen together for a while. He said that he had seen Charles Hale a few days after the bombing and that Hale had told him the investigators had been to the State Highway Department questioning him. A week or so later, McCrary met again with Hale, who now wanted to be paid. McCrary said he and Hale then went to Tom's Restaurant and met with Bynum, who agreed to the payoff. McCrary said he followed Bynum to Bynum's burned house on Mountain Street while Charles Hale waited for them in town. He said that Bynum got an envelope containing twenty hundred-dollar bills from the trunk of the Buick Electra. After the payoff was completed, Bynum again suggested they not be seen together for awhile. McCrary testified Bynum told him, "Don't get nobody else right now. Let them wait awhile. Let things kind of die down." McCrary told the court that later that day he met with Hale and gave him $400, keeping $1,600 of the payoff money for a drug debt that Hale owed him.

Although Al Bowen and Roderick Beddow continued to object that any conversations McCrary reported having had with Charles Hale constituted hearsay testimony, Judge Sullivan allowed McCrary to relate a conversation with Hale when the young man told McCrary what had happened the Sunday night he planted the bomb. "Charles Hale told me he went up to Bob Collins's house first, and a dog scared him away. He couldn't put a bomb on Bob Collins's car. He said he left there and went down on Hamlin Street, down at Loy's place. He didn't say where he parked his car. He said he parked it near and got out, opened the door, and pulled the latch hood, and raised the hood. And he said he couldn't get the dynamite on the car; he couldn't wire it up without taking the breather off, laid it down beside the car, and forgot it. He fastened the hood back down and forgot the breather. And he happened to think about he left the breather off. He went back and got the breather and carried it somewhere near the school and hid it in some bushes or honey-suckle or something close to the school."

McCrary said that not long after the bombing, Bynum began coming around, sometimes three or four times a week, to wher-ever McCrary was and continued to talk to him about killing the four men. McCrary said this went on for two years. "Every time he would come around he said, 'Well, you ain't got nobody to kill them?' And I said, 'No, I ain't found nobody yet, Hugh.' And he said, 'Looks like Charles ain't going to do nothing else.' He said, 'Looks like Charles laid down on me.' That's all the man wanted to talk about was killing somebody."

At this point, the cocky felon, feeling at home on the witness stand, leaned back in the witness chair and propped his feet on the railing of the witness box. This gesture infuriated Baxley. He knew that McCrary's arrogant attitude would not help his credibility in the eyes of the jury.[2]

"Take your foot down, Billy Ray," Baxley snapped.

"It's kind of boring sitting here."

"Well, you sit up there and tell what conversations you had, now."

"Every time the man would come around," McCrary resumed, "he would ask me if I found anybody to kill Bob Collins and finish the job on Loy Campbell and Mayor Reid and Jay Black."

"Would he say anything, or did he have an additional reason to be mad at them or talking about the same reason, or what would he say, if anything?"

"He said, 'Reid's trying to run the town.' He said his people was responsible for this town."

"Whose people, now?"

"Hugh Otis Bynum's people."

McCrary testified that Bynum had become obsessed with the Campbell case and that he kept all newspaper articles written on the case. "Anything he would find concerning the case, he would bring it up there, and he said the very time to get John T. Reid was on First Monday. He said to get him right after a First Mon-day. When all these merchants were around here causing all this trouble about parking spaces. He said they were all kicking about Reid and he said, 'Somebody would think some of that bunch done it.' "

Then McCrary detailed for the jury how, just two or three weeks before his arrest on the liquor violation, he and John Poarch, a jewelry salesman out of Huntsville, had hoaxed Bynum out of $3,000. McCrary told the jury he had introduced Poarch to Bynum as a hitman who would be willing to do what Bynum wanted done. McCrary recalled Bynum telling the salesman, "I want, especially want, Bob Collins killed and I want him killed bad. I don't care how he's dead, just so you kill him." McCrary said Poarch told Bynum that for $3,000 he would drill holes in the floor of the sheriff's house and gas him.

In response to Baxley's questioning, McCrary said he recalled a specific conversation he had had with Bynum about Loy Campbell shortly after Campbell had returned home the first time from the hospital.

"Tell what that conversation was," said Baxley.

"He said something about there wasn't no use in bombing Loy no more. He said, 'He ain't got no legs,' and Hugh Otis said, 'Just catch him and cut his throat.'"

At this point Billy Ray McCrary had been on the witness stand for nearly two hours. Anticipating a lengthy cross-examination, Judge Sullivan excused the jury for lunch. However, following lunch, the court learned that Beddow and Bowen were not yet ready to conduct their questioning of McCrary. Bill Baxley was left to round up witnesses to fill out the day's testimony. Baxley called Jimmy Dewayne Evett, the part-time janitor at Caldwell Elementary School, to the stand. Evett testified to finding the breather cap assembly from the Campbell car in some bushes by the school.

The prosecution next called BATF agents Larry Luckey and Robert Miller to the stand. The two agents substantiated much of what Donald Barrett had said concerning the physical evidence gathered at the scene of the explosion. Agent Luckey described finding the fragments of the blasting caps and the fragments of the blasting cap leg wires found on what was left of the car's engine. He said that investigators had taken these pieces of evidence to the BATF laboratory in Atlanta and had turned them over to the chief chemist, Clarence Paul, for analysis.

Agent Miller testified that it was he who had gone with Donald Barrett to the State Highway Department bunker in Scottsboro and that he and Barrett had gotten three of the M-6 military style blasting caps kept there. He said that he and Barrett had sent the blasting caps to the laboratory in Atlanta, where technicians had exploded one of them for comparison with the fragments found at the scene. Miller also described how he and Barrett had removed the carburetor from the Campbell car, and that scratches on the air filter assembly found at the school matched scratches found on the carburetor.

BATF fingerprint expert Frank Kendall testified that fingerprints found on the air filter assembly did not match those of Charles Hale or Billy Ray McCrary. Kendall also testified that he could find no latent fingerprints on the two hundred-dollar bills taken from McCrary's shirt pocket the night Bynum was arrested. In response to questioning by John Yung, Kendall told the jury that when he took the bills from the evidence envelope, he noticed they had been folded in an unusual way. He said both bills had been folded once lengthwise and again crosswise.

Wendell Britt, an office clerk at the State Highway Department bunker in Scottsboro, next took the stand. He testified that in the weeks prior to the bombing, Charles Hale had worked for the highway department and had been on projects where dynamite had been used. Britt's testimony established that Hale had easy access to dynamite and blasting caps while working at the highway department.

It was now time for Sheriff Bob Collins, one of the four men whom Hugh Otis Bynum was accused of conspiring to kill, to take the stand. The sheriff began his testimony by telling the court that he had known Hugh Otis Bynum for about eighteen years. He said that until the shooting of the two black teenagers, Willie McCamey and Claxton Green, his relationship with Bynum had been good. The two men often met at Tom's Restaurant, and Bynum frequently came by the sheriff's office for social visits. After Bynum's arrest for shooting the two teenagers, however, he stopped coming by the office, and whenever Collins saw Bynum at Tom's and spoke to him, Bynum left the restaurant without saying a word. The sheriff also testified that he had known Billy Ray McCrary for about fifteen years and that he had often seen McCrary and Hugh Otis Bynum together. Collins told the court that on the night Bynum was arrested and charged with the bombing of Loy Campbell the old man had $331 tucked in his shirt pocket. He said each of the bills was folded lengthwise and then folded again in the middle.

Roderick Beddow knew that the sheriff's testimony concerning his relationship with Bynum was intended to support the prosecution's motive theory. Beddow had to show the jury that there was nothing unusual about the strained relationship between Bynum and Collins. Beddow also planned to use the cross-examination of the sheriff to discredit Billy Ray McCrary.

"Now, you have seen Mr. Bynum, you have seen him in the company of many people over there in front of Tom's Restaurant," Beddow said to Collins.

"Yes."

"And you have seen Billy Ray McCrary with the company of many people at the Sisks'?"

"Yes, sir."

"The square is his home, isn't it? I am talking about McCrary."

"His home?"

"Yes, sir. He is up and down and around this square and in and out the courthouse all the time?"

"He is down here a lot, a whole lot."

"And he is driving a big, long, red and white Cadillac when he comes to town, doesn't he?"

"Yes, sir."

"And he pulls up and stops and walks in and out of the courthouse and acts like he owns it?"

"I couldn't tell you about that."

"Well, he walks a little taller since Hugh Otis Bynum was arrested than he ever has before, hasn't he?"

"I hadn't noticed it."

Then Beddow stiffly questioned the sheriff about his relationship with Bynum. "Well, sheriff, to hold a political office, most all political animals have to have a rather thick skin, don't they, to be a good law enforcement officer?"

"It helps."

"Or good D.A. Sometimes they are criticized and sometimes they are not, isn't that true?"

"Yes, sir."

"And during the course of your tenure of some eight or nine years, I will ask you, as a matter of fact, aren't there several people that used to frequent your office that don't frequent it anymore?"

"I imagine there are. I can't think of any."

"That's nothing strange about politics, is it?"

"I don't know about that."

"Well, on those occasions where you say you have seen Mr. Bynum and tried to start some conversation with him and he remained mute, he made no overt act or no overt gesture to your person, did he?"

"No."

"You say on other occasions, he just got up and walked out, and it's a free country, isn't it?"

"Well, I would think so."

"If a fellow wants to get up and walk out of a cafe or restaurant, you couldn't quarrel with that, could you?"

"No."

"That is a right, and that is a privilege?"

"Yes."

The prosecution next called Billy Ray McCrary's brother Virgil to the stand. Unlike his brother, Virgil had not run afoul of the law and had made his living at a local factory. In response to John Yung's questioning, Virgil said that within a week or ten days after McCrary had gotten out of the federal penitentiary, Hugh Otis Bynum had visited his brother at their father's house in Hollywood. Virgil also testified that McCrary had given him two hundred-dollar bills on the day of their father's funeral, two weeks after the bombing. Virgil said his brother had told him he had gotten the money from Hugh Otis Bynum. In his cross-examination of Virgil McCrary, Beddow succeeded in bringing out for the jury that Billy Ray McCrary had been arrested forty-seven times and that he had been in and out of prison.

The second day of the trial ended with the testimony of Annie Ruth McCrary, Billy Ray's mother. Following his pretrial interview of Mrs. McCrary, John East had told Baxley she would make a convincing witness. "She had that clear, strong, mountain voice of a hard-working woman with conviction," East said of her.[3] Just as Virgil McCrary had, Mrs. McCrary told the court that Hugh Otis Bynum had come to her home and talked with Billy Ray shortly after her son had been released from prison. She also said she had seen Billy Ray and Bynum together on the courthouse square several times.

During one of the breaks during this second day of the trial, Loy Campbell met with John East. "Do you really want to find this Poarch fellow?" Campbell wanted to know. East told Campbell that he and Baxley felt it was imperative to find the ring salesman in order to corroborate Billy Ray McCrary's testimony. Campbell told East there was an attorney in Huntsville who might be able to help find Poarch. The lawyer's name was Herman "Buck" Watson, Jr.[4]

Buck Watson had been friends with Loy and Bunk Campbell for years. The Campbell brothers had grown up just a block away from Watson's home in Fort Payne. Watson had played football for Vanderbilt University, and the Campbell brothers often had gone to watch Watson play.[5] That Tuesday afternoon, Watson was sitting in his office when he got a phone call from Bunk Campbell. Campbell explained to his friend what Baxley and East needed and asked for his help. Watson said he had a private investigator by the name of Artie Wooten who was an expert at locating folks that didn't necessarily want to be found. That afternoon Watson put Wooten on the job. "Don't spook him," Watson recalls telling Wooten. "The attorney general's office has been looking for this guy for several months and they need him in Scottsboro."[6]

Watson placed a condition on his promise to help, however. He sent word to the attorney general that he was not doing this to help out the young prosecutor. "I am not doing this for Baxley," Watson told Bunk Campbell.[7] At the time of the Bynum trial, Watson and Baxley were bitter enemies. At the start of Baxley's first term as attorney general, Watson and his law partner at that time, Jack Giles, had entered into a land transaction with the State Highway Department. Baxley had claimed that the land deal had been done improperly, and he vowed to investigate it. A lower court and later the Alabama Supreme Court ruled there had been nothing improper about the land deal. Eventually, the two men were reconciled, and today Baxley counts Buck Watson among his closest friends. But in 1975, there was no love lost between the two lawyers.[8]

Following the court's adjournment after the second day of the trial, Baxley and some of his staff drove from Scottsboro to Huntsville to meet with Linda Darlene Sullivan. It was the first meeting between the attorney general and the girlfriend of Charles Hale. Sullivan was due to testify against Hugh Otis Bynum, and Baxley wanted to review her story. He came away with the impression the woman was telling the truth. More important, he felt she would make a strong and convincing witness.[9]

Baxley and his staff also used the trip to Huntsville as a chance to relax. Following the meeting with Linda Darlene Sullivan in the Huntsville jail, Baxley took the staff members to dinner and drinks. It gave them time to review the day's testimony. Billy Ray McCrary's testimony was now the backbone of the prosecution's case. But McCrary now had to face Bynum's attorneys, and Baxley knew how hard Roderick Beddow would try to shake McCrary from his testimony.[10]

15   *Like a Child That Has Seen a New Toy*

On Wednesday, 26 March 1975, the third day of the trial, it was Roderick Beddow's turn to question Billy Ray McCrary. It was his job to try to cast doubt on McCrary's previous testimony, and it was a job he took on with enthusiasm. Beddow knew that the defense of Hugh Otis Bynum in part depended on discrediting McCrary's testimony. McCrary was no newcomer to the halls of justice, however. He had been on the witness stand many times over the years, and he proved to be a stubborn and combative witness.

In order to paint for the jury a portrait of a man who would do anything to save himself, Beddow began his cross-examination by asking McCrary about his being sentenced in 1970 by U.S. District Court Judge Clarence Allgood on the charge of illegally distilling whiskey. McCrary denied he had threatened to kill Robert Reed, the mayor of Hollywood and McCrary's partner in the illegal still venture, when he found out that Reed would testify against him. He also denied that he told authorities he would help them prosecute former Jackson County Sheriff Fred Emmett Holder and Ed Pepper of Montgomery if they reduced his sentence for the moonshining conviction.

Beddow's questioning of McCrary produced an amusing exchange. "And during your tenure of time in the Atlanta penitentiary, you told authorities that if they would reduce your sentence, you would help them implicate Fred E. Holder, didn't you?" asked Beddow.

"I didn't do ten years in the penitentiary."

"I said tenure, t-e-n-u-r-e, tenure."[1]

McCrary denied that he had initiated contact with Hugh Otis Bynum while in prison or in the days following his release on 15 November 1972. Beddow continued to ask him if he had repeatedly called Tom Sisk's restaurant by telephone looking for Bynum. "Well, I will ask you, as a matter of fact, prior to seeing Mr. Bynum, you called Tom's Restaurant on the morning you saw him, four or five times inquiring or asking about Mr. Bynum?"

"I don't remember."

"And after the five or six calls, if you didn't get him on the phone and make a request of Mr. Bynum to come to your father's house?"

"I don't remember that either."

"Did you tell him that you wanted to see him but you had no transportation?"

"No, sir."

"You didn't make that statement?"

"No, sir."

Then Beddow wanted to know about the alleged meeting between McCrary and Bynum at the home of McCrary's father. "After you got in the car, what was the first thing said or done by you or the first thing said or done by Mr. Bynum?"

"Hugh Otis said he had some guys he wanted to get killed."

"He just came right to the lick log. Y'all sat down in the automobile and Mr. Bynum said, 'Look, I have some guys I want killed'?"

"He said, 'I have been looking around and I can't find anyone.'"

Beddow questioned McCrary about his divorce from his first wife, Lilah, and his subsequent marriage to his young, attractive mistress, Joyce Turner. Beddow also wanted to know if McCrary had used his paternal love for his children as a way to get parole from prison. Beddow was attempting to paint for the jury a portrait of a man without morals and without a conscience. "Well, as part of this offer that you made to the federal government, you told them you wanted to go home and live with your wife and six kids, didn't you?"

"No, sir."

"Well, now, Mr. McCrary, you didn't tell them that your children were the only thing you had to live for?"

"I don't think so."

"And that you had been working in that cotton mill while in prison?"

"Yes, sir."

"And every cent you made, you sent home to them?"

"The money, I didn't even see. The check that I got in the penitentiary, it was sent to Joyce."

"Joyce received the check?"

"Yes."

"It wasn't sent to your family, not your six kiddies?"

"Sure wasn't."

"In fact, you haven't given them anything since the 15th day of November, 1972, have you?"

"Yes, sir."

"And paying $244 a month for a big Cadillac, aren't you?"

"Yes, sir."

At another point in his testimony, McCrary admitted that he didn't know the birthdays of his children and wasn't quite sure of their ages. He also denied that he had given one of his sons several matchboxes filled with marijuana to sell and that later he had told Lilah the boy "was too dumb" to sell the dope.

Beddow now turned his questioning to the meeting McCrary had testified had taken place between him, Charles Hale, and Hugh Otis Bynum. In response to Beddow's questioning, McCrary recounted how he and Hale had come to the courthouse square and met Bynum in front of Tom's Restaurant. He said the three of them got into Bynum's car.

"After you got in Mr. Bynum's car, what, if anything, did you say, and what, if anything, did Mr. Bynum say, and what, if anything, did Mr. Hale say?"

"Well, Hugh Otis said, 'Here's old Charles back,' and asked Charles how he was getting along. And I said, 'Hugh Otis, Charles said he would do your job.' Hugh Otis said he was ready and said, 'Charles, I got $2,000 for each one—Loy Campbell, Bob Collins, Mayor Reid, and Jay Black.' "

"And what did Mr. Hale say at that time?"

"He told him he would get on the job."

Beddow used this line of questioning to attack McCrary again for his lack of conscience while talking about killing four people. "What did you say, if anything?"

"I didn't say nothing at that time. I was sitting there listening."

"Well, when Mr. Bynum said he would offer him $2,000 for these men, did you say, 'Well, now, wait a minute, fellows. Maybe this has gone too far'?"

"No, sir. I didn't."

"Did you say, 'I don't want to be a party to this thing'?"

"No, sir."

"Did you importune upon either one of them not to commit this act?"

"No, sir. I didn't."

"Did you, in fact, call the sheriff and tell him that there was two people sitting out here on the corner talking about assassinating him?"

"I sure didn't."

"Did you call Mr. Campbell, who had previously been your lawyer, or ask him or advise that someone was talking about killing him?"

"Sure didn't."

"Did you call the D.A. of this county and advise him anything about it?"

"Sure didn't."

"Did you call Mayor John T. Reid?"

"I didn't call nobody."

"You were sitting there listening?"

"Yes, sir."

"You didn't tell them not to do it?"

"No, sir."

"Did you tell them to go ahead with it?"

"No, sir."

"You found Charles and had done your part of the deed?"

"Yes, sir."

Beddow questioned McCrary at length about the alleged meeting he had had with Hale the night before the bombing. McCrary repeated the story of how Hale came to Lilah McCrary's house and called him outside. "Charles Hale told me that he had ten sticks of dynamite, said he had five sticks for Bob Collins and five for Loy Campbell and said that he was going to get Black, but 'I am going to get Bob Collins and Loy Campbell tonight,' " McCrary told the court. McCrary denied that he had ever told his ex-wife, Lilah, that he was the one who wanted Bob Collins and Loy Campbell killed.

Beddow asked, "Well, on this occasion when you were there at Lilah's house, I will ask you whether or not you made this statement to her: 'I am going to kill some son-of-a-bitches. I am going to blow them up and I am going to make them suffer the way they have made me suffer'?"

"No, sir."

"And if she didn't tell you, 'Billy, you can't kill nobody. Only God has the right to give life and take it away'?"

"I know that wasn't said."

"And if you didn't say this, Mr. McCrary: 'You will see, if you put enough dynamite under those son-of-a-bitches, you can blow them into hell'?"

"No, that was not said."

"And if she didn't tell you this, Mr. McCrary: 'Billy you are going to destroy yourself trying to get revenge'? And if you didn't say, 'I am willing to die and go to hell to get them son-of-a-bitches'?"

"Nothing like that was said."

" 'I am going to get Loy Campbell and the sheriff'?"

"No, sir."

"Did you tell her, 'I laid awake while I was in prison thinking about ways to get rid of those son-of-a-bitches'?"

"No, sir."

McCrary also denied ever bringing home the blasting caps that Lilah McCrary claimed she had discovered in his coat pocket. He also denied telling his ex-wife on the night before the bombing that their children who attended Caldwell School could not go to school the following day and that he allowed them to go to school only after he found out their recess would not be held until after 10 A.M.

Beddow then wanted to know about the payoff McCrary said took place between him, Bynum, and Charles Hale. "Well, at this time and on that occasion, Hale told you, didn't he, 'Hey, man, when am I going to get paid'?"

"No, sir, that was the next time I saw him, I believe."

"I will ask you if you didn't say, 'You owe me $1,600 already, man'?"

"Yes, sir."

"When did Hale borrow this money?"

"He didn't borrow no money from me."

"He didn't borrow no money?"

"No, sir."

"What were the circumstances of him owing you $1,600?"

"He owed me $1,600 for some pills."

"Some pills?"

"Yes, sir."

"Did you describe that during the preliminary hearing as dope?"

"I believe so." McCrary went on to say that he had bought the pills for $400 shortly after he had gotten out of the penitentiary. He then sold the drugs to Hale for $1,600, making a $1,200 profit. Pressed for the name of the person who had sold him the pills, McCrary was evasive at first, but then reluctantly identified George Hunter Payne, a Scottsboro pharmacist, as the man who had met him on the square one night and made the transaction. Of the money he said he got from Bynum as the pay-off for the bombing, McCrary described some of the hundred-dollar bills as being "old, yellow-looking money."

Beddow wanted to know how Sam Holland's name had come to be among those whom McCrary said Bynum wanted dead. "Well, did you tell him at that time that, the investigator or the individual that was interrogating you, that Bob Collins and Sam Holland were the ones, they stole and burned his house and cost Hugh Otis around $92,000, and he wanted them dead? Did you tell them that?" asked Beddow.

"Yes, sir. He later brought Sam Holland in. He sure did."

"Well, Sam Holland was right in there at the first by your original statement. Isn't that true?"

"Well, he mentioned him all along."

"He mentioned him and it hasn't been up until now that you thought to tell this jury about Sam Holland?"

"Sir, I don't believe you have asked me about Sam Holland, have you?"

Beddow then turned to one of the critical points in his cross-examination—the meeting between Bill Baxley and McCrary in Montgomery, the day before Bynum was arrested. Under intense questioning, McCrary admitted he had been granted immunity for his testimony and that he had lied about the immunity during the preliminary hearing before Judge John Haislip.

"You lied to Judge Haislip, didn't you?" Beddow asked.

"Yes, sir."

"You sat there under oath in that very chair and lied, didn't you?"

"Yes, sir."

"On three or four separate occasions, isn't that true?"

"I suppose so."

"You suppose so. Well, did you lie to him so many times that you can't remember the number you told?"

"No, sir."

Baxley knew McCrary's admission about his lying dealt a huge blow to the man's credibility. Beddow, sensing his advantage, pressed on.[2]

"Do you remember being asked this question, Mr. McCrary, during the preliminary hearing, 'As a matter of fact, to stay out of jail, to keep your probation from being revoked, you told Mr. Baxley you would tell him anything?' And didn't you tell Judge Haislip, under oath, just like you are today, 'Nobody promised me anything'?"

"Yes, sir."

"And you knew you were lying on that occasion, didn't you?"

"Yes, sir."

"Do you remember this question being asked you, 'Your bond was granted after having this conversation with Mr. Baxley'?"

"Yes, sir."

"And you didn't say, 'I don't know what Mr. Baxley done. All I have been asked to do is to tell the truth, and that's what I am up here for,' is that right?"

"Yes, sir. I suppose so."

McCrary admitted that it was not out of any compassion for his fellow man that he had made the statements to Baxley about Hugh Otis Bynum and he agreed with Beddow that he would have said anything to save his own hide.

"In fact, you told an agent here in the month of February of 1975 'that if it comes to me going to jail or you going to jail, then, brother, you can bet you are going to jail.' Did you tell him that?"

"Yes, sir."

"Only you didn't use that language, did you, Mr. McCrary?"

"I don't remember. I don't remember who it was."

"When you were talking to him, you were talking about one's posterior, weren't you?"

"No, sir. I couldn't say that."

"You didn't say, 'If it means my ass going to jail or your ass going to jail, then you can better believe it's your ass going to jail'?"

"I may have said that."

Baxley, in his redirect examination of McCrary, would not let the testimony about the immunity deal go unchallenged.

"Mr. Beddow asked you, 'Well, were you told, "Well, we ain't going to charge you with nothing"?' and stop right there?"

"Yes, sir."

"And to refresh your recollection, could that sentence have been, 'Well, we ain't going to charge you with nothing as long as you tell the truth'?"

"Right."

"And do you remember what you answered?"

"Yes, sir."

"What was that if you remember?"

"I told you that's what I was down there for was to tell the truth."

"Did you say, to refresh your recollection, 'I say I came down here for the truth. I didn't come down here for no bullshit or to tell no lies or nothing and to the best of my knowledge, that's the way it is'?"

"Yes, sir."

Baxley had some questions of his own for McCrary concerning Sam Holland. "Were you asked in the sentence that Mr. Beddow was reading to you about what Sam Holland, in substance, what Sam Holland had to do with it, do you remember that?"

"Yes, sir."

"Do you recall what your answer was at that time?"

"He said Sam Holland was helping steal his cattle."

"To refresh your recollection, do you remember stating at the later part of the conversation—Mr. Beddow asked you about Sam Holland—'Ain't got a thing in the world to do with nothing and that's some of Bynum's old crazy idea he's got. Sam Holland ain't had nothing to do with nobody'?"

"Yes, sir."

Then McCrary described for the court the time Bynum had

given Charles Hale a rifle. "Charles Hale pulled up over there," said Billy Ray, "and Hugh Otis, I was sitting in the car with Hugh Otis and I said, 'There is Charles,' and he said, 'Yeah, I got a gun here for Charles,' and Charles got out and said, 'Hugh, where is that gun?' And he said, 'I got it here,' and he got it out."

"Who got it out?" Baxley asked.

"Hugh Otis."

"Where was the gun?"

"In the trunk of his car."

"What was it?"

"A .30–06 Remington."

"What did he do or say?"

"He told Charles, 'I want you to take this gun and go up on Bob Collins' farm,' he said. 'He will be coming up there this evening to feed, and you kill him when he comes up there.' And Charles started to get back in the car and Charles says, 'Wait. You didn't give me no shells.' He got a box of shells and a paper sack, and he put them back there and give them to Charles. And Hugh Otis said, 'Oh, yeah, wait a minute, Charles, I got a scope here, too,' and he got a scope out of a little leather pouch."

After nearly five hours of questioning, McCrary stepped down from the witness stand and returned to the witness room. Baxley knew that Beddow had succeeded in damaging McCrary's credibility with the admission of how McCrary had lied about the immunity. Still, McCrary had not faltered in his testimony concerning what had taken place between himself and Hugh Otis Bynum. Nevertheless, Baxley was worried that all the jury would remember was McCrary lying to Judge Haislip. Local newspapers covering the trial touted the fact that McCrary had lied. An article in *The Huntsville Times* detailing the testimony of the third day of the trial carried the headline, "McCrary Admits That He Lied About Immunity," and Scottsboro's newspaper, *The Daily Sentinel,* carried a similar banner.

At 5 A.M. that Wednesday morning, lawyer Buck Watson was awakened at his home by a phone call from Artie Wooten, the private investigator. Wooten had found John Poarch, the jewelry salesman whose testimony the prosecution needed to corroborate what Billy Ray McCrary had said about hoaxing Hugh Otis Bynum out of $3,000.

"Where is he?" Watson wanted to know.

"He's sitting on the sofa across from me," Wooten said. "I am at his house."

Wooten had heard the man might be staying in Tennessee. He had spent the previous night looking all over that portion of Tennessee bordering Alabama, north of Huntsville, but he had no luck finding the man. Finally, Wooten called a friend who worked with the Huntsville utility department and asked the friend to check the records to see if someone named Poarch had perhaps requested that his utility deposit be transferred to another person. It was a long shot.

The persistent Wooten was able to talk his friend into going to the utility department during the early morning hours. After a brief check, his friend discovered that Poarch had indeed transferred the deposit. The private investigator's long shot paid off. Wooten drove to the address given him by his friend in the utility department, and John Poarch answered the door.

"Do you think he will run?" Watson wanted to know.

"All I can tell you," said Wooten, "is that he is here right now."

Watson called Bunk Campbell in Scottsboro with the news. The man had been found, but there might be a problem. Poarch did not want to come back to Scottsboro without first talking with his lawyer. Watson told Campbell that the lawyer's office was located just off the courthouse square in Huntsville and that Baxley should send someone to Huntsville right away. They should look for a Cadillac parked in front of the lawyer's office, Watson told Campbell.[3] Bunk Campbell relayed the message to Bill Baxley, who in turn sent John East and Chief Sheriff's Deputy Paul Mount to Huntsville. Armed with a subpoena, East was told to bring the man back to Scottsboro.[4]

Back in the courtroom, the prosecution called grocer Lonnie Grider to the stand. Grider had operated a family-owned grocery store in Scottsboro called the Blue Bonnet, named for its distinctive blue-tiled roof. He had only recently retired and moved to the small town of Attalla, south of Scottsboro.

In response to questioning by John Yung, the grocer testified that he had seen Billy Ray McCrary and Hugh Otis Bynum pass the store while riding in Bynum's car several times before the bombing of Loy Campbell. He said he often saw the two together as they drove towards some pastureland Bynum owned in the area behind the store. He told Yung that whenever he saw the two men, it was always during daylight hours. He also told

Yung that on the day of the bombing he had told Loy Campbell's brother, Bunk, about seeing McCrary and Bynum together. Under cross-examination by Roderick Beddow, Grider said he could not remember the month or the year he had seen the two together, but that he remembered it was just before the First Monday bombing.

The prosecution called Loy Campbell, the man who over two years earlier had lost his legs in the car explosion, to the witness stand. Campbell told the jury that over the years he had done legal work for Hugh Otis Bynum on a number of occasions. He said he had prepared Bynum's will. In answer to questioning by Bill Baxley, Campbell told of representing the two men charged with burning the house that belonged to Lucy and Jessie Sue Bynum, and he recalled the time Bynum was tried for shooting the two black teenagers. He recalled helping Roderick Beddow, Bynum's defense lawyer in the shooting case, to choose jurors. Campbell described seeing Bynum after he had been convicted of the assault on the two boys. He said he told Bynum he thought he had come out pretty good, " . . . didn't you Hugh? And Bynum said, 'Not so damn good,' and just walked on." Campbell said that after Bynum's trial for shooting the two boys, he never had any legal dealings with him.

Then Baxley asked Campbell to describe what had happened on the morning of 4 December 1972—the day his life was changed forever.

"Okay. I got up about 7 A.M., probably. I sent my daughter, she was six years old at the time, going to school at Caldwell, just across the street. She went to school about 8 A.M. and I stayed around the house, got dressed, and started to work. It was a First Monday and I went out to get my car around 9 A.M., and I got in the car and turned the switch on and boom! It was the only thing I can remember. I was trying to get out of the automobile. I thought it was on fire. The flames had shot up into my face. The next thing I remember, I was at the hospital and Dr. Hodges was slapping around on my face and trying to wake me up and telling me he had to take my legs off."

Baxley then asked Campbell about speaking with Hugh Otis Bynum at the Liberty Restaurant after he had gotten out of the hospital in April 1973. "Now, Loy, after you got back from the hospital, after the bombing, when was the next time that you saw the defendant, Hugh Otis Bynum?"

"I would guess about a month or maybe six weeks later in Liberty Restaurant up on Highway 72 up here."

"Who were with you?"

"My brother, Bunk."

"Did you observe Hugh Otis Bynum at the time?"

"Yes, sir. I was sitting at a big table back on the left as you go in and when I sat down, I was facing right directly towards him."

"Did he come over to speak to you or say anything to you on that occasion?"

"When he started out, he said something about 'You won't run any more races,' or something to that effect, something about I wouldn't run anymore."

"Hugh Otis Bynum said that?"

"Yes, sir."

"Did you understand him plainly?"

"No, sir, I didn't. He kind of mumbles when he talks and it had to do with that. I wouldn't be running anymore."

Baxley wanted to know if Bynum had shown any emotion when he made the ambiguous remark about running.

"Well, ordinarily," said Campbell, "he has absolutely no expression on his face at any time about anything. But then at the first time he looked up from eating and saw me, his face just kind of lit up like a child that has seen a new toy or something."

There had been another incident between the two men at the Liberty Restaurant. Baxley wanted to know about that incident. "Well, the next time you saw him and had a conversation with him, you say this was also at the Liberty Restaurant?" asked Baxley.

"That's right."

"Tell the court and jury, please, sir, everything that was said between you and Hugh Otis Bynum on that occasion."

"All right. He came by the table that my brother and I were eating lunch and again, he had been eating over at the big table where he had the first time I saw him. And he came by and stopped, and he was a little bit behind me and he said, 'Your buddy sent Barrett to see me,' and he said yesterday or sometime. I don't know. It had been within a few days."

"Did you know what he was talking about?"

"No, sir. I believe he said, 'buddy' something, and he said, 'the sheriff.' And then he said, 'Barrett said the sheriff told him that I hired Billy Ray McCrary to blow you up.' And I said, 'Hugh,

I hadn't heard that.' And I said, 'Did you?' And he just smiled and turned around and walked on up to the cash register and walked on out. He didn't say 'yes' or 'no' or make any kind of reply. And he smiled and just grinned kind of, he is a little paralyzed or something, you know, and he kind of sideways-type grinned, and turned and walked off."

"He didn't say anything?"

"He didn't say 'yes' or 'no.' He didn't admit it or deny it."

In his cross-examination of Campbell, Al Bowen tried to shake him from his testimony concerning the conversation at the Liberty Restaurant. "Now, the conversation you had at the Liberty Cafe with Mr. Bynum, I believe you testified that the first time he came over and said something concerning you not being able to run?"

"That's right. He said something about 'You won't be running anymore.' "

"But you don't know. You say it was mumbled and you just didn't understand?"

"No, sir. I didn't then and I don't now."

"And I believe you testified that quite some time later, again at the Liberty, he came by your table and stopped and said something about Barrett had told him that the sheriff had said that Hugh Otis had hired somebody to do this to you?"

"And hired Billy Ray McCrary to do it."

"And you asked him, 'Did you?' "

"I said I hadn't heard he hired Billy Ray McCrary. I heard he hired Charles Hale. I said, 'I hadn't heard that, Hugh Otis. Did you?' And he smiled and turned around and walked off."

"Loy, could you possibly have mistaken that Mr. Bynum said, 'No, I didn't,' and turned around and walked off?"

"He did not. He did not say anything," Campbell insisted.

Bowen then asked Campbell if he had ever made a statement that he had never had any problems with Hugh Otis Bynum.

"I could have. I didn't know that me and Hugh Otis had any problems. I didn't realize it until I found out that he had me blown up, and I decided we had a problem."

The prosecution next called Scottsboro Police Captain Keith Smith to the stand. Smith testified that in the days just before the bombing of Loy Campbell he had been to look for Billy Ray McCrary at McCrary's father's house near Hollywood. Smith said that while he was there, Hugh Otis Bynum drove up to the house. He also said he saw McCrary and Bynum together, sitting in Bynum's car at a trailer McCrary owned on the lake. He said this took place in the summer of 1974.

Smith testified that on another occasion in the summer of 1974, he and his partner, Raymond Bell, were talking with McCrary at the location of a second trailer McCrary owned when Bynum drove up. He said McCrary walked to Bynum's car and talked to him for about fifteen minutes before returning to where the officers were waiting. He said that during routine patrols of Scottsboro, he often had seen McCrary and Bynum talking together in front of Tom's Restaurant.

During cross-examination by Roderick Beddow, Smith admitted that Bynum had not tried to hide himself on any of the occasions he was seen with McCrary. He also said that it was common to see Bynum in front of Tom's talking with several different people. Most important, Smith told the court that he would not put it past McCrary to lie under oath.

After Judge Sullivan excused Smith from the witness stand, Baxley touched off a rhubarb when he called Linda Darlene Sullivan as his next witness. Outside the hearing of the jury, defense lawyer Al Bowen strenuously objected to Sullivan's testifying. Bowen made his objection on the grounds that any statements Charles Hale had made to Sullivan had been made after the bombing of Loy Campbell and after any so-called conspiracy had already ended. He also included in his objection the fact that Hugh Otis Bynum was being charged with assault to commit murder and was not being charged with conspiracy to commit murder. Bowen's objection, however, only succeeded in delaying the testimony. After studying a case brief prepared by Baxley's staff concerning the admissibility of a coconspirator's statements to another person, Judge Sullivan ruled that the witness could testify.[5] She was scheduled to begin the next day's testimony.

In the meantime, the prosecution called to the stand Deputy Troy Ferguson, who had taken Billy Ray McCrary to Montgomery and returned with him to Scottsboro. Ferguson testified that before he had taken McCrary to Montgomery, McCrary had been searched and that he had been searched again after he was brought back to Scottsboro. Ferguson said McCrary did not have any money on him—with one exception.

"Do you know he did not have any money on him that trip?" Bill Baxley asked the tall, red-haired deputy.

"He had some change in his pocket."

"Other than the change?"

"Well, the night we put him in Montgomery jail, he got ten dollars."

"From who?"

"Off the chief deputy to play some poker on." At this the courtroom erupted in laughter and the embarrassed Ferguson's face turned as red as his hair.[6]

"Who is the chief deputy?" Baxley continued when the laughter had faded.

"Paul Mount."

"And other than the ten dollars and some change, did he have any money?"

"That's all. When we got to the jail, they searched him and told him he couldn't take any money back and he gave the money back and he said, 'I don't need it if they are going to keep it out here.' So he had some change in his pockets."

"In other words, he turned and gave the ten dollars back right then."

"Yes, sir," said Ferguson.

The prosecution recalled Sheriff Bob Collins to the stand, and his testimony concluded the third day of the trial. Collins testified that on the night Bynum had been arrested, he had taken two hundred-dollar bills out of Billy Ray McCrary's shirt pocket when McCrary had returned to the Holiday Inn. Collins said the bills were folded in half lengthwise and then folded again in the middle. He testified that the money that the arresting officers had taken from Bynum when they took him into custody was folded in the same way. Collins also testified that he owned a dog, an Eskimo spitz named Mitzy, the night of 4 December 1972.

After Judge Sullivan excused Collins from the witness stand, Baxley announced that Linda Darlene Sullivan would be his next witness. Judge Sullivan released the jury to return to their rooms at the Holiday Inn. After the judge discussed with the lawyers some points of law concerning Sullivan's testimony, the third day of the trial came to a close.

Later that afternoon, in Huntsville, John East and Paul Mount waited in a car parked across the street from the office of John Poarch's lawyer. A Cadillac was parked a short distance from them. After a while, a man appeared and began walking toward the Cadillac. "This must be our man," East told Mount, and he got out of the car and headed across the street. He met the man in the middle of the street.

East identified himself and then asked the man if he were John Poarch. The man acknowledged that he was John Poarch, and East told him he wanted to talk to him. The two men got into Poarch's Cadillac. East told him that the attorney general needed his testimony in Scottsboro. "We can put you in the car with the deputy over there or you and I can ride to Scottsboro in your car," East told him. Poarch told him he would drive his own car to Scottsboro and East signaled Mount to follow them.[7]

Just before 7 P.M. that Wednesday, John Poarch met with Bill Baxley at the Jackson County Courthouse. Loy Campbell was with Baxley when John East brought the jewelry salesman in. Baxley questioned Poarch, and then the man made a formal statement and signed it.[8]

Baxley told Poarch, "As a material witness, we can put you in jail here until time for you to testify or we can take your word that you will come back over from Huntsville tomorrow morning." Interestingly, the salesman was more worried about trouble with the Internal Revenue Service than he was worried about legal troubles stemming from the hoax of Bynum. Baxley assured him he would be questioned only about his part in the Bynum incident. Poarch vowed he would return the next day and he was released to return to his home in Huntsville.[9]

But Campbell and Baxley harbored fears that they might never see the man again.[10]

16   *We Have a Job to Do*

Linda Darlene Sullivan appeared poised and calm as she seated herself in the witness box at the start of the fourth day of the trial. Dressed in a brown skirt and a full-length knitted vest, the tall, attractive, dark-haired woman did not appear to be a bank robber or the moll of accused murderer Charles X. Hale.[1] But the calm appearance masked the danger the woman faced. Few people realized the courage Sullivan had to muster to take the witness stand. It was a dangerous thing to implicate a man as treacherous as Charles Hale. The authorities had not captured her former lover, and he could be hiding anywhere, even in Scottsboro.[2]

Roderick Beddow and Al Bowen had tried desperately to block Sullivan from taking the stand against Bynum. They argued strenuously that her testimony was that of a third party and that anything she might say was not directly related to the attempt on Loy Campbell's life. Bill Baxley and his team, however, argued just as vigorously that her testimony would substantiate the conspiracy theory. Judge Sullivan ruled in Baxley's favor, but that did not prevent Beddow and Bowen from repeatedly raising objections during the woman's testimony.

Sullivan began her testimony by saying she had never met Billy Ray McCrary or Hugh Otis Bynum and would not recognize either of the men if she saw them. She recounted how, in February 1974, Charles Hale had brought a .30–06 rifle and a scope to her home in Pisgah and that together they had mounted the scope on the rifle.[3] "I asked him where he got the gun and he said, 'That doesn't matter right now,' and he gave me $150 and told me to put it up."

"Do you remember what denomination the bills were?" Baxley asked.

"Three fifty-dollar bills."

"Do you remember whether they were rolled up or loose?"

"They were folded in a certain way. You take and fold them half in two and back."

"Did he tell you where he got the money?"

"No, sir, not then."

"Later on in the day, did you or he do anything with that rifle?"

"We took the rifle out and went up on Tupelo Pike and we discussed everything, that he had planned to kill the sheriff and told me where he had gotten the gun and where he got the money."

"Where did he tell you he got the gun and money?"

"Hugh Otis Bynum."

Sullivan described how they had driven to a hillside overlooking Sheriff Collins's cattle ranch and how Hale had gone into the woods toward the ranch. During the drive to the ambush site, she testified, Hale made an admission to his girlfriend. "He told me that Hugh Otis had paid him to kill the sheriff," she told the jury, "and during the trip up there, we had discussed the bombing of Loy Campbell and he told me he was the one that put the bomb in there."

Baxley turned his questioning to the day Sullivan said she came to the courthouse square with Charles Hale. Sullivan told the jury how she and Hale had parked on the square and she had seen Hugh Otis Bynum's car parked in front of Tom's Restaurant. She said Hale went into the restaurant while she waited in the car. In a few minutes, Hale returned and gave her $150. She said each of the three fifty-dollar bills had been folded the same as the other bills, lengthwise and again in the middle.

"When Charles Hale came back to the car on that time and on that occasion, what, if anything, did Charles Hale say?" Baxley asked.

"He told me he had $150, and he said, 'We have a job to do tonight,' and I asked him, 'What?' And he said, Hugh Otis had put $500 on Billy Ray's head."

"Did he say anything about why Billy Ray was supposed to be killed?"

"He said Hugh Otis told him that Billy Ray knew too much and he was afraid he was beginning to start talking and he wanted him out of the way before he got both of them in trouble." She told the jury she had tried to talk Hale out of the killing of McCrary but found out later Hale intended to carry out the assignment Bynum had given him.

Sullivan testified that, on one occasion, Charles Hale had wanted to know where Jay Black, the district attorney, lived. "He asked me if I knew Jay Black," she said, "and I told him, 'Yes.' And he asked if I knew where he lived, and I said, 'Yeah.' And he asked if I would show him and I told him I would. I asked him why and he said, 'Hugh Otis was wanting Sheriff Collins, Loy Campbell, and Jay Black, and one more.' He never did tell me the fourth name, so I took him to Fort Payne and showed him where Jay Black lived." She then described for the jury the night Hale had hunted for the dynamite hidden behind the Carriage House Apartments. She told the jury it had been too dark that night for Hale to find the dynamite, and she told how she had drawn a map of the area behind the apartment complex for John East and Don Barrett.

Then Baxley asked Sullivan what had taken place between Hale and Bynum during Hale's prison stay during most of 1973.

"Charles told me he didn't have to worry about anything while he was in prison because Hugh Otis was sending him money. He told me that he never had to worry about money, because he could go to Hugh Otis and get any amount he wanted, just for any needs he had because Hugh Otis knew he would do the work for him."

Baxley asked her to describe for the jurors what Hale had told her about the night he wired the bomb to Loy Campbell's car.

"We had discussed it," she began, "and he told me he went by the sheriff's house to put the dynamite in the sheriff's car and a barking dog scared him off. And he went on down to Campbell's and got up under the car and put the dynamite in and he almost got caught. He cut his leg when he crawled out from under the car."

"Now, by almost getting caught, what did he say about that?"

"A city cop car came down the street and he backed up and he got out from under the car on the other side and he went on behind the garage. They shined a flashlight over the yard and drove on off."

"All right, did he say anything during this same period of time about any conversation he had with Hugh Otis Bynum about Loy Campbell after the bombing took place?"

"He was afraid that Hugh Otis wouldn't pay him and he talked to Hugh Otis about it. Hugh Otis told him that Loy Campbell was as good as dead and he had suffered enough so he was satisfied and he went ahead and paid him."

"Even though Loy wasn't dead."

"Right."

Despite an intense cross-examination by Al Bowen, Linda Darlene Sullivan remained composed while in the witness box. She steadfastly denied that Bill Baxley had promised her anything for her testimony. At one point, Bowen sarcastically called her "no deal Sullivan." In an effort to cast doubt on her character, Bowen asked about several crimes in which she might have been involved, including the robbery of the fishermen at Mink Creek, the burglary of a veterinary clinic in Fort Payne, and the murder of the man in Florida. Sullivan again denied that the authorities had promised her immunity in exchange for her help in solving those crimes.

In spite of Bowen's stiff cross-examination, Linda Darlene Sullivan remained unshaken in her testimony. Hers was some of the most damaging testimony against Hugh Otis Bynum given thus far in the trial. She insisted that Charles Hale had admitted to her that he had put the bomb on Loy Campbell's car and that he had done so at the request of Hugh Otis Bynum.

Sullivan had accomplished something more for the prosecution: her testimony corroborated much of what Billy Ray McCrary had said. Her statement that she had never met McCrary was significant because it showed she could have learned the details of the bombing only through her relationship with Charles Hale.

Elsewhere in the courthouse, John Poarch awaited his turn to testify. He had returned to Scottsboro bright and early that morning, just as he had promised Bill Baxley. In the years after the trial, Loy Campbell always suspected that it was the showman in Poarch that caused him to come back to Scottsboro to testify against Bynum. But Poarch spent that Thursday waiting. It was not until the next day that he got his chance to play out his part in the drama that was unfolding in the Jackson County Courthouse.[4]

Following Linda Darlene Sullivan to the stand was Charles Hale's uncle, Isaac Roberts. Roberts was one of those rare witnesses whose honesty and forthrightness was immediately apparent. There were few observers who could ever doubt that what the man said was the truth. But beyond the evident honesty of the witness, the testimony of Isaac Roberts proved to be significant in another way.[5] Roberts told the court that on four separate occasions, Hugh Otis Bynum had stopped at his home on Tupelo Pike asking Roberts if he knew where Charles Hale was. Roberts said that on each occasion he had told Bynum he hadn't heard from Charles since the young man had left Alabama. Roberts vividly remembered the third time Bynum had come to see him.

"He pulled in my yard one Sunday morning," Roberts said. "He says, 'Isaac, have you read the paper?' And I said, 'What paper?' I said, 'I don't even take a paper, and I don't read the paper hardly ever.' And he said, '*The Birmingham-Post Herald.*'

And I said, 'No.' And he said, 'Well, I seen in the paper where Charles got caught, and his girlfriend, robbing a bank in Florida.' That's the first I knew where he was at, and I said, 'That's where he is at.' And he says, 'I think Charles got away, but they caught his girlfriend.' And he says, 'If he got in touch with you some way—.' And I said, 'Hugh Otis, he won't get in touch with me.' And he said, 'Well, if he does get in touch with you and tells where he is at, tell him to keep going and not to come back.' He said, 'Go to Mexico, if he has to,' and that's the last words he said."

Roderick Beddow, through his cross-examination of the witness, was unable to confuse Roberts or catch him in a contradiction. At one point, Beddow wanted to know about the conversation involving Mexico. "Well, did Hugh Otis say, 'If this is true, he would be better off to keep on going to Mexico'?" asked Beddow.

"No, he didn't say that."

"Didn't he say, 'If, what had happened down there in Florida, he would be better off in Mexico'?"

"I don't know that."

"Is that what he said, in substance?"

Roberts would not stray from his earlier testimony. "Hugh Otis said, 'You tell the boy to keep going, to go to Mexico if he can," Roberts told Beddow emphatically.

His testimony completed, Isaac Roberts stepped down from the witness stand and stood for a moment facing the packed courtroom. He threw his fist into the air before turning and walking from the courtroom. It was hard to tell if the man's gesture was meant to be one of defiance or one of victory.[6]

Isaac Roberts's testimony was important not only because of the genuine honesty the man projected but because the testimony had a direct link to Hugh Otis Bynum. This was not secondhand hearsay. The man had told the court what he remembered Bynum telling him personally.[7]

Harold Wilson, the state trooper whose duty it had been to pose as a killer for hire, was sworn in and took the stand. Under the direction of Bill Baxley, the undercover agent recounted the events of 6 December 1974, when he and Billy Ray McCrary had met Hugh Otis Bynum at Tom's Restaurant after the agent had been wired with a radio transmitter. He told the jury that Bynum had come to the table where he and McCrary sat and that

McCrary had introduced him to Bynum by saying, "Hugh, this is a man here I have been hunting to do the job that you want done."

He detailed how the three of them had gotten into the car parked outside Tom's and how the conversation had turned to the proposal to kill Sheriff Bob Collins. The price for having the murder committed was set at $5,000, Wilson told the jurors. He said that Bynum had told him that the destruction of his barns and cattle had cost him $92,000 and that he blamed the sheriff for that loss. Wilson also told the jury that at one point Bynum had said, "Yeah, I want it done. I wouldn't give a damn if it would have been done a month ago," referring to killing the sheriff. Wilson described how the three men had returned to Tom's Restaurant, how McCrary and Bynum had gone to a bathroom at the rear of the cafe and how, only seconds later, McCrary had returned with two hundred-dollar bills stuffed in his shirt pocket.

Baxley ended his questioning of the agent by asking about the times Hugh Otis Bynum laughed during the conversation. Over the objections of Al Bowen, Judge Sullivan permitted Wilson to answer. "The times he would laugh would be when we talked about killing somebody. He would always laugh after we talked about killing a man," he said.

Roderick Beddow, in his cross-examination of the undercover agent, led Wilson word-for-word through the entire conversation between the three men. He seized every opportunity to portray the agent as a menacing figure out to intimidate a harmless old man, and he forced Wilson to repeat for the jury the profanity he had used that night.

"How big are you?" Beddow asked Wilson.

"Six feet, one inch."

"How much do you weigh?"

"225."

"You were talking pretty bad when you got in that car?"

"Yes, sir. I wasn't posing as a preacher."

"I see. You were posing as a snitch?"

"No, sir. I was posing as a hitman."

At another point in the testimony, Beddow wanted to know where Wilson was seated in the car. "Where were you seated in the back seat?" he asked.

"Right behind Mr. Bynum."

"Right behind him?"

"Yes, sir."

"All hunched up over him?"

"No, sir."

"You were leaning up back towards the front of the automobile, front seat, talking to them?"

"No, sir. I was sitting normal in the car."

"You were sitting back normal in the car?"

"Yes, sir."

"You were sitting back. You weren't leaning up close to the front seat?"

"No, sir."

"Breathing down his neck?"

"No, sir."

Beddow had some questions about when the trio had returned to Tom's Restaurant and about the conversation concerning the killing of four people. "And you were told by McCrary outside Tom's Restaurant to, 'Just wait here at the door'?"

"I was told by Mr. Bynum, 'You just wait here at the door.' "

"Well, from the time he told you to sit in the car and you wait here at the door, the first orders he has ever given you, he was pretty well going with everything out there in that automobile and that dark place, wasn't he?"

"Yes, sir."

"He was very noncommittal, wasn't he?"

"Yes, sir."

Beddow ended his cross-examination of the agent by asking him specifically who was marked for death during the conversation in the car. "Mr. Wilson, did Mr. Bynum ever say that he would pay you for killing the sheriff?"

"No, sir."

"Did he ever mention the name of Loy Campbell?"

"No, sir."

"Did he ever mention the name of Jay Black?"

"No, sir."

"Did he ever mention the name of John T. Reid?"

"No, sir."

"Did he ever say anything about more than one person?"

"He mentioned something in there about Morgan Weeks, meaning he was looking for Billy Ray."

"Morgan Weeks was looking for Billy Ray?"

"Yes."

"All right, did he say he wanted Morgan Weeks dead?"

"No, sir. He just told him that Morgan was looking for him."

"Well, did he say he wanted to kill anybody?"

"No, sir."

"Did he make this statement or this statement in substance, 'All four of them, all four of them need to be killed'?"

"No, sir."

" 'All four of them need to be dead,' he never did make that statement?"

"No, sir."

In his redirect examination of Wilson, Bill Baxley endeavored to point out to the jury that Beddow had conveniently omitted portions of the taped conversation between the agent, McCrary, and Bynum during his cross-examination. With a transcript of the conversation in hand, Baxley asked the agent to recall that part of the conversation in which Bynum discussed his feelings for the sheriff.

"On page 5," Baxley began, referring to the transcript, "right after the part where Mr. Beddow was questioning you about where Mr. Bynum said, 'Because everybody knows I don't like the S.O.B.', what was the next statement and by who?"

"Mr. Bynum said, 'Yeah. They know it because everybody knows that I don't like the son of a bitch.' "

"What was the next statement and by who?"

"The next statement is by me," Wilson answered.

"What did you say then?"

"I said, 'You want him or you want four. I will do just him.' "

"What was the next?"

"Mr. Bynum: 'Well, I haven't got any money right now. That's the reason I told Billy.' "

Baxley succeeded in bringing out that Bynum had not resisted the proposal to kill four people but instead had used his lack of funds as a reason for not consummating the deal. Baxley then directed Wilson's attention to that part of the conversation wherein the agent jokingly had suggested the sheriff was worth more to kill.

Said Wilson, "Mr. Bynum said, 'It ain't a question of worth. It's just a question of getting the money. I can get any amount of money but if I was to get it. You had that poor sheriff killed they would say old Hugh had the old sheriff killed.' " Wilson said that Bynum, and only Bynum, laughed about killing the sheriff.

Baxley then wanted to know what Bynum had said when the undercover agent had named the price for killing the sheriff.

Wilson said, "And the next one talking is Mr. Bynum, 'Well, that's a reasonable price, but I ain't got any money. I could give you all or any amount of money but I know what they will say if I go get it and borrow it. Why, that poor sheriff, if something happened to him, then boom, they would be on my ass.' "

"He said, 'That's a reasonable price'?"

"Yes, sir."

Baxley again wanted to know about the times when Bynum laughed during the conversation. "Now, when you mentioned laughing," Baxley asked Wilson, "there was some time, I believe you said, when all of you or both of them laughed?"

"Yes, sir."

"Were there times when just one person laughed?"

"Yes, sir."

"Was there ever a time when you laughed by yourself, nobody else laughed?"

"No, sir."

"Was there ever a time when Billy Ray McCrary laughed by himself?"

"No, sir."

"Was there ever a time when Hugh Otis Bynum laughed by himself, a time or times?"

"Yes, sir."

"When was Hugh Otis Bynum laughing and no one else laughing?"

"Well, I would talk about killing the sheriff."

By the time he stepped down from the witness box, Harold Wilson had testified for over three hours. His testimony had been damaging to Bynum, but the defense had managed to neutralize that damage by bringing out the fact that Bynum had never openly agreed to the killing of the sheriff or four people. The agent had admitted, too, that Loy Campbell's name had never surfaced during the conversation.

At the completion of Wilson's testimony, Bill Baxley rested the state's case against Hugh Otis Bynum. Roderick Beddow wanted to recall Billy Ray McCrary to the stand for further questioning, however.

Beddow began his reexamination by questioning McCrary closely about where he had spent the night before the First Monday bombing. McCrary insisted he could not remember if he had spent the night of Sunday, 3 December 1972, at his then-wife's house on Hembree Street or at his father's home in Hollywood. Beddow pointed out that McCrary had told Judge John Haislip during the preliminary hearing that he had indeed been at Lilah McCrary's home that night. McCrary admitted he could have said that but went on to tell Beddow, "Like I say, I can't say I was staying there and I can't say I didn't."

Beddow then wanted McCrary to repeat what he had done with the money he had gotten from Bynum as a payoff for the bombing. McCrary said, once again, that he had given $400 to Charles Hale. He said that with a thousand dollars of the remaining $1,600 he had bought a lot and trailer and had spent the remainder on a used car. At Beddow's prompting, McCrary again described some of the hundred-dollar bills as being "old and yellow."

Beddow turned his questioning to the meeting between McCrary and Bill Baxley in Montgomery the day before Hugh Otis Bynum was arrested. "You saw Mr. Baxley, and you were the one that suggested to Mr. Baxley when you were down in Montgomery that if they would wire you up, or wire some man up, or wire the car up, that you could go and could produce, isn't that true?"

"I don't remember."

"Well, you made a suggestion to them down there about putting a transmitter on you?"

"There was something said about that. I don't remember how it was said."

"But you were the one that told Attorney General Baxley and his agents that this could be done, that you could go produce, didn't you?"

"I think so."

Then Beddow questioned McCrary about what he and Bynum had said when they were in the back room at Tom's Restaurant. "And I will ask you, as a matter of fact, didn't he tell you, Billy Ray, 'I don't want no part of this'?"

"No, sir. I can't say that he said that."

"He didn't say, 'I don't trust that man'?"

"I don't remember him saying that either."

"Did he make a statement, 'He is big enough and ugly enough to be what he says he is. I don't trust him, Billy'?"

"He said something about big enough and ugly enough."

" 'And you are going to get in trouble following around with him, worlds of trouble'?"

"No, sir. He didn't say that."

"Well, did you tell him this, 'Hugh, you have got money. Everybody knows you carry money with you.' Did you tell him that?"

"No, sir."

"Did you tell him, 'I have just gotten out on bond'?"

"I don't remember if I told him I just got out on bond or not. I told him I got out. I don't know if bond was mentioned or not."

"Well, you told him this fellow Tally wouldn't set you any bond, but that man over in Fort Payne was the one that set your bond."

"Yes, sir. I said that."

"Did you tell him, 'I just got out on bond and I am broke and I haven't even seen Joyce'?"

"I don't remember."

"Did you tell him this, 'Lend me $200 for gas money until I get on my feet. I need it'?"

"No, sir."

"Well, you have gone to him on other occasions and gotten money to get on your feet when you needed it, haven't you?"

"No, sir."

"Well, you told those people down there in Montgomery, on occasions, that you beat him out of, you guessed, $130,000?"

"Yes, sir. I said that."

Toward the conclusion of Beddow's questioning of Billy Ray McCrary, there occurred this interesting exchange.

"And your probation revocation case is still pending," Beddow said.

"Yes, sir."

"But that's to be fixed?"

"I don't know about that."

"Well, that was part of the deal, wasn't it?"

"I ain't been before the judge yet."

"Well, that was part of the deal. It was going to be fixed. You were going to get your own judge, I believe that's what you told me yesterday?"

"No, there was nothing said about a judge. I don't own a judge."

"Well, thank God for small favors," Beddow said.

"Yeah, same back to you," McCrary retorted.

It was now late in the afternoon and now it was the defense's turn to present its case to the jury. However, the attorney general still had one actor left waiting in the wings. John Poarch, the humorous and flashy ring salesman, had yet to testify.

17   *Truth and Veracity*

Before the defense called its first witness to the stand, Al Bowen stood before Judge Sullivan and entered a lengthy motion to throw out the testimony of Linda Darlene Sullivan and the undercover agent, Harold Wilson. Bowen argued that the prosecution had produced no evidence, other than the testimony of Sullivan, to prove that there had been a conspiracy to kill Loy Campbell or any others. Bowen also argued that if in fact there had been a conspiracy to commit murder, it had ended some two weeks after the bombing of Loy Campbell when the alleged payoff for the bombing took place. Therefore, Bowen reasoned, any statements made by Charles Hale to Linda Darlene Sullivan were made after the so-called conspiracy had ended and should not be allowed.[1]

Bowen's motion to exclude the testimony of Harold Wilson hinged on the fact Loy Campbell's name had never been mentioned during the conversation between Wilson and Hugh Otis Bynum. It was on a charge of intent to murder Loy Campbell that Bynum now stood trial and he was not being tried on a charge of conspiracy to commit murder, Bowen argued. Bowen also pointed out for Judge Sullivan the fact that Bynum, during the conversation with the agent, never agreed to hire someone to kill another person. "Bynum did not pay any money to anyone to kill anyone and the only evidence of any money transpiring is testimony of Billy Ray McCrary, who is an accomplice," Bowen said. Bowen also argued that any statement made by Hugh Otis Bynum to the undercover agent was the result of entrapment. Judge Sullivan was not swayed by the eloquent argument, however, and overruled Bowen's motion to exclude the testimony.

After a brief recess, the defense called its first witness, H. Jack Milnes, to the stand. Milnes was the personnel director at the Tennessee Valley Authority's nuclear plant under construction at Bellefonte outside of Scottsboro. He produced for the defense a job application dated 30 December 1974, and filled out by Billy Ray McCrary. On the application, McCrary had listed his first job choice as "powder man," one who handles and detonates dynamite. Milnes testified that during a job interview, McCrary claimed he had a great deal of experience as a powder man. Milnes testified that McCrary had gone to work at the construction site on 22 January 1975, as a drill operator. The TVA later fired McCrary when it learned that he had lied on the application about his criminal record. Milnes's testimony was intended to show that McCrary had experience of his own in the use of explosives and that it might have been McCrary who planted the bomb on Loy Campbell's car.

The defense next recalled Bureau of Alcohol, Tobacco and Firearms agent Donald Barrett to the witness stand. Al Bowen asked Barrett about the times he had questioned Billy Ray McCrary, and Barrett testified that he had questioned McCrary a few days after the bombing and again about a month after the first round of questioning. Barrett said that on both occasions McCrary denied involvement in the bombing. Bowen then asked Barrett about the search of Hugh Otis Bynum's house following his arrest when agents confiscated a .30–06 rifle. Barrett testified that the rifle had not been fitted with a scope and that investigators had found no fingerprints on the rifle. With that, Bowen turned Barrett over to Bill Baxley for questioning.

Baxley asked Barrett to describe the events of the night of 6

December 1974, when Hugh Otis Bynum was arrested. Barrett described how officers had spotted Bynum driving his Buick Electra 225 and had followed him to McCrary's service station at Martintown Hill.

"When we stopped Mr. Bynum," Barrett said, "I approached him on his driver's side and advised him he was under arrest. And while getting him out of his car, he wanted to continue to sit in his car and he acted like he wanted to sit back down in it. . . . He made the motion of sitting back down, and I pulled him away from the car and turned him over to the custody of investigator George Tubbs." Barrett went on to say that a search of Bynum's car turned up a pistol that had been hidden under the front seat. Barrett also told Baxley and the jury he had difficulty getting fingerprints from Hugh Otis Bynum. "Mr. Bynum, for me, is a hard person to print," Barrett said. Baxley wanted the jury to know that because of the old man's scleroderma, it was unlikely he would have left fingerprints on anything he touched, including the rifle.

Tom Sisk, the longtime friend of Hugh Otis Bynum and owner of Tom's Restaurant, took the stand for the defense. Sisk testified that shortly after Billy Ray McCrary had gotten out of prison in November 1972, McCrary called the restaurant by telephone looking for Bynum. He said McCrary called the restaurant four or five times on that morning asking for Bynum. Sisk told the jury he told Bynum about the phone calls and that Bynum told him he would see McCrary. The defense intended the testimony about the phone calls to plant the notion that it was McCrary, not Hugh Otis Bynum, who had initiated the visit that took place after McCrary was released from prison.

Al Bowen then asked Sisk how Bynum carried his money. "Have you ever observed the way Mr. Bynum carries his money?" Bowen queried.

"Yes, sir. I think so."

"Does he fold it any particular way?"

"Yes, sir."

"Show me how he does it."

Sisk then took a dollar bill and demonstrated how Bynum folded his money. "Well, he takes it and turns it all the same way and folds it like this," said Sisk, "folds it like that, and bends it over like this." What Sisk demonstrated matched how Linda

Darlene Sullivan had described the folded money Charles Hale had told her had come from Hugh Otis Bynum and it also matched how Sheriff Bob Collins described the two hundred-dollar bills taken from Billy Ray McCrary the night Bynum was arrested.

"How long has he done that, to your knowledge?" Bowen asked Sisk about the folding of the money.

"Ever since I can remember. It's been a long time," Sisk answered. Like many of the witnesses called for the defense, Sisk said Billy Ray McCrary's reputation was bad and that he could not be believed under oath.

Under cross-examination by Bill Baxley, Sisk testified that he had often seen McCrary and Bynum together around the courthouse square. He also said he was a close friend of Bynum, that Bynum had often lent him money, and that he had taken Bynum's meals to him while Bynum was in jail. Baxley wanted the jury to know that Sisk was not an entirely impartial witness.

In a further effort to discredit the testimony of Billy Ray McCrary, the defense put on a parade of no fewer than twenty-two witnesses who testified that McCrary's reputation in the community was bad and that his word could not be believed under oath. But Baxley's cross-examination of some of the witnesses produced some noteworthy facts. Baxley asked Mickey Wright if he knew McCrary's general reputation for "truth and veracity and honesty." Wright answered he thought it was bad.

Baxley wasn't sure, however, that the man understood the question. "Mr. Wright, lawyers sometimes use words that I don't know what they mean. What does veracity mean?" asked Baxley.

To the amusement of the courtroom, Wright answered, "I would imagine it means always raising Cain around town, doesn't it?"

Ray McLaughlin, an acquaintance of McCrary, had testified McCrary told him that he could get someone to kill Loy Campbell's brother, Bunk, for $1,500. McLaughlin also testified he had heard McCrary after the First Monday bombing say, "There was going to be some more of them son-of-a-bitches blown up around town if they didn't straighten up." But under cross-examination by Baxley, McLaughlin admitted that he disliked Bunk and Loy Campbell because they had represented his wife during the couple's recent divorce.

"As a matter of fact, you have quite a bit of ill will for the Campbells," said Baxley.

"Well, yes, sir, I guess. If somebody beat you out of thirty or forty thousand dollars, you would too."

"As a matter of fact, the ill will was over your wife's divorce settlement, and they were her lawyers?"

"They were her lawyers, yes, sir."

"And the judge and Bunk Campbell kept telling you to get you a lawyer, and you wouldn't do it?"

"I believe you are supposed to have justice without a lawyer."

Baxley also brought out the fact that McLaughlin was ordered by the court to seek psychiatric help after he threatened to kill Bunk Campbell. "As a matter of fact, on six different nights you called Bunk Campbell's house and threatened him and told him you were going to kill him. Didn't you call Bunk Campbell's house?" Baxley wanted to know.

"Certainly."

"And didn't you say you were going to kill him?"

"No."

"Didn't he tell you the telephone call was taped?"

"I told him I knew it was taped."

"And didn't you tell him, quoting you directly, 'that the same thing was going to happen to him as happened to his brother'?"

"I don't remember anything to that effect, no."

"Did you tell him that? Did you say, 'Do you want it like your brother got it or how'?"

"Is it on the tape?"

"Did you say that or not?"

"I don't remember."

In an apparent effort to show there was no hard feelings between Bynum and Loy Campbell, Jimmy Gilliam testified that after the bombing, he had been referred to Campbell by Bynum to have some legal work done. However, under cross-examination, Gilliam said he was a son-in-law to Tom Sisk and was a distant cousin to Billy Ray McCrary's ex-wife, Lilah.

Mark Scott Skelton admitted during cross-examination that he was a first cousin to Bynum and was one of the four landowners who had helped make Bynum's bond. Eb Cornelison said he was in the cattle business with Bynum and was also one of those who had signed Bynum's bond. Fred Casteel, the owner of the Variety Bake Shop, said he was close friends with Bynum and that he had taken Bynum his meals while Bynum was being held in the jail.

Like the other character witnesses, Elbert Hubbard, a Scottsboro car dealer, said he wouldn't put it past McCrary to lie under oath. However, under cross-examination by Baxley, Hubbard gave a different view of McCrary.

"In other words," began Baxley, "what you would say is that you would check pretty close what he said before you decided to believe him or not?"

"I believe what he tells me," answered Hubbard.

"You do believe what he tells you?"

"Yes, sir. Of all the dealings I have ever had with him, it's always been straight."

The last of the witnesses called for that day of the trial was the circuit clerk of Jackson County, Charles William Wann, who, in response to questioning by Roderick Beddow, testified that there had been a charge of grand larceny lodged against McCrary but that the case had never gone to court. In cross-examination, Wann said the larceny case involved the alleged theft of a 1973 Buick Electra 225 from Joyce McCrary. He said the incident was the result of a domestic dispute and that the case was later dropped. He said that it was not uncommon for a wife to drop a case against her husband after the couple resolved their dispute.

It was now late in the afternoon on the fourth day of the trial, and Roderick Beddow informed the court that the defense's next witness would take some time to question. Judge Sullivan excused the jury and ordered the trial recessed for the day.

The first witness to be called on Friday, the last day of testimony, was to be Lilah McCrary, the ex-wife of Billy Ray McCrary.

18　　*I Wouldn't Do a Thing Like That*

Friday, 28 March 1975, was Good Friday, the day on which Christians remember the crucifixion of Jesus Christ and traditionally turn their thoughts to Easter and the celebration of Christ's resurrection. Good Friday 1975 was the last day of testimony in the trial of Hugh Otis Bynum. Separated from their friends and families, the jurors had now endured four days of testimony by dozens of witnesses. Many of the jurors had begun to tire from the ordeal.[1] The testimony they were about to hear on that Good Friday, in that courtroom in the Jackson County Courthouse, was some of the most dramatic and most powerful given during the entire trial.

At 9 A.M., Billy Ray McCrary's ex-wife, Lilah, took the witness stand for the defense. She began her testimony by saying she had married Billy Ray McCrary when she was sixteen and remained married to him for eighteen years until they divorced in January 1973.[2] She said she remembered that after McCrary had been released from the federal prison in November 1972, he stayed at her house three or four nights a week. She said she remembered that McCrary was filled with hatred after his release from prison and she remembered his saying, "I am going to kill some son-of-a-bitches. I am going to blow them up, and I am going to make them suffer the way they have made me suffer."

Defense lawyer Al Bowen asked her, "Did he make this statement to you: 'I am going to get Loy Campbell and the sheriff. I laid awake while I was in prison thinking about ways to get rid of those son-of-a-bitches'?"

"Yes, sir."

"Now, between the dates of November 16 and December 4 of 1972, on the occasions that he spent the night with you during that period of time, nearly every night he was there, did you have a discussion with him concerning this matter?"

"Yes, sir. We argued continuously. When he come home from prison he was filled with hate and revenge and he talked continuously of getting even with people that had made him suffer.

And he said that he was going to kill Loy Campbell and the sheriff for making him suffer. That's the words he put it."

"Did he state to you any reason that he hated Loy Campbell and the reason he wanted to get rid of him?"

"Yes, sir. He told me that Loy Campbell and Bob Collins had kept him from getting an early parole and he said that Loy had refused to represent him in cases."

Bowen then questioned the witness about the events that took place at her home the night before the bomb exploded in Loy Campbell's car. She said that some guests at her home had left to go to the courthouse square, leaving her, McCrary, and Charles Hale alone at the house.

"In a few minutes, Charles Hale got up and looked over at Billy and said, 'I better go. I have a heavy date.' And Billy looked at him and winked and sort of grinned and he said, 'You better be careful, you S.O.B.' "

Mrs. McCrary also related how McCrary had insisted their children not go to school on that First Monday of December 1972. "He told me I better not let the kids go to school. And I asked him, 'Why not?' And he said, 'Well, I am just telling you, you better not let them go. There is going to be a big boom, a lot of excitement, and a lot of talk in town.' He called our son in the bedroom and said, 'What time do y'all get out for recess?' And the boy said, 'Ten.' And Billy said, 'Okay, you can go to school then.' "

Lilah McCrary then recalled the night her ex-husband had come home with what she described as "some shiny objects," dynamite caps, in his coat pocket. "Billy came home one night and he was undressing, and he pulled his jacket off and hung it on the bed post. And he said, 'Look in my pocket,' and I run my hand in his jacket pockets. I pulled out some shiny objects and I said, 'What are these?' And I put them back real quick, and he said, 'You'd better be careful. You will blow them S.O.B.'s up.' "

The witness insisted that after McCrary's release from prison, he had often told her that he hated Jay Black and that he hated Robert Reed, the mayor of Hollywood, and that he was going to get even with Reed for testifying in federal court against him. She said McCrary once warned her, "You and the children had better not mention Charles Hale's name or y'all would get blowed up too."

Over the continued objections of Bill Baxley, Al Bowen asked Mrs. McCrary about several crimes in which Bill Ray McCrary might have been involved, including the burglary of a post office in a small town south of Scottsboro.

Said Mrs. McCrary, "Well, one night this man pulled up in front of our house, we lived at Grant, and Billy told me it was a man that he had met in prison. And they left and didn't come back until after midnight. It was in the early morning hours, and he had a lot of change in a sack, and he told me that him and his man had robbed the Grant Post Office."

Al Bowen asked Lilah McCrary to describe an incident that took place at her house a few days after the bombing of Loy Campbell.

"Well, it was one night after dark," she said, "and Billy Ray came running in the house and he had a long gun in his hand and he said, 'Turn off the lights and close the curtains.' And we went around closing the curtains and he had an insane look in his eyes, he looked wild. And he said, 'They are after me.' And I said, 'Who?' And he said, 'Them s.o.b. law,' and I said, 'What for?' And he said, 'About that Loy Campbell deal,' and I said, 'Billy, you can't shoot in the house with these kids in here,' and he said, 'I will if they come after me'." She concluded by saying McCrary had threatened her when he learned she would testify for the defense.

In his cross-examination, Bill Baxley wanted to know more about the shiny objects Lilah McCrary said she had found in her husband's pocket.

"Now, Mrs. McCrary, these dynamite caps, did they have short wires, long wires, on them, or no wires?"

"I don't remember any wires. I just—"

"You don't remember any wires being on them?"

"No."

Under intense questioning by Baxley, Lilah McCrary told the jury she had suspected her former husband was involved in the bombing but had been afraid to tell the authorities. Only after the arrest of Hugh Otis Bynum did she go to Scottsboro Police Chief Ed Cotten and tell him she suspected McCrary.

In an apparent effort to shed light on the woman's motivation for testifying, Baxley asked her about McCrary's relationship with his present wife, the former Joyce Turner. "Now, when did Billy Ray take up with Joyce Turner?" Baxley asked.

"Around eight or nine years ago."

"When did he finally move in with her for good?"

"When he come home from prison this last time."

"About how long after he came home did he move in with her for good, please, ma'am?"

"To the best of my knowledge, a couple of months after we separated."

"A couple of months after you separated."

"Yes."

"It was when he went out and he got a tattoo. A big old 'Joyce' tattooed on his fist, didn't he?"

"Well, I noticed it when he came home from prison."

"And he's pretty rough, and the times you have been separated, he's been flaunting that around to you and being ugly to you?"

"No, sir."

"He hasn't been ugly to you?"

"He hasn't been nice."

The testimony of Lilah McCrary was clearly an attempt by the defense to direct suspicion toward Billy Ray McCrary and away from Hugh Otis Bynum. The crux of the defense was that Billy Ray McCrary and Charles Hale had conspired to kill Loy Campbell and Bob Collins, and that McCrary was now attempting to frame Hugh Otis Bynum, Jr., to save his own hide.[3] It was yet to be seen if the jury believed Lilah McCrary's story that Billy Ray McCrary was behind the bombing of Loy Campbell or believed, as Baxley hoped they would, that her testimony was being fueled by jealousy and vindictiveness.

The defense called the Scottsboro pharmacist, George Hunter Payne, to the stand. Payne denied he had ever sold Billy Ray McCrary any pills. He, like so many of the defense witnesses, testified McCrary could not be believed under oath. However, through cross-examination by Bill Baxley, Payne admitted he was a close friend to Hugh Otis Bynum and that he was one of the four people who had signed Bynum's bond.

It was now mid-morning and the defense had one more witness to testify. Hugh Otis Bynum, the man accused of masterminding and financing the attack on Loy Campbell, took the stand. Dressed in the brown khaki shirt and pants that were his trademark, Bynum showed little emotion as he prepared to defend himself. The packed courtroom was hushed as Bynum spoke in a voice barely above a whisper.[4]

Bynum began his testimony by describing his routine on First Monday, 4 December 1972. He said he awoke at 5:30 that morning and after reading a cattle magazine went to the Variety Bake Shop at about 7:30 to eat breakfast. Following his morning meal, he went to his cattle farm at Tupelo Pike and then shortly drove back to the courthouse square, where he parked in front of Payne's Drugstore, next to Tom's Restaurant. He said that he went into Tom's Restaurant and that Tom Sisk's wife, Lala, informed him that there had been an explosion near the Caldwell School. She suggested Bynum drive over in that direction to see what was going on, but he declined, saying he did not want to lose his parking space to the First Monday crowd. He stayed at Tom's Restaurant for about an hour and a half and then drove to the Liberty Restaurant for his midday meal.

He said he returned to Tom's Restaurant shortly after noon and saw Billy Ray McCrary, George Hunter Payne, and John Frank Hurt standing together near the restaurant. He said he overhead them talking about the Tennessee Valley Authority. In direct contrast to how McCrary had described the events of that day, Bynum said he never spoke to any of the men who were standing in front of Tom's. Under questioning by Roderick Beddow, he flatly denied talking to McCrary about the bombing.

"At that time and on that occasion, Mr. Bynum, did you nod or motion for Billy Ray to come somewhere or come away from these gentlemen and have a conversation with you?" asked Beddow.

"I did not."

"Did you make a statement to amount to this, 'Well, we got him now'?"

"I did not."

"And did McCrary tell you at this time and on that occasion, 'He might live'?"

"He did not."

"Did you say anything like, even this, Mr. Bynum, 'Well, he's going to bleed to death'?"

"No, sir."

Bynum said he then went to the barber shop located on the square and at about 1:10 P.M., went back to his cattle farm, where he met two friends, Billy Charles McCord and Eb Cornelison. He said he returned to Tom's Restaurant about 3:15 P.M. and ate his dinner. He said that he returned home at about 6 P.M. and, after reading awhile, went to bed. In response to Beddow's questions, Bynum denied seeing McCrary during the course of the day, other than the one time on the square. He said he did not see Charles Hale at all that day.

Beddow wanted to know how many times Bynum had seen Billy Ray McCrary from the time McCrary had gotten out of prison in November, 1972 until the first of the year, 1973. Bynum testified that he saw McCrary four times during that course of time. Bynum said that on the morning of 16 or 17 November 1972, there had been several telephone messages from McCrary at Tom's Restaurant. He said he received a phone call from McCrary, who told Bynum he needed to see him. Bynum said he went to McCrary's father's house at about eleven o'clock that morning and met with McCrary who, according to Bynum, told him he was broke and needed a loan. He denied ever talking to McCrary about killing anyone.

"Mr. Bynum, at that time and on that occasion did you tell Billy Ray, 'Billy, I want four people killed'?" Beddow asked.

"No, sir."

"Did you say, 'Billy, I want to kill the sheriff'?"

"No, sir."

" 'Billy, I want to kill Mr. Loy Campbell'?"

"No, sir."

" 'Billy, I want to kill Jay Black'?"

"No, sir."

" 'Billy, I want to kill John T. Reid'?"

"No, sir."

"That 'I want these people dead'?"

"I did not."

"That 'I would give $2,000 apiece for having each one of them killed'?"

"I did not."

"Did you ask him at that time and on that occasion if he would seek someone out or find someone that would kill these four individuals?"

"No, sir."

Bynum testified that the next time he saw McCrary was on a Sunday afternoon about a week after meeting with McCrary at his father's home. He said McCrary and Charles Hale were sitting in a parked car on the courthouse square near Tom's Restaurant. He said he only waved at the two men and did not speak to them. Bynum said the third time he saw McCrary was on the day of the bombing on the square. He said the fourth time he saw McCrary after his release from prison was about a week after the bombing. He said McCrary had come to him asking him to sign for about $10,000 worth of bonds held against McCrary in DeKalb County. Bynum said he told McCrary, "I am sorry. I don't go on any bonds."

Bynum went on to deny ever asking McCrary if he'd gotten someone to kill the four men, denied that McCrary ever told him that Charles Hale would do the job, denied ever offering Hale $2,000 apiece to kill the men, denied ever paying McCrary $2,000 after the bombing of Loy Campbell, and denied ever giving Charles Hale $150, as Linda Darlene Sullivan had claimed. Bynum did say that sometime in February or March of 1974, Hale had met him in Tom's Restaurant and he had loaned Hale $100. But he went on to deny that he had ever given Hale a .30–06 rifle or had asked Hale to murder Billy Ray McCrary. Bynum said that some three or four months after loaning Hale the $100, he sought Hale out to demand repayment of the loan. He said he went to Hale's uncle, Isaac Roberts, seeking the man's whereabouts.

"I said, 'Charles has done messed up. They have got him accused of bank robbery and murder, and if I was him and was guilty and done what they said he did, I would go to Mexico'," Bynum told the court.

"Did you ever tell Isaac Roberts, 'If Charles contacted you to tell him to keep running and to go on to Mexico'? Did you make a statement like that?"

"No, sir. I said, 'If he was guilty, I would go to Mexico'."

"If he were guilty, you would go to Mexico?"

"Right."

Beddow then questioned Hugh Otis about the peculiar way he folded his money. "Mr. Bynum, how long have you carried your money like that?"

"Since I got crippled up with scleroderma."

"What is that?"

"That's a rare type of rheumatism. I've carried it that way since 1950."

"And what are the reasons you carry it that way?"

"It's easier for me to handle."

"And I will ask you to tell his honor and this jury whether every merchant or friend or everybody on this square knows that you carry your money like that?"

"Absolutely."

"And you have been doing it for twenty-five years, is that right?"

"That's right."

Beddow wanted to know about the alleged conversations between Bynum and Loy Campbell at the Liberty Restaurant. Bynum said he did not remember ever mumbling something to Loy about not running again. Bynum did remember, however, what was said during the second conversation with Campbell at the restaurant.

"Loy was sitting in front because he couldn't get around very well, and I went to the checkout counter. I stopped by and told him his friend told me or put Don Barrett on me and wanted me to give him my fingerprints. And Mr. Barrett told me that it was said that I give Billy Ray McCrary a lot of money to bomb Campbell."

"And what was said when you said that?" Beddow asked.

"Bunk Campbell said, 'I hadn't heard that,' and Loy said, 'Are you right sure you didn't?' And I said, 'No, I wouldn't do a thing like that,' and went on out."

"Now, when you saw him, did you smile like a child that had a brand new toy?"

"No, sir."

"When he asked you, 'Are you sure you are not,' or 'Did you, Hugh?', did you just stand there and smile and not make a statement, Mr. Bynum?"

"No, sir."

Curiously, in his questioning of Bynum, Beddow pointed out to the jury that Bynum went to his sister's house nearly every night and that this sister lived in a new house across the street from Loy Campbell. Beddow did not attempt to explain for the jury the purpose of the questioning but it was clear he intended to show that had Bynum so desperately wanted Loy Campbell killed, he could have done it himself and not had to turn to someone like Billy Ray McCrary.

Beddow turned his questioning to the events of the night of

6 December 1974, when Bynum met with McCrary and the undercover agent, Harold Wilson. The lawyer once again used the testimony to portray the agent as threatening Bynum.

Asked Beddow, "Would you describe, enroute to the Holiday Inn, what the big man [Wilson] in the back was doing and how he was doing it?"

"Well, he wanted me to give him some money to kill the sheriff."

"And what, if anything, did you say to that?"

"I said, 'No.' I said, 'I hadn't got the money and I am just through with the conversation.' "

"Did the man appear to be angry after he tried and tried again to tell you to give them some money?"

"He did."

"Now, did you enter into any discussion with them about the fact that you wanted the sheriff to be killed?"

"No, sir."

"Did you make any statement like this: Billy Ray said, 'We want four of them,' and you said, 'Yes, we want four of them'?"

"I don't think I did."

"At any time, on any occasion, did you tell that man out there that you wanted four people killed?"

"No, sir."

"Was the name of Loy Campbell ever mentioned in that automobile?"

"No, sir."

Bynum told Beddow and the jury that even though he had been raised around a mule barn, he had never heard the type of foul language the agent used that night and at one point described the agent as "breathing down my neck."

Beddow questioned Bynum closely about what took place between himself and McCrary when they had returned to Tom's Restaurant that night. Bynum said he called McCrary to the restroom at the rear of the restaurant and warned McCrary to stay away from Wilson, that he would be getting into "worlds of trouble" hanging around with the man. Bynum then gave his version of how the $200 came to change hands.

"Did McCrary say this to you, 'Hugh, you have got money. Everybody knows you carry money with you'? Did Billy say that?" Beddow asked.

"Yeah, he did that."

"Did McCrary tell you this, 'I have just gotten out on bond. I am broke and I haven't even seen Joyce'?"

"That's right."

" 'Lend me two hundred for gas money or walking-around money until I get on my feet. I need it'?"

"Yeah, that's what he told me."

"Did he beg you for the money, Mr. Bynum?"

"Same as begging me."

"Did you tell him, 'All right, Billy, but you remember what I said. You don't want no part of that son-of-a-bitch [Wilson]'?"

"That's what I told him."

Bynum told the jury that later that night, still concerned about McCrary's welfare, he drove to McCrary's service station at Martintown Hill to warn him again. "I got to thinking about that big guy," Bynum told the jury, "and about Billy wanting to get somebody killed. So I went up there to tell him not to fool with that guy under any circumstances." Bynum denied ever telling McCrary "that Loy Campbell was crippled. He had his legs blown off. Don't blow him up. Just go out to his house and cut his throat." He also denied ever telling Charles Hale, "Loy Campbell has suffered enough, so you don't have to worry about killing him."

Before turning Bynum over to Bill Baxley for questioning, Roderick Beddow finished his examination by asking two questions. "Mr. Bynum, at any time between the 15th day of November, 1972, and through this very day, have you acted in concert with anyone in an effort to kill Loy Campbell?"

"I have not," was Bynum's answer.

"Between the 15th day of November, 1972, through this very day, have you entered into a conspiracy with anyone to kill Loy Campbell?"

"No, sir."

The defense's examination of Hugh Otis Bynum had been a carefully orchestrated attempt to refute the testimony of Billy Ray McCrary and the other prosecution witnesses. Roderick Beddow had used a gentle approach, directing Bynum to address each point of the prosecution's case. Bill Baxley's cross-examination of Hugh Otis Bynum, however, was far from gentle.[5]

Bynum began by telling Baxley and the jury he had known McCrary since McCrary was a kid and that he had known Charles Hale most of Hale's life. Bynum said he knew the two men were pretty rough fellows. He said he had spent a good deal of time with McCrary and with McCrary's friends, such as John Frank Hurt, Brent Gant, and C. W. "Bighead" Johnson. Baxley wanted to know if, while hanging out with McCrary, Bynum had ever heard foul language like that used by the undercover agent.

"And you are telling this court and jury that hanging around people like that, you're telling us that you have never heard language used like that until you heard this agent?" Baxley asked.

"I never did," was the man's reply.

"You mean, Billy Ray, all this time, never did use language like that?"

"Never did use language like that," Bynum said.

"He talked like he was in Sunday school?"

"No, sir. He didn't talk like he was in Sunday school."

"You never heard Billy Ray use the words the agent used?"

"No, I never did hear him."

"Now, you would have washed his mouth out with soap if you had of?"

"Well, he didn't use that type language."

Bynum said he had not heard language like that used by the agent even while in the U.S. Army, which prompted Baxley to observe, "You must have been in a different army than I was in."

Baxley turned his questioning to the times Bynum staked McCrary in poker and crap games. Bynum said he put the cash up for McCrary to gamble but somehow McCrary always, in his words, "managed to lose." How much, over the years, had McCrary managed to lose? Baxley asked him.

Bynum answered, "I guess he's lost about $10,000."

"About $10,000? And Billy Ray, as a matter of fact, would go back in the corner and they would give him half back after you would be gone?"

"They might have."

"Not too long ago, Billy Ray said he knew he had been losing your money and had something or some way to get it back for you. He said he had a gambling machine?"

"I don't know about that."

"Do you recall him telling you that he had some fixed dice, where they had the electronic button and the dice would stop and you would always win?"

"Yeah," Bynum answered.

"And he sold that to you, didn't he?"

"Yeah."

"And how much did he pay for that? $25,000?"

"Yes, sir."

"And then Billy told you were going to have to be the house, and it was fixed so you could win all the money?"

"Yeah."

"So he had you to put up some money to be the house, didn't he?"

"No, sir."

"But he said you were the house?"

"He said I was the house."

"And then, lo and behold, he's fixed it where the player would win?"

"The house won."

"You won some of that money back?"

"Yes."

"And you gave Billy Ray $25,000, is that what you just said?"

"Yeah."

John East recalls that with Bynum's admission about his use of the rigged gambling device, a murmur went through the packed courtroom. East said he could sense, for the first time, the opinion of the crowd swing decidedly against Bynum when he openly admitted that he had cheated people. For many of those observing the trial, it was the first time they had seen the mysterious side of Hugh Otis Bynum that for so long had been hidden from the people of the town.[6]

Baxley asked Bynum how many rifles he had owned. Bynum replied that he had bought two rifles over the years. When asked how many rifles he currently had, Bynum answered, "I got no rifle at home now."

"No rifle at home now?" asked Baxley.

"No."

"The sheriff or ATF agents has one, is that right?"

"That's right."

"You didn't trade that other rifle in on something, somebody stole it?"

"Yes, sir."

"I figured that's what happened," Baxley replied sarcastically.

Bynum said he had considered himself to be a friend of Loy Campbell until October 1974, when Donald Barrett began to question him about the bombing. But Baxley pressed on and

Bynum admitted he had ill feelings for Campbell before the 1974 incident with Barrett.

"But you say you haven't been unfriendly towards Loy Campbell?" Baxley asked.

"I haven't."

"Do you remember when Mr. Barrett came and got your fingerprints and you were talking about the lie detector you were telling Mr. Beddow about?"

"Yeah."

"Do you remember Mr. Barrett asking you about whether or not you hated Loy Campbell?"

"Yeah."

"What did you tell him?"

"I told him, 'No'."

"Did you say you didn't like him?"

"No, I didn't say I didn't like him."

"You didn't say that? I will ask you whether or not, when an ATF agent, Barrett, came to see you that you stated to him that you did not hate Loy Campbell, but you sure didn't like him, when Loy represented those men in burning your house? Did you say that?"

"I might have said that. I don't know."

"Did you further say, 'No, I don't hate him but I don't like him, and I ain't ever going to give him no business'?"

"Yeah, I said I wasn't going to give him any more business."

"You said you weren't going to give him any more business because he represented those two that had been charged with bombing that house?"

"That's right, not bombing it, though."

"And that was when? 1969?"

"I think so."

Bynum said he had been close friends with Sheriff Bob Collins, had even given Collins's daughter a diamond necklace, but admitted he turned against the sheriff when he was arrested for shooting the two black teenagers and Collins failed to make an arrest for the burning of Bynum's barns.

"You gave the sheriff a list of some people you said that burned your houses right about that time, and you wanted him to investigate it, didn't you?" Baxley asked.

"Yes."

"And he didn't arrest anybody?"

"No."

"And you turned against him right then, didn't you?"

"That's right."

"And, in fact, he did investigate it, didn't he?"

"He didn't, no."

"And he didn't arrest no one?"

"Yeah."

"And that really set you off, didn't it?"

"Yeah."

"And you haven't had a bit of use for the sheriff since then?"

"I haven't."

Bynum said he did not have any hard feelings toward Mayor John T. Reid, but admitted he had resented the fact that the city had condemned some Bynum property to build a park in the black section of town. He said there had been a conflict between himself and the city when one of his cows had been found dead on city property. Baxley persisted, and Bynum admitted his true feelings for the mayor.

"You haven't, since then, been complaining about first one thing and then another?" asked Baxley.

"Well, John T. Reid is not a friend of mine."

"John T. Reid is not a friend of yours?"

"He is an acquaintance but not a friend."

"You don't like him, really, do you?"

"No, I don't like him."

"That's not what you said about five minutes ago, is it?"

"Yeah."

"It is what you said from the start, before we got into all this business, that you didn't like John T. Reid?"

"That's right."

"You have said that all along?"

"Yeah."

"Now, you went around and got mighty, mighty mad at John T. Reid about some events that happened the night that you were in the Jackson County Jail here, when they burned some buildings, didn't you?"

"I didn't get mad at him about that."

"John T. went and made some speeches trying to quiet down some trouble, didn't he?"

"Yeah."

"You didn't like that, did you?"

"I didn't like it."

"And you resented it very much, didn't you? You thought John T. was out of place to do that?"

"I did. I thought he was out of place."

Bynum denied he had ever called Isaac Roberts by telephone and denied ever telling him to tell Charles Hale "to keep running and go to Mexico." He also denied ever talking to a man at McCrary's service station about killing the sheriff and denied ever giving the man $3,000 to carry out the murder. Bynum also flatly denied ever talking to McCrary the morning of the First Monday bombing.

In direct contrast to what he had testified earlier, Bynum said he had only seen McCrary three times after McCrary was released from the federal prison in November 1972.

"Now, how many times did you say you had seen Billy Ray between the time he got out of the federal penitentiary and the time Loy was blown up?" Bynum was asked.

"Three."

"Didn't Mr. Beddow ask you and you said four?"

"Three."

"You said 'three' all along?"

"Yeah."

Throughout his examination of Bynum, Baxley repeatedly brought Bynum back to the conversation with the undercover agent on the night of 6 December 1974. The attorney general then took Bynum, once again, through the details of that night's conversation. In response to Baxley's intense questioning, Bynum admitted to many of the statements attributed to him. Bynum admitted saying, "Why, hell, yeah, I could, I could have done it myself before the news got out on him, anytime, myself, damn near," referring to the killing of the sheriff. He admitted that on more than one occasion, he had told the agent and McCrary that he could get any amount of money he wanted, but that it might be traced back to him and that if the sheriff were killed, he would be a suspect. And he admitted telling the undercover agent, Harold Wilson, about the burning of his barns.

Asked Baxley, "And did Billy Ray say, 'Just tell him . . . by God, how they done you, Hugh,' remember that?"

"No, sir."

"And didn't you immediately answer, 'Well, I shot these two damn niggers, they were in my cattle, and they put me in jail'?"

"That's right."

" 'I lost my house and two barns and had to sell my cattle at a commercial price while they were registered cattle. In all, it cost about $92,000.' Did you say that?"

"That's right."

Bynum also admitted saying to the agent, "Yeah, I wouldn't give a damn if it was done a month ago," again referring to killing the sheriff. Asked by Baxley if he had said, when the agent quoted a price for murdering the sheriff, "Well, that's a reasonable price, but I ain't got any money, that's my trouble," Bynum told the jury, "I remember saying that."

At one point in the examination, Baxley asked Bynum if he feared the undercover agent. "Were you afraid he was an undercover agent?"

"No, I wasn't afraid of him."

"You were afraid he was a mean man?"

"No."

Hugh Otis Bynum had been on the witness stand for more than four hours. As Baxley neared the end of his examination, one of his aides handed him a slip of paper. After reading the message, he turned back to Bynum for one more series of questions. "When was the last time that you heard from Charles X. Hale?" Baxley wanted to know.

"I read in the newspaper that he got in trouble in Florida," Bynum said.

"When have you heard from him?"

"I haven't heard from him."

"You haven't heard from him?"

"From him, I haven't."

Baxley then delivered a startling revelation to the packed courtroom. "Do you know that two weeks ago he was arrested in Bowling Green, Kentucky, under a fake name and by the time his prints came back, he made bond and got loose again?"

Over the murmur of the crowd, Bynum's answer barely could be heard. "No, sir, I didn't know that," Bynum whispered.

So there it was. The elusive fugitive had been captured but allowed to go free through a breakdown in communication. The man accused of wiring the bomb to Loy Campbell's car was still loose. Little did anyone know that Charles X. Hale would continue to elude the authorities for many more months.

Hugh Otis Bynum's testimony in defense of himself had been a litany of denials. It had also been a testimony of contrasts and contradictions. Bill Baxley later told his staff he had never been so pleased by the examination of a defendant.[7]

At the conclusion of Bynum's testimony, the defense rested its case. However, Baxley had one more witness he wanted to put on the stand. Late in the afternoon on that Good Friday, 1975, John L. Poarch took the stand to testify against Hugh Otis Bynum.

19   *Putting On a Front*

If the trial of Hugh Otis Bynum, Jr., had been a Shakespearean play, John Poarch surely would have played the part of Falstaff. "I have never seen a more comical witness," Bill Baxley recalls. "He was a natural comedian." His testimony was interrupted by laughter from those watching the proceedings. It was not so much what he said, but how he said it.[1]

Bynum's defense attorney, Roderick Beddow, Jr., is less flattering in his assessment of the jewelry salesman. "Poarch was a joke," Beddow said nearly twenty years after the trial. Beddow was not amused by Poarch's antics.[2]

At the time of the trial, Poarch was making his living as ring salesman. He traveled throughout seven states selling inexpensive imitation diamond rings that he passed off as more expensive jewelry. "Now, this ring is not stolen," was an opening line Poarch often used. He was telling the truth, but the implication was that the ring was in fact stolen. He used this premise to explain to the buyer why he was asking such a small amount for such an expensive ring. During one of the breaks in the trial, the inveterate salesman tried to swap one of his personal rings for a snappy sportscoat worn by Oliver Laney, one of the bailiffs assigned to the Bynum jury.[3] A big hulking man, at the time of the trial the salesman wore his brown hair long, combed over his ears and over his shirt collar. His speech was tinged with a hint of a lisp, but that did not hinder the man's gift of gab.

Poarch began his testimony by relating how he had stopped at Billy Ray McCrary's service station at Martintown Hill. He had never met McCrary before that time, he told the court. He said McCrary approached him about making some easy money. "I stopped and was going to get some gas and going to sell him a ring," Poarch said, "and we got to talking and McCrary said, 'You are a fast talker,' and he said, 'I know where we can make some money.' And I said, 'Well, I am in for making some money, you know.' "[4]

Poarch told the jury that a few weeks after the initial meeting with McCrary, he stopped by the service station on his way to Chattanooga with the intention of selling some more rings. It was then he first met Hugh Otis Bynum. "Billy said, 'There is that Bynum guy I was telling you about,' and so he told me to come on inside the trailer, that is what he was using for a station office, and commenced talking, and was talking to me and telling about how bad I was."

"Who was doing that?" Baxley asked.

"Billy."

"Billy Ray?"

"Yes, and telling about how rough I was, what all I had done, and me and him had been in prison together, which I didn't know he had ever been in. And he was telling him all this stuff and I was going along with it. And the old man was standing there watching me, and I was watching out of the corner of my eye, standing there listening. And Billy Ray was talking about how they wanted to kill, you know, the sheriff and three or four more and I was going along with him and he was telling how bad I was and I was going right along with it, you know, and I would do anything, you know, and so after a while then, he got him out and talked to him."

"Billy Ray left with the old man?"

"Outside the door and talked to him, and then he was telling me, you know, the old man would give me so much money."

Roderick Beddow interrupted Baxley's examination with a question of his own. "Was Mr. Bynum present during all this?" Beddow asked Poarch.

"Yes, sir, during all this talk about me being a bad guy, he was.

And then, Billy got in hisself talking, and come back to me and told me how much money Bynum would spend."

Baxley resumed his questioning. "How much money did Billy say he would spend?"

"He said he would give me $5,000 walking money and $5,000 in thirty days. Of course, it was going to be thirty days before I could come back anyway."

Poarch said the three of them went to another trailer belonging to McCrary and at that time, McCrary and Bynum got into Poarch's car. "We went down to his trailer, and Mr. Bynum got in my car and sat there and talked. Mr. Bynum said, 'I can't get no money until tomorrow. The banks won't be open until 10:00 tomorrow.' And Billy Ray said to Bynum, 'I will tell you what. I owe you $2,000. I will go ahead and give him $2,000. I am going to show him around the town,' you know, and I was to come back tomorrow and pick it up, pick the money up."

"Pick up the rest of the five?"

"Yeah, the other $3,000."

"All right."

"And in thirty days, I was to go back to the station and get the other $5,000 from Billy Ray. I wasn't supposed to see him anymore, so Mr. Bynum was going to follow me down to his house. He was going to show me where his house was. He said, 'When you come in the morning, you pull around here to the back.' "

"This man over here said that?" Bill Baxley asked pointing to Bynum sitting in the courtroom.

"Yes, sir," Poarch answered.

He said he returned to McCrary's trailer where the two men laughed about their plot to hoax the old man. The next day he returned to Scottsboro and drove to Bynum's house, taking pride in the fact he was there promptly at 10 A.M. He testified that Bynum came out of the house after he had pulled his car to the back of the house as he had been instructed. "He came walking out the back door, walked up to the car door. I rolled the car window down and he said, 'Well, I've changed my mind.' And I said, 'You did?' And I said, 'Well, let's go up there and tell Billy Ray,' and he said, 'Okay.' I said, 'You go with me,' you know, and he got in the car with me and we started driving on up that way and we got up there two or three miles and he said, 'Turn around'."

"Who is 'he'? This man here?" Baxley asked, again pointing to Bynum sitting at the defendant's table.

"Yes. And I said, 'Which way?' And he said, 'I am going to go ahead.' And I said, 'Okay.' And I drove back down, and he showed me how to get back down to his house and I pulled right back in the same place, and he said, 'I will be back in a few minutes.' He said, 'I got to go to the bank,' that's what I understood him to say. So he got his Buick out and I got backed out of the way there and he went on and was gone, I would say, fifteen minutes, and he came back with an envelope."

"What was in the envelope?" Baxley wanted to know.

"Three thousand dollars. Thirty one-hundred-dollar bills."

Poarch said that at that time, McCrary, apparently nervous the salesman might abscond with the entire amount, pulled into Bynum's driveway. Together, he and McCrary pulled their cars away from Bynum's house and met a short distance later, where they split the $3,000.

Poarch testified he never had any intention of killing the sheriff or anyone else. Asked if there had been any conversation between himself and Bynum while riding in the car, Poarch said, "Well, he wanted to, but I wouldn't let him. I told him I knew everything. Don't worry about a thing."

"Tell what he would say or start to say," Baxley instructed.

"He would start to tell me, 'Now, you are going to get the sheriff and these other two or three people's names,' and I would say, 'Now, listen. Me and Billy Ray's done worked this out.' I said, 'Don't tell me nothing. Just don't tell me nothing.' And he said, 'You know where he lives?' And I said, 'Now, Billy Ray is going to show me everything'."

"Do you recall anybody that was mentioned, that the old man mentioned, that you were supposed to kill?"

"Well, the sheriff and he named two or three or four more. I don't remember."

"But you don't know who the others were?" Baxley asked.

"No, I done forgot the other names, but they were two or three important people in town he was mad at."

Poarch said he did not see Billy Ray McCrary again until after McCrary had been taken to Montgomery and Hugh Otis Bynum had been arrested. He said he stopped briefly at McCrary's service station and learned then about the bombing of Loy Campbell. He told Baxley and the jury, "I done found out I was at the wrong place and I didn't go back."

Poarch testified he had only met Bill Baxley on the Wednesday of the week of the trial. He said the attorney general had instructed him to find something that might show the date he had gotten the money from Bynum. Poarch said he found receipts from when he had purchased a necklace on that day for his wife using some of the money he had gotten from Bynum. He said the receipts were dated 15 November 1974.

Attempting to find weaknesses in the man's testimony, Roderick Beddow cross-examined John Poarch using of a series of probing questions. He asked Poarch if he ever used credit cards or kept receipts for the rings he sold. Poarch told Beddow and the jury he preferred to deal in cash, did not use credit cards, and rarely gave receipts for the rings he sold. He could not, consequently, say for sure the date he first met Billy Ray McCrary. He insisted, however, he had not known McCrary before stopping at the service station for gasoline.

At one point, Beddow questioned Poarch at length about a rifle the man said he had with him the second time he stopped at McCrary's service station. This was the day he first met Hugh Otis Bynum. Poarch said he left the rifle with McCrary as he drove on to Chattanooga because he feared he might be breaking the law by carrying the rifle in his car. He said he later retrieved the rifle from McCrary and that he then gave it to his son.

Beddow then led Poarch through the conversation in which he, McCrary, and Bynum allegedly had discussed the plot to kill the sheriff. "And what was said or done by either of you or Mr. Bynum or Mr. McCrary?" Beddow asked.

"Well, McCrary was talking to Bynum about that, and he got him out and talked to him and come back, both of them did, and talked to me about, you know, what he was wanting done, how much money he would pay."

"Now, you say 'talking about what he was wanting done.' Was Mr. McCrary talking to you about what he was wanting done?"

"Well, they both was."

"What did Mr. McCrary say?"

"He was just telling about how bad I was, to him, one thing and another."

"What did McCrary tell you he wanted done?"

"They just wanted the sheriff killed."

"Wanted the sheriff killed. Did you advise them at that time and on that occasion how you were going to kill the sheriff?"

"Well, something was said about gassing and something was said about shooting." Poarch went on to say that the suggestion was to drill holes in the walls of the sheriff's home and gas him.

Beddow pressed Poarch to discover whether the suggested means of murder had come from Billy Ray McCrary. "Well, let's get back to this gassing," said Beddow, "that intrigues me. Who determined that you could bore holes in the wall and gas the sheriff?"

"I don't know. I might have said it myself," Poarch answered. Poarch then repeated his assertion that he had no intention of carrying out the murder plot. "It was just talk, putting on a front for him. There wasn't nobody going to do nothing," he said.

"You didn't enter into any conspiracy with McCrary or Mr. Bynum to kill anybody?"

"No, I wasn't going to bother anybody."

"Well, was it McCrary's idea to make this statement to Mr. Bynum and get $3,000?"

"Well, he said you had to talk rough and make him think you would do anything. That was the talk and that was why he was bringing up this stuff, you know."

In response to Beddow's questioning, Poarch said the first time he told anyone about the hoaxing of Hugh Otis Bynum was on Wednesday night of the week of the trial, when he met with Bill Baxley in Scottsboro. Beddow questioned Poarch at length about how he had come to be called to testify. Poarch told the story of how he had been initially contacted by John East, how he had refused to cooperate with East, how he had been tracked down by Buck Watson and Artie Wooten, and how, finally, East and Paul Mount had found him in Huntsville and brought him to Scottsboro.

Poarch repeated for Beddow and the jury how he had come to find out about Hugh Otis Bynum, Billy Ray McCrary, and the bombing of Loy Campbell. "He was telling me about being in the penitentiary one day and being in Montgomery, over this one thing and another," Poarch said of his final meeting with McCrary. "And then, he told me all about who this Bynum was and all this stuff that had been going on. And so, I was in a hurry to get out of there and so, I didn't stay no longer than I had to."

Referring to McCrary's previous testimony about the "old and yellow" money, Beddow asked Poarch to describe the money he said he had gotten from Bynum.

"They were thirty one-hundred-dollar bills," the man said.

"They weren't old and yellow, were they?"

"No, sir, they were pretty new. I had to ruffle them up a little to keep them from sticking together."

"When you went to split the loot?"

"I wanted to be sure I didn't give him one too many."

Poarch's remark about how he was careful not to be outconned by McCrary drew a round of laughter from the courtroom.[5] Obviously, there was no honor or trust between the two thieves.

In response to Beddow's final question, Poarch again insisted he never intended to carry out the murder.

"But it was never your intention to kill anyone?" Beddow asked.

"No, sir."

"And you didn't enter into any agreement with McCrary to kill anyone?"

"No, sir."

In all, the defense had done nothing to shake Poarch from his testimony. Beddow had done little to show that the man was not telling the truth.

Following up on Poarch's testimony, the prosecution called George H. Gibson to the stand. Gibson was a senior vice president at a Scottsboro bank where Bynum did business. Gibson produced records showing that at 10:30 A.M. on 15 November 1974, Hugh Otis Bynum had visited a safe-deposit box. This date matched the date on which Poarch said he had gotten money from Bynum, and the time noted on the bank records fit the time of day Poarch said Bynum had gone to the bank.

Defense lawyer Al Bowen, in his brief cross-examination of the banker, could do nothing to show that the records might have been altered. Over the objections of Bill Baxley, Bowen asked Gibson to go to the bank and bring the safe-deposit box back to the courtroom. Judge Sullivan never ruled on the objection, and Gibson never brought the box to the courtroom.

The last witness called by the prosecution was the insurance agent, Norman Farrior, who testified to seeing Hugh Otis Bynum and Billy Ray McCrary on the courthouse square the morning of the First Monday bombing. He said he saw the two men standing together and apart from anyone else on the sidewalk near Tom's Restaurant. During cross-examination, Farrior said he had first told Bunk Campbell about seeing Bynum and McCrary together shortly after the bombing. He said he told Alabama Bureau of Investigation agent Marvin Bryant about the incident shortly after Bynum was arrested. Farrior admitted he was a close friend of Bunk Campbell and had known Loy Campbell for more than fifteen years.

Following the testimony of Norman Farrior, the prosecution rested its case against Hugh Otis Bynum. However, in light of the testimony of John Poarch, the defense was now obligated to offer further witnesses. As a part of their rebuttal of Poarch's testimony, the defense entered into a lengthy and tangled discussion of how and when the salesman had been subpoenaed. The defense called to the stand John East, the investigator with the attorney general's office, who testified that Billy Ray McCrary had first told him about John Poarch during an interview on 19 December 1974. He said that at first McCrary remembered the man's name as being "Henry" but that later McCrary produced the man's true name and a telephone number. Poarch had testified he had written his name and telephone number for McCrary thinking McCrary would help him to sell some more rings.

East went on to say that he contacted Poarch by telephone sometime in January 1975 and that the man was evasive and would not cooperate with the investigation. He said the first time he got a statement from Poarch was on Wednesday, 26 March, the week of the trial. He said he had a subpoena from the Jackson County district attorney when he met Poarch in Huntsville outside the office of the man's lawyer.

The defense next called Jackson County Circuit Clerk Bill Wann. Wann testified that according to his records, the first subpoena for Poarch was issued on 26 March. But in response to questioning by Bill Baxley, Wann pointed out that the district attorney and the sheriff have blank subpoenas they sometimes use. He said if those subpoenas had failed to be delivered to someone living outside the county, it would not necessarily be in his records.

Sheriff Bob Collins testified that prior to the subpoena issued on 26 March, there had been two subpoenas issued for Poarch. He said one of the subpoenas had never been returned from the Madison County Sheriff's Department. He said the second subpoena had been served on Poarch by John East, and that a third subpoena, the one recorded by the circuit clerk, was given Poarch on the Wednesday night he was brought to Scottsboro. The clerk's subpoena was given Poarch to compel him to return to Scottsboro and testify.

The final rebuttal of Poarch's testimony came from the defendant himself. The defense returned Hugh Otis Bynum to the witness stand, and Bynum categorically denied ever meeting Poarch at McCrary's service station. He denied he had ever talked to Poarch about killing Sheriff Bob Collins, denied ever meeting him at his house in Scottsboro, and denied ever giving the man $3,000.

In response to the testimony given by banker George Gibson, Bynum said he kept cattle registration papers in the safe deposit box and that on the day recorded at the bank, he had retrieved some of those registration papers. In an effort to substantiate this claim, the defense produced a check written by Bynum on 23 November 1974, to the American Angus Association for the registration of some cattle.

John Poarch's testimony, beyond providing comic relief, had been a serious and damaging attack on the defense. His testimony was significant because it tended to substantiate Billy Ray McCrary's testimony about the hoaxing of Hugh Otis Bynum and, more important, it showed how obsessed Bynum had become with the killing of Bob Collins.

In the courtroom where the trial was taking place, a hallway leads from the judge's bench and witness stand to an anteroom that served as the chambers for Judge John B. Tally, the man whose attempted assassination had focused Bill Baxley's attention on Scottsboro. Tally's office was within earshot of the witness stand, and the judge occasionally leaned his high-back swivel chair into the doorway leading to the hallway and listened in on the testimony. Following the testimony of the jewelry salesman, Tally had chance to pass John East in the hallway. "That's some mighty powerful testimony," East recalls the usually reticent judge as saying.[6] Some four months after the conclusion of the trial, Roderick Beddow admitted to John East that he had been so unnerved by Poarch's testimony that it had made him physically ill. He told East he had gone back to his hotel room and vomited.[7]

It was now late in the afternoon on that Good Friday and all the testimony in the case against Hugh Otis Bynum was in. The trial had spanned five days and had generated over 750 pages of testimony. A total of fifty-five witnesses had testified during the week. The trial had become the longest criminal trial in Jackson County's history. All that remained was the lawyers' closing arguments to the jury. Knowing that these arguments would be time-consuming, Judge Sullivan excused the jury for the day. The Saturday before Easter would be given over to the final statements from the prosecution and the defense. The burden would then fall to the jury to decide the fate of Hugh Otis Bynum.

The issue of Bynum's character had not surfaced during the trial. At the conclusion of the testimony on that Friday, Bill Baxley told John East to turn his notes documenting Bynum's past acts of violence over to a reporter with *The Birmingham News* by the name of Peggy Roberson. Little did Baxley know that the generous act was to threaten the final outcome of the case.[8]

20   *Lay Down with Dogs*

The closing arguments of a trial are that phase of the proceedings during which the defense and the prosecution are given the opportunity to go over for the jury the facts of the case. It is also an opportunity to make appeals to the emotions of the jurors. It can be the most dramatic part of a trial and often can be overtaken by theatrics. It is the final struggle in the effort to prove a person's guilt or innocence. Because the closing arguments of a trial so often are based on emotion, in most Alabama cases the lawyers' statements do not constitute part of the trial record and are not included in the final transcript.

John Yung took the lead in the prosecution's closing arguments. Yung labeled much of the defense's case as a legal smoke screen, an effort to draw the jury's attention away from the facts in the case. He methodically went over the testimony of the many witnesses and told the jurors that, as reasonable people, they could very easily tell which witnesses were being truthful.[1]

In spite of his college professor appearance, John Yung was not above appealing to the emotions of the jury. At one point, he compared Loy Campbell to Alabama's governor, George Wallace. Wallace was popular in Jackson County, and both he and Campbell had been crippled by assassination attempts. The comparison drew an angry objection from Roderick Beddow.

"Wait a minute, please," Beddow said. "Governor Wallace, he hasn't been brought into this trial, and it's an appeal and it's bogus and we ask the court to instruct the jury that Mr. Campbell's liken unto Governor Wallace doesn't have anything to do with this lawsuit."[2] Judge Sullivan sided with Beddow and instructed the jury to ignore Yung's remark.

At another point in his argument, Yung drew an objection from Beddow when he again tried to appeal to the jury's emotion by pointing out that Campbell's six-year-old daughter, Ramona, surely would have been killed by the explosion if she had not walked to school on that First Monday. Judge Sullivan again ordered the jury to ignore the remark.[3]

But there was one bit of John Yung's histrionics the jury could not ignore even if they had been ordered to do so by the judge. Throughout the trial, it had been the prosecution's concern that Loy Campbell might not be seen by the jury as a victim. Campbell had never wanted to be pitied. Even though he wore the artificial legs and walked with the aid of crutches, as he sat at the prosecution table dressed in a business suit there was no outward appearance that he had suffered a terrible explosion. During his appeal to the jury, and with no advance warning to anyone except Loy Campbell, Yung reached down, picked up one of Campbell's crutches and began to bang on the man's artificial legs. Bill Baxley's assistant, Bill Bowen, remembers hearing the metallic sound echo through the hushed courtroom.[4] Yung then pointed the crutch at the defendant and delivered a scathing indictment. "Hugh Otis Bynum bought this for Loy Campbell for $2,000," Yung told the jury.[5]

Loy Campbell, the man whose life had been changed forever by the vicious attempt on his life and who was now the subject of the jury's attention, showed no emotion during Yung's dramatic use of the crutch. However, Bill Baxley recalls that a few moments later, he looked at Campbell and noticed that a single tear made its way down the man's cheek.[6]

John Yung did not remain in Scottsboro for the jury's decision. Upon completion of his closing argument, Yung slipped out of the Jackson County Courthouse for the four-hour drive south to Montgomery in order to serve as pallbearer at the funeral of a friend that Saturday afternoon.[7]

The task of the defense, in their closing arguments, was to tear away at the prosecution's conspiracy theory and to cast doubt on the alleged motive. It was also the task of the defense to discredit the testimony of Billy Ray McCrary, the state's chief witness against Hugh Otis Bynum. In his closing statement, Roderick Beddow wasted no time in viciously attacking the character of Billy Ray McCrary. "He is a bootlegger, a dope pusher, and a man who burns homes and upon whom the oath given him was a waste of time," Beddow said. He pointed out to the jury McCrary had been given immunity for his testimony and that he had been free to drive around in a big Cadillac while Hugh Otis Bynum was locked in jail for two months.[8]

Referring to the testimony of Lilah McCrary and her statements about the dynamite caps she said she found in McCrary's pocket, and referring to the TVA job application where McCrary had put "powder man" as his first job choice, Beddow asked the jurors if they were not sure McCrary himself hadn't planted the bomb on Loy Campbell's car. Beddow also pointed out apparent conflicts between the testimony of McCrary and Linda Darlene Sullivan. He pointed to the fact that McCrary had testified Bynum had told him to go to Campbell's house and cut his throat. But Linda Darlene Sullivan had testified that Charles Hale had said Bynum was satisfied because Campbell had suffered enough. Beddow also brought to the jury's attention the fact that McCrary had testified Charles Hale had gotten paid $400 for the bombing but that Linda Sullivan had said Hale had been paid $1,000. Beddow also told the jury that only McCrary had testified about some of the payoff money as being "old and yellow" looking.[9]

Beddow attacked the testimony of John Poarch, the ring salesman, saying, "birds of a feather flock together." Beddow said the whole story of the two men hoaxing Bynum had been conjured up. He said it was ridiculous to believe Hugh Otis Bynum would have been foolish enough to pay a man like Poarch $3,000 to drill holes in the sheriff's house and gas him.[10] Beddow also tried to cast doubt on the motive theory. He said that the prosecution had offered no substantiated evidence that there had been any ill will between Hugh Otis Bynum and Loy Campbell. And as far as a conspiracy, Beddow pointed to the fact that there had been no acts of violence against Campbell or any of the other men on the so-called hit list since the First Monday bombing in December 1972.[11]

Finally Beddow attacked Bill Baxley. He questioned the reason the attorney general of Alabama had gotten involved in the case and said the only reason Baxley came to Scottsboro was for political gain. The only reason Hugh Otis Bynum had been arrested, Beddow told the jury, was "because he makes good newspaper copy."[12]

Al Bowen is a big man with a commanding voice. He took up the attack on the prosecution's case and repeated the assertion that Billy Ray McCrary had framed Hugh Otis Bynum.[13]

Perhaps to counter Bynum's poor performance on the witness stand, Bowen insisted that Bynum had told the truth and said the man had taken the stand even though "he knew a lot of stuff would come out he'd rather didn't." Bowen admitted that in his younger years, Bynum had been "a cutter and a rounder. He drank and gambled and wasn't afraid of the devil." But since being afflicted with scleroderma, Bowen said Bynum was unable to do what he once had done. He said Bynum was now forced to relive his younger years vicariously by associating with men like Billy Ray McCrary. But in spite of his association with known criminals, Bowen said, there had been no evidence showing that Bynum was not an honest man.[14]

Bowen launched an attack on the prosecution's witnesses. He said the insurance agent, Norman Farrior, because of his friendship with Bunk Campbell, had conveniently remembered seeing Hugh Otis Bynum and Billy Ray McCrary together in the days preceding the bombing. Bowen's attack on Linda Darlene Sullivan was especially harsh. Recalling for the jury the woman's sordid past and appealing to the jurors' sense of morality and evoking the southern concept of "poor white trash," Bowen said of Sullivan, "Her testimony is the rankest sort of testimony coming from a briar patch whore."[15]

Bowen turned his attention to the conversation between

Bynum and the undercover agent, Harold Wilson. He portrayed Wilson as a thug who had threatened Bynum and said Bynum had been afraid of the agent but "wouldn't tell you that if his life depended on it." He repeated that Bynum was an innocent man who was being falsely accused by his former friend, Billy Ray McCrary.[16]

It was now Bill Baxley's turn to argue the state's case. As a prosecutor, Baxley had earned a reputation for delivering fiery summations to juries. It was said that if he could ever get to a jury he could win a seemingly unwinnable case.[17] On the wall in his Birmingham law office hangs a plaque with a quote from the poet Dante that reads, "The hottest place in hell is reserved for those who, in a time of moral crisis, maintain their neutrality." Throughout his life, Bill Baxley has been surrounded by controversy. A man with a distinct belief in right and wrong, he never has shied away from or compromised those beliefs. He was far from being neutral when he stood before the jury in that Jackson County courtroom. His closing argument was that of a man convinced that Loy Campbell had been the victim of violence brought on by an old man's sick and twisted mind.

Much of Baxley's closing statement was given over to answering and refuting the arguments raised by the defense. He began by answering Beddow's charge that he was in Scottsboro to prosecute the case solely for political gain. "I hate that I even have to waste time talking about it," he told the jury.[18] Then, referring to the attempted bombing of Judge John B. Tally, Baxley told the jury, "Around 'bout August or September or something of this past year, '74, something happened up here and the courthouse and the bar association got in an uproar and said there wasn't enough help coming up here and they had to have some help with this situation. We came in it full force. I personally got in it.

"Sure I got a job as a political officer. But I consider myself a prosecutor and an attorney general under your constitution and under your laws as the chief prosecutor in this state. I know enough about politics, if all I was interested in was politics, there'd be a lot better ways of gettin' it than gettin' in a controversial situation, 'cuz you don't do nothing but make some people mad. In the time I spent on this case, if all I was interested in was making political hay, I could have gone around and made a hundred political speeches and shaken ten thousand hands and made speeches being against dope and waving the flag and not made a soul mad. That's got no place in this trial."

In his closing remarks, Roderick Beddow had talked about McCrary lying to Judge John Haislip during the preliminary hearing in December 1974. Beddow had pointed out to the jury that the attorney general had remained silent as McCrary lied. Baxley had an answer for the jury. "Beddow said, 'Mr. Baxley was sitting right over here, just a few feet away when Billy Ray testified and never uttered a word,' like I was implicated in Billy Ray's lie. Gentlemen of the jury, if a lawyer is supposed to jump up every time a witness on the stand tells something that is not true and he knows it, when Hugh Otis Bynum was on that stand, Mr. Beddow would have looked like a jack-in-the-box over there. He'd a been popping up every time he answered a question."

Addressing the issue of McCrary's immunity, Baxley said he would take the blame for making the deal with McCrary and asked the jury to use common sense. "I think that you have enough common sense," he told the jurors, "to realize that if we could try this case, and try Billy Ray McCrary, and try Hugh Otis Bynum, and try Charles Hale all, we much prefer to do that and put every one of them in a cell together. . . . Finally it came down where a decision had to be made. Whether or not you're going to let all three of them continue to run loose, continue to plot and run the risk of it maybe happening again or go ahead and deal with one of them even though you feel you want to wash your hands when you get through dealing."

Then Baxley speculated for the jury about what might have happened had he taken a different approach to the case. "I wonder what would have happened," he said, "if we arrested Billy Ray and Charles Hale and not arrested Hugh Otis Bynum. And maybe that week, Billy Ray had gypped Hugh Otis out of some money or he'd sold some pills or he'd stolen something and he had enough money to hire a lawyer like Mr. Beddow."

Then, his voice rising to a shout, Baxley pressed on. "Can't you imagine how Mr. Beddow or any other good lawyer would have hollered about it? 'You mean the man who planned it all, Hugh Otis Bynum, where's he? The rich man! They always try the poor folks! Where's the man who had the money? That thinks he can do anything he wants to because he's from an old family and 'cuz he's got land and 'cuz he's got money. They never do fool with people like that. They try the minnows and the slime like Billy Ray and Charles Hale!' Don't you know Bed-dow'd a hollered about it? If Mr. Beddow had been up here, he'd been jumping up so his head would have hit that rooftop!"

Baxley told the jury the motive seemed so crazy he feared they would not believe it. "But lo and behold, Mr. Bynum got up there and owned up to everything we said about motive." He said Bynum said he had been friends with Loy Campbell, Sheriff Bob Collins, and Mayor John T. Reid, but that there had come a time when the friendships soured. "The friendship turned to hate," Baxley said. "No logical reason. A rational person wouldn't have allowed that to happen! Somebody that's so blinded for what reason, I don't know, inside of his mind is so blinded by hatred, he developed these reasons and he set out on revenge.

"And I want you to remember the date. It all culminated in April of 1971 [when Bynum was tried for shooting the two black teenagers] . . . that was the cutoff date . . . and he hired an intermediary from the federal prison. And he walked around these streets and stayed in that house and plotted for eighteen months, a year and a half, Hugh Otis Bynum just thinking, 'Just wait 'till my man gets out of the penitentiary! I'll fix these so-and-sos! Oh, I can't wait! There'll be a day, there'll be a day!' Soon as Billy Ray gets out of the penitentiary, Bynum got his man to do his dirty work."

Turning to the defense claim that there was a conflict between what McCrary had said about cutting Campbell's throat and the testimony from Linda Darlene Sullivan that Bynum was satisfied that Campbell had suffered enough, Baxley pointed out that these two statements by Bynum had come nearly a year apart. "What happened in the intervening time?" Baxley asked the jury. "Hugh Otis saw Loy Campbell out at the Liberty Restaurant and he saw some of the results of his handiwork. And after he saw that, it satisfied that mind of his. He'd done had a payday for those imagined wrongs. So he could turn his attention somewhere else. So in '74, he told Charles Hale, 'No, don't fool with Loy no more. I'm not mad at you. He's suffered enough. Move on with the sheriff.' "

Countering Beddow's claim that McCrary could have done the bombing himself, Baxley told the jury, "Their own witness, Lilah, says he went to bed over there and didn't get up 'till the next morning." He scoffed at the idea that John Poarch, the jewelry salesman, and McCrary fabricated the story about hoaxing Bynum out of $3,000 to kill the sheriff and told the jury, "If that man would have been conjuring up something with Billy Ray, we wouldn't have had to issue three subpoenas for him. Wouldn't have had to wait until Wednesday to talk to him. Soon as Billy Ray told Mr. East, Mr. Poarch would have marched himself in and spilled it out if they would have conjured something up."

With his deep south Alabama accent booming throughout the courtroom, Baxley then delivered his blistering indictment of the wealthy landowner. Standing in front of Hugh Otis Bynum, the attorney general said, "Mr. Beddow starts talking something about his mama. He's got a fine mama and she told him the absolute truth when he was a young boy on her knee. She said, 'Birds of a feather, flock together.' She said, 'Show me your friends and I'll tell you what you are.' I'll add one more to it." And now with his voice rising to a shout and pointing at Hugh Otis Bynum, "If you lay down with dogs, you get fleas, and Hugh Otis Bynum has been laying with the biggest dogs in this county and he got fleas.

"That's the kind of man he is 'cause he told you who his friends were. He told you who the Boys were. 'Up there with the Boys playing cards. I just rode up there to see the Boys.' Who? Who? 'Uh . . . Uh . . . Billy Ray.' Who else? 'Uh . . . Uh . . . Bighead Johnson.' Who else? And he named them. Yeah, you show me who a man's friends are and I'll tell you what you are and Miz Beddow was right. You know who Hugh Otis' friends were."

Then, referring to the defense claim that only McCrary described the payoff money as being "old and yellow," Baxley told the jury, "I submit to you, Billy Ray McCrary has gotten so many hundred-dollar bills from Hugh Otis Bynum, he's gypped him out of so many at so many different times, he's probably gypped him out of a suitcase full of yellow, old ones and a suitcase full of new ones!"

Baxley began to go over the specific evidence in the case. Baxley took the jury back to the night Hugh Otis Bynum had been arrested after meeting with the undercover agent and giving Billy Ray McCrary two hundred dollars. Bynum had claimed repeatedly that the money given McCrary had been a loan. But Baxley reminded the jury that during the conversation, McCrary had told Bynum more than once that he could get three hundred dollars of the down payment to the agent if Bynum could come up with the rest. The claim that it was a loan was just too far-fetched to be believed, Baxley said. "If that was just an innocent loan, why didn't Hugh Otis say, 'Well, Billy, you must not need any traveling around money, or gas money, 'cause you just said you can get three hundred up'?"

Referring to Al Bowen's statement that Bynum was not dishonest, Baxley reminded the jury that Bynum had admitted to buying the rigged dice machine and had, in fact, used it to cheat people. Then Baxley launched into an attack of the testimony of the defense's chief witness, Billy Ray McCrary's ex-wife, Lilah. He pointed out to the jury that the woman had said she had not seen any electric wires on the dynamite caps she claimed she saw in McCrary's coat pocket. However, Baxley reminded the jury, the experts in the case said the detonating caps always came with wires attached.

"Oh, for some reason," Baxley said, "she took what she knew about Billy Ray being involved and then because of revenge or some reason she started either to convincing herself or just plain making it up. Ain't a thing in the world she knows about this case one way or the other, except that Billy Ray is a helluva sorry fella, and all of us know that."

Baxley talked about the peculiar way Bynum folded his money. He noted that Tom Sisk, during his testimony, had demonstrated the way Bynum folded his money and it matched the way the money had been folded the night Bynum was arrested and the way Linda Darlene Sullivan described the money Bynum had given Charles Hale.

Baxley admitted to the jury that most of the evidence against Hugh Otis Bynum was circumstantial, but he told them that in many instances circumstantial evidence can be better than eyewitness testimony. He then gave them his own classic examples of circumstantial evidence.

Appealing to the agrarian background of the jurors, Baxley said, "Can't say it this year because it's been raining too much. But there's been years, I don't know if any of you farm, where it's been mighty dry. Ground be dusty and cracked. You go to bed really worried you ain't going to make nothing that year. Ain't got any rain and you're really worried. Sleep hard all night long, you get up the next morning, you walk out there and everything looks like it's got new life to it, it's just sprung up. You see little puddles all around and little things trickling off slopes. . . . Now, you slept all night long. You didn't see it rain but you know it rained just the same. How do you know it? By circumstantial evidence and you know it beyond a reasonable doubt, even though you wasn't there and saw it.

"Maybe some of y'all's wives might wax the kitchen floor one night and put a board or something, a chair in the door and tell you, 'Stay out of there till it's dry.' You go on to bed, sleep all night. The next morning you come in there and there's rat tracks all over the kitchen. You wasn't up and saw that rat in there but you know he was there just the same as if you had a saw him. You know it how? By circumstantial evidence and beyond a reasonable doubt.

"You know what happened on that night before the bombing just the same as if you were watching Charles Hale do it and you know it beyond a reasonable doubt."

He told the jury that even though Billy Ray McCrary had a sorry reputation, there were at least a dozen points of circumstantial evidence that pointed to the fact that McCrary and the other witnesses were being truthful. He said the testimony of Wendell Britt from the State Highway Department substantiated that Charles Hale had gotten the dynamite there, just as McCrary and Linda Darlene Sullivan testified that Hale had told them. The discovery of the rotted dynamite at the Carriage House Apartments also substantiated what Sullivan had told the agents in Florida and again substantiated what Hale had told her and McCrary about trying to assassinate Bob Collins the night he planted the bomb on Loy Campbell's car.

Baxley said the testimony of Lonnie Grider, Annie Ruth McCrary, Virgil McCrary, and Captain Keith Smith substantiated what McCrary had said about meeting with Bynum after getting out of prison in November 1972. Baxley also reminded the jury about the testimony of Isaac Roberts, the uncle of Charles Hale, who said Bynum had told him to tell Hale to flee to Mexico. Bynum, in his testimony, had denied ever telling Roberts that.

"You've either got to say Hugh Otis Bynum is lying," Baxley told the jury, "or Isaac Roberts is lying. I asked Hugh Otis, did it happen like Isaac said. He said, 'No. No.' Isaac Roberts told you exactly what happened. If all you had to say, whether Billy Ray was lying or Hugh Otis was, it would be an easy decision.

But if you say Hugh Otis was telling the truth, you got to say, not only is Billy Ray lying, not only is Linda Darlene Sullivan lying, not only is Virgil McCrary lying, not only is Annie Ruth McCrary lying, but that Keith Smith lied, that Loy Campbell is lying about that conversation at the restaurant, that Isaac Roberts had lied, that Mr. Farrior had lied, that Poarch had lied."

Baxley then directed the jury's attention to the victim, Loy Campbell. "Oh, it's easy to have sympathy. Easy to have sympathy for anybody, I reckon, especially an old man that looks so harmless just looking at him. But if you're going to have sympathy, rather than direct it to Hugh Otis, direct it to this man right here. Think about it. Oh, it might have been a game with the town clown like Poarch, like he thought it was, until you look at those stumps over here. It's easy, in the subjective, to talk about a man getting his legs blowed off. But think about what that means. What does that mean? Means he'll never walk again. Every time he uses the shower or the bathroom or everything for the rest of his life . . . "

Al Bowen had had enough. He jumped to his feet and said the attorney general's emotional remarks were uncalled for. Judge Sullivan told Baxley his time had run out. But Bill Baxley was determined to have the last words. Leaning on the jury box railing and speaking in a low voice, barely audible to anyone else in the courtroom, he told the jurors, "I know you're going to do your job. I know you're going to try the case on testimony. I want to talk a little bit about Jackson County. I'm going to be back in Montgomery, but you're going to raise your children here. But you can start by making a place where they can live. You can start by a verdict of guilty in this case."

It had been a dramatic and emotional display by the attorney general. Many of the observers who sat through the trial remembered few of the details of the testimony. But most remember the closing speech by Bill Baxley.[19]

In all, the closing arguments in the case had taken nearly four hours. The task now fell to Judge Sullivan to instruct the jury in its duty. Soon, the fate of Hugh Otis Bynum would be in the hands of the twelve men seated in the jury box.

21   *The Verdict*

The weather turned sour on that Saturday before Easter, 1975. An unseasonably cold rain began to fall, threatening to cancel the many Easter sunrise services planned for Sunday morning. The gloomy weather added to the seriousness of the proceedings taking place inside the Jackson County courtroom.

Following the attorneys' final arguments, Judge Sullivan began his charge to the jury. As is true of all jury trials, it is the responsibility of the presiding judge to go over the points of law the jurors are to consider as they decide their verdict. In the case of Hugh Otis Bynum, the judge's instructions to the jury were lengthy and complex.

Sullivan read for the jury the grand jury indictment that had brought Hugh Otis Bynum to trial. "The grand jury of said county charge that before the finding of this indictment, Hugh Otis Bynum, Jr., and Charles X. Hale, whose names to the grand jury are unknown otherwise than as stated, unlawfully and with malice aforethought, did assault Loy Campbell with the intent to murder him, contrary to law and against the peace and dignity of the State of Alabama," the indictment reads. Sullivan cautioned the jurors not to consider the indictment as evidence of Bynum's guilt. He also told the jury they could find Bynum guilty of the lesser charge of assault and battery.[1]

Sullivan told the jurors that much of the state's case was based on the theory that Bynum had entered into a conspiracy with Billy Ray McCrary and Charles Hale to kill Loy Campbell. Under Alabama law, Sullivan told the jury, anyone involved in the conspiracy is just as guilty as the person who actually carries out the deed. Sullivan pointed out to the jury that it was an undisputed fact that Billy Ray McCrary and Charles Hale were accomplices in the bombing of Loy Campbell. Because of the conspiracy theory, statements attributed to Hale had been admitted into evidence through the testimony of Linda Darlene Sullivan and McCrary. However, before the jurors could consider those statements, Judge Sullivan said, they would have to determine if a conspiracy actually existed, what the purpose of the conspiracy was, and how long the conspiracy lasted. If the jurors reached

Judge William Sullivan
(Courtesy *The Jackson County Advertiser*)

the conclusion that any conspiracy had ended before Hale told his girlfriend about his part in the bombing, those statements could not be considered as evidence.[2]

Sullivan told the jury that much of the state's case rested on circumstantial evidence and that evidence must be found to be compelling and convincing before a guilty verdict could be rendered. He also defined "beyond a reasonable doubt and moral certainty" for them. Said Sullivan, "When I say the state is under the burden of proving guilt beyond a reasonable doubt and to a moral certainty, that does not mean the state must prove an alleged crime beyond every imaginable or speculative doubt or beyond all possibility of mistake, because that would be impossible. But a reasonable doubt means an actual substantial doubt arising out of the testimony, or it could arise from a lack of testimony in the case. It is a doubt for which a reason can be assigned, and the expression to a moral certainty means practically the same thing."[3]

Just before 2 P.M. on that Saturday afternoon, Judge Sullivan completed his instructions to the jurors and sent them to the jury room to begin their deliberations. Outside the Jackson County Courthouse, a cold, hard rain began to fall.

It was Bill Baxley's habit not to remain in the courtroom while a jury deliberated. During one of the first trials he prosecuted in Dothan, Baxley had remained in the courtroom as the jury deliberated and they had returned with a not guilty verdict. As a result, Baxley had developed a superstition and refused to stay in the courtroom while the jury was out. When Judge Sullivan had completed his charge to the jury, Baxley left Scottsboro to meet his fiancée, Lucy Richards.[4] Richards had been Baxley's secretary when he was district attorney in Dothan, and he had asked her to come with him to Montgomery after being elected attorney general. The working relationship blossomed into romance, and on 11 July 1976, in a quiet ceremony, they were married. Baxley and his bride-to-be spent Easter Sunday, 1975, relaxing in New Orleans as the twelve men debated the guilt or innocence of Hugh Otis Bynum.[5]

Shortly after beginning their deliberations, the jurors took their first vote. Only two, Grady Roberts of Pisgah and John H. Graham of Stevenson, voted for acquittal. The other jurors were convinced of Bynum's guilt.

Basing his assessment on some key points in the testimony, jury foreman Doug Farmer was certain of Hugh Otis Bynum's guilt. He had been particularly impressed with the testimony of Linda Darlene Sullivan. "There was no link between the Sullivan woman and Hugh Otis Bynum," Farmer said. "There was very little reason for her to lie."[6] Farmer had also been struck by the testimony concerning the way Bynum had folded his money. Each time money from Bynum changed hands, it was folded the same way—once lengthwise and then again in the center. "If it had not been for the way the money was folded, I doubt Linda Darlene Sullivan would have ever remembered so vividly being given that money by Charles Hale," Farmer said. Sullivan had testified that the money had come from Hugh Otis Bynum.[7] Farmer was impressed by the testimony of the jewelry salesman, John Poarch, also. It was during the salesman's testimony, Farmer remembers the only time Bynum had shown any emotion. Farmer said a distinct look of surprise came over Bynum's face when the man was called to the witness stand. He believes the salesman's testimony also caught the defense lawyers off guard. "I don't believe they had any notion that the man even existed," Farmer said.[8] But, according to Farmer, the testimony of Hugh Otis Bynum itself was just as damaging as any of the other evidence against him. "He just could not help but let his hatred show through," the jury foreman said. "During his testimony, you could tell from his looks that the animosity was there. You could tell he would have done anything to get his revenge."[9]

The jurors began to go over the testimony in order to resolve the doubts of Graham and Roberts. Graham in particular, was concerned about the circumstantial evidence in the case and a lack of physical evidence. But there was something about Graham that troubled the other jurors. Doug Farmer remembers that from the very outset of the deliberation, Graham kept talking about the jurors being deadlocked. "He just kept talking about a hung jury," Farmer remembers.[10]

Farmer relayed his concerns by way of a note to Judge Sullivan. The jury had reached an impasse, Farmer told the judge, and one juror in particular was convinced the jury would not be able to reach a unanimous decision. Shortly after receiving the note, Judge Sullivan ordered that the jury be brought back to the courtroom.[11]

Experienced trial judges rarely accept a jury's first notion that they are deadlocked. As is the custom, Judge Sullivan emphasized the jurors' responsibility to try to resolve any differences of opinion. The trial had been an expensive process for the state of Alabama and some of the witnesses might not be available for a second trial, he told them. Doug Farmer remembers the judge adding one admonition. "It will be three days after hell freezes over before I will accept a hung jury," the foreman recalls the judge saying.[12]

The jurors returned to their deliberations and began to tick off the evidence against Hugh Otis Bynum. They particularly emphasized the testimony of John Poarch as revealing Bynum's obsession with killing the men.

"Poarch's talking about drilling holes in the sheriff's house and gassing him was just downright silly," said Farmer. "How could anyone imagine that it would be possible to do that in the middle of the night and with people asleep in the house. Bynum buying into that showed he had become so possessed with hatred he had lost touch with reality."[13]

Late in the evening, Judge Sullivan inquired about the jury's progress and was told that little had been made. He again brought the jurors before him. He asked them if they wanted to continue their deliberations or to call it quits for the day. The problem, he told them, was if they chose to recess, it would be Monday before they could continue their deliberations. They would have to spend Easter Sunday at the Holiday Inn.[14] The jurors returned to their deliberations and took another vote. This time, John Graham was the only one to vote for acquittal. Grady Roberts, after listening to the other jurors, had become convinced of Bynum's guilt.[15] Shortly after 9 P.M., Judge Sullivan summoned the jury and recessed them for the weekend. They were told they would resume their deliberations Monday morning.[16]

In north Alabama, as is true throughout the rigidly religious South, Easter is a particularly significant day of observance. Many pastors use this time to rekindle the Christian spirit of their flocks. Often, the week preceding Easter Sunday is given over to a time of revival, with nightly services designed to bolster belief and win new converts. It is a time of great emotion and religious fervor. Itinerant evangelists are called upon to preach emotionally charged services and to beseech followers to "come as thou art" and to accept "the blood of the Lamb." The week culminates with predawn Easter sunrise services held at high school football fields and in open pastures. The church services that follow are used to baptize newly saved souls. Within the Christian South, Easter symbolizes a new beginning. It marks the true start of a new year.

In 1975, the weather had cleared for Easter Sunday. The rains of Saturday had ended and, although colder than normal, that Sunday dawned clear and bright with sunshine.[17] The jurors spent the day resting or passing the time playing cards. During the day, while in the company of the bailiffs, two of the jurors at a time were allowed to spend a few minutes with their families. Doug Farmer recalls that his seven-year-old daughter, Adrienne, was disappointed and angry that he had not been allowed to go to church with her that morning. She had a new Easter outfit and she had looked forward to showing off the dress with her father at Easter services.[18] Farmer remembers that John Graham kept to himself that Sunday. Though none of the jurors showed any ill will toward Graham, the man did not take part in any of the social pastimes.[19]

Elsewhere in the world on that Easter Sunday, the fall of South Vietnam was imminent. Hundreds of thousands of refugees took to the sea to flee the onslaught of North Vietnamese troops. A planned airlift of refugees was suspended when the airport at Da Nang came under rocket attack as the North Vietnamese pushed toward the capital of Saigon. The United States was only days away from experiencing one of its most humiliating defeats. A chapter in American history was coming to a close.

The flight of refugees from Da Nang was chronicled in that Easter Sunday's edition of *The Birmingham News.* That same newspaper also chronicled the trial of Hugh Otis Bynum. On the front page, an article written by Peggy Roberson carried the headline, "Bynum following old habits as jury works." A photograph of Bynum in front of Tom's Restaurant on the courthouse square in Scottsboro accompanied the article. Though the jury was not allowed access to the newspaper, the papers were placed in the newsstand just outside the motel where they were staying. Defense lawyer Roderick Beddow was furious when he saw the article.[20]

Roberson had used the information John East had given her in writing the article, which detailed many of Bynum's past acts of violence. Roberson described Bynum's attack on the man at the chicken fights, the shooting of Ray Webb, the attacks on lawyer Harold Foster and newspaper editor Fred Bucheit, and the shooting of the black boy's puppy in the article. Neither the prosecution nor the defense had introduced testimony about the incidents during the trial. If a juror were to read the article, it could be argued that he had been prejudiced by the news account.

The ever-vigilant Roderick Beddow had hired an observer for that Sunday evening. He gave Robert G. "Garland" Campbell (no relation to Loy Campbell) the task of watching the jurors' rooms during the night. From 6 P.M. that Sunday evening until 7:30 the next morning, Campbell stayed in room 300 of the Holiday Inn and watched through a window to see if any of the jurors left their rooms or had visitors. Beddow was seeking anything that he might use in an appeal should his client be found guilty.[21]

At 8:30 A.M., on Monday, 31 March 1975, the jury resumed its deliberations and immediately took another vote. Once again, eleven of the men voted to convict Hugh Otis and, once again, John Graham voted for acquittal. According to Doug Farmer, the jurors were resolved to stay as long as necessary to obtain a conviction. "We knew," said Farmer, "that if Hugh Otis were set free, there would be no telling what he would do."[22]

They again went over the testimony and again pointed to the evidence that so strongly proved Hugh Otis Bynum had conspired with Billy Ray McCrary and Charles Hale to kill Loy Campbell and had paid to have the murder carried out. After about an hour, John Graham was ready to change his vote. "Ah, let's hang the son of a bitch," Farmer remembers Graham saying when he made the decision to convict. Graham's son recalls his father telling him that he was convinced all along of Bynum's guilt and Graham told Loy Campbell after the trial that he had wanted to make sure that everything was done properly.[23]

At 9:40 A.M., one hour and ten minutes after they had resumed their deliberations, the jury returned to the courtroom to deliver its verdict. Bill Bowen remembers the mood of the courtroom was somber as the jury delivered the guilty verdict.[24] Immediately, Bynum's lawyers asked that the jurors be polled to ensure that their decision was unanimous. Judge Sullivan ordered the jurors to stand before him. One by one, the twelve men told the judge that they believed Hugh Otis Bynum was guilty and that they had not been pressured to reach their decision.[25]

Judge Sullivan thanked the jurors for their time and apologized for the length of the trial and the inconvenience it had caused them and their families. Their part in the drama was now played out; Judge Sullivan dismissed the jurors, and for the first time in a week they were free to return to their homes. Judge Sullivan then ordered Bynum to stand before him as he pronounced sentence. Sullivan's voice was filled with emotion as he told Bynum and his lawyers, "I have pondered the evidence in the case. I know the great harm that has been done to the injured party in this case and I know of no mitigating circumstances." Sullivan then ordered that Bynum be imprisoned for the maximum sentence of twenty years.[26] As was the case throughout much of the trial, Hugh Otis Bynum, his stony face frozen by scleroderma, showed no emotion as the judge pronounced the sentence. He was taken into custody by Sheriff Bob Collins, one of the four men he had wanted killed. Bynum was released later that same day after he posted a $50,000 appeal bond.[27]

Don Valeska remembers that at the conclusion of the trial, many of those who had been openly hostile to the prosecution team during the course of the trial now came to them and said, "Yeah, we knew he was guilty all along. We're glad you got him."[28]

Though the work of the prosecution, Judge Sullivan, and the twelve jurors was complete, the case of Hugh Otis Bynum, Jr., was destined to be argued in yet more courtrooms.

Except among a handful of Bynum supporters, the mood of Scottsboro upon hearing the news of the conviction was one of relief. The town's business community, the chamber of commerce crowd, was relieved that the negative attention focused on the town because of the case would now dissipate. Part of the legacy of the the Scottsboro Boys case had been to make the town unduly sensitive to media attention. At such a time of economic boom, it would not do to have the image of the Friendly City tarnished by macabre tales of an eccentric man seeking revenge. Scottsboro did not want to be part of the perverted South as depicted by William Faulkner.

But others in the town were truly relieved that the menace of Hugh Otis Bynum was now subdued. His many acts of violence and intolerance and perversity, once tolerated and excused, were now openly vilified. Few doubted that Hugh Otis Bynum was an evil man who had used his heritage and position in the town to further his obsession of revenge.

The conviction of Hugh Otis Bynum signaled the beginning of a new era for Scottsboro. As in much of the South, the tradition of the elite, moneyed, old-family aristocracy was broken. No longer could wealth and social insulation ensure immunity from the law.

22   Aftermath

On 1 May 1975, Roderick Beddow filed a motion for a new trial for Hugh Otis Bynum. In his motion, Beddow cited more than forty reasons why Bynum should be given a new trial. Beddow claimed that Bynum had been unfairly convicted based on what he called the uncorroborated testimony of Billy Ray McCrary, an admitted conspirator in the plot to kill Loy Campbell. Beddow also argued that Judge Sullivan had erred when he failed to declare a mistrial after the jury foreman told him that the jury was deadlocked.[1] Judge Sullivan set a hearing for 30 May but delayed the hearing until 27 June at the request of Bynum's lawyer. The hearing was again postponed and finally took place on 7 July. As a matter of procedure, Beddow had appealed the case to the Alabama Court of Criminal Appeals.

During the 7 July hearing, defense lawyer Al Bowen closely questioned nine of the jurors, James Westmoreland, John Graham, Grady Roberts, Roy Shaw, James Bell, Homer Johnson, Gaylon Stone, Wesley Allen, and John Wann, concerning their actions during the trial. The mother of Roderick Beddow died at the time of the hearing, and Beddow therefore was unable to take part in the hearing.[2] Bowen asked the jurors if they had received any telephone calls or received visitors while sequestered at the Holiday Inn. He also asked them if they had seen or read *The Birmingham News* article of 30 March that carried the headline, "Bynum Following Old Habits as Jury Works." The jurors said they had not seen the newspaper article nor received any phone calls or visitors during the trial. They insisted they had not discussed the case outside the courtroom and had not seen anyone passing notes during the trial.

One of the jurors, Grady Roberts, said that his mother was ill during the time of the trial and that he had asked bailiff Bill McNeese to check on her condition. McNeese took the stand and told Bowen he had indeed inquired about the condition of Roberts's mother and had reported back to Roberts. McNeese and bailiff Oliver Laney both testified they had not witnessed any improper action on the part of the jurors. Another juror, John Wann, testified that on Tuesday evening of the trial he had visited a co-worker who was staying at the Holiday Inn. But, he insisted that the trial of Hugh Otis Bynum was never mentioned during the thirty-minute visit with his friend. Three of the Bynum trial jurors, Allison Wynn, J. L. "Buck" Strickland and jury foreman Doug Farmer did not appear at the hearing. However, each of the three men had provided signed affidavits to the court. In their statements, they, like the other jurors, insisted they had no outside contact during the trial nor had witnessed anything improper by any of the jurors during the course of the trial.[3] Over the strenuous objection of John Yung, Al Bowen succeeded in having *The Birmingham News* article entered into the record.

Bowen's gallant effort to find something amiss with the jury's action was for naught. On 12 August 1975, Judge Sullivan denied the motion for a new trial. In his order denying the new trial, Judge Sullivan said he could find nothing improper in the way the trial had been conducted. He said there was no evidence that the jurors had been influenced adversely. He also said that the court had acted properly in urging the jurors to continue with their deliberations even after being notified they were deadlocked.[4]

Roderick Beddow remains adamant the jurors had been prejudiced by *The Birmingham News* article. In an interview for this book, Beddow said he believes some of the jurors must have seen the newspaper, in spite of their statements to the contrary. "They were staying at the same motel we were staying at, and that newspaper was available at the newsstand," said Beddow.[5]

As the appeal process for Hugh Otis Bynum was beginning, Billy Ray McCrary was having legal problems of his own. On Friday, 20 June 1975, the star witness of the Bynum trial was arrested at his home by a team of Scottsboro police officers. McCrary was accused of stealing twenty-five sheets of paneling from a Scottsboro lumber yard. Also, while the officers were searching his home, they found a large stash of beer, and McCrary now faced an additional charge of bootlegging.[6]

On Monday, 23 June, County Judge John Haislip set bond for McCrary at $2,500 but ordered him to remain in jail on a charge of violating his probation. McCrary had applied for and had been given probation in 1973 after he was sentenced to two years in prison for illegally transporting alcoholic beverages. After McCrary's arrest for bootlegging and for stealing the paneling, Jackson County District Attorney Tommy Armstrong immediately set about having his probation revoked.[7] During a six-hour hearing on 30 June before Calhoun County Judge Edwin W. Harwell, McCrary and his wife, Joyce, testified that McCrary had been granted immunity from the probation by Bill Baxley in return for his testimony against Hugh Otis Bynum. Joyce told the Court that Baxley had told her "my word is my bond" when granting the immunity.[8]

The argument didn't wash with Judge Harwell. On Wednesday, 9 July 1975, Harwell ordered McCrary back to state prison to begin serving the two-year term for the transporting conviction. In his order, Harwell said he was satisfied that McCrary had broken the law in direct violation of his probation condition. He also said he was not aware of any state law that gave the attorney general the authority to grant immunity for all future criminal acts.[9] So it was that, for the time being, Billy Ray McCrary was off the streets of Jackson County and back in the state penitentiary.

On 27 April 1976, Bill Baxley and his assistant, James S. Ward, filed a 236-page argument urging the Alabama Court of Criminal Appeals to uphold Bynum's conviction. The argument eloquently detailed the evidence against Bynum and cited dozens of cases in support of the use of witnesses such as Billy Ray McCrary and Linda Darlene Sullivan. On 29 June 1976, the Alabama Court of Criminal Appeals upheld Bynum's conviction. Roderick Beddow immediately petitioned the Alabama Supreme Court to hear the case. However, the court ruled that Beddow should again appeal to the Criminal Court of Appeals. Undeterred, Beddow again asked for a hearing before the state's highest court, and on 15 November 1976, the Alabama Supreme Court agreed to review the case.[10]

At about the same time, the case of Hugh Otis Bynum took another bizarre turn. Charles Xavier Hale, the man who was alleged to have wired the bomb to Loy Campbell's car, was arrested in Eau Claire County, Wisconsin.[11] Except for the botched arrest in Bowling Green, Kentucky, Hale had managed to elude authorities for nearly two years. In November 1975 however, his luck ran out when he opened fire with a pistol in a tavern. In addition to the bombing charge in Alabama, Hale was wanted for murder in Florida and was wanted by the federal authorities for bank robbery. It was a contest between the different agencies to see who would get Hale first.[12]

Bill Baxley wanted to talk to Charles Hale. Any information about the bombing Hale could give the attorney general might prove valuable in the event that the state's high court granted Bynum a new trial. Baxley sent Jack Shows and John East with Sheriff Bob Collins to Wisconsin.[13] Hale had little to say when East and Shows met with him. However, he agreed to be brought back to Alabama and tell what he knew about the bombing. But something soon occurred to make Hale change his mind.[14] As

Hale was being moved in the Eau Claire Jail, he happened to spot Sheriff Bob Collins standing at the end of a hallway smoking a cigarette. He had not been told the sheriff was in Wisconsin. "Hell, no," he told Shows. "I ain't going back to Alabama with that son of a bitch. Just take me back to Florida."[15] Hale's hatred of Collins stemmed from an earlier arrest in Jackson County. Jay Black, then the district attorney, determined that Hale had violated parole and obtained a judge's order for Hale to be returned to prison. Black had instructed Collins to take Hale directly to prison and not to even let him see his family members waiting in the Jackson County Courthouse. Hale always blamed Collins for the incident.[16]

In August 1977 Hugh Otis Bynum's appeal process came to a close. In a move that shocked Roderick Beddow, the Alabama Supreme Court reversed itself and refused to hear the case. Bynum's conviction stood, and he was ordered to begin serving the twenty-year sentence. On 8 February 1978, more than five years after the car bomb exploded and shredded Loy Campbell's legs, Bynum entered prison.[17]

In a great twist of fate, Bynum was assigned a cell with Robert Edward "Dynamite Bob" Chambliss, the man Bill Baxley had prosecuted for the bombing of the Sixteenth Street Baptist Church in Birmingham. Chambliss had been convicted in November 1977 for planting the bomb that had snuffed out the lives of four young black girls.[18] Apparently, Bynum was not thrilled by having Chambliss as a cellmate. Roderick Beddow distinctly remembers that during one of his visits to Bynum in prison, Bynum told him, "Get me out of this cell with this guy. I am tired of his crying and whining about being innocent."[19]

Several of Bynum's friends from Scottsboro visited him while in prison. His longtime friend Fred Casteel, the baker, remained loyal to Bynum and made regular trips to visit him. To his attorney and to his friends Bynum continued to maintain he was innocent. In spite of his profession of innocence, however, there is evidence that prison life did nothing to lessen his thirst for revenge. In 1979, J. D. White, the deputy warden of Staton Prison in Montgomery where Bynum was being held, called Loy Campbell and Bob Collins in Scottsboro. White told the two men that he had been told by a reliable prison informer that Hugh Otis was continuing to plot to kill the two men. White told them Bynum had placed a $10,000 bounty on their heads and had made arrangements with someone in Scottsboro to make the payoff. In 1994 White said of his former prisoner, "I recall that he did not have an assigned duty either because of his age or illness. It was a real challenge for me to find a way to occupy his time so he wouldn't have an abundance of time to plot his revenge."[20]

In December 1975, nine months after the Hugh Otis Bynum trial, Loy Campbell was appointed circuit court judge in Jackson County. At that time, Chief Justice Howell Heflin of the Alabama Supreme Court wanted to revamp the state's court system. State Senator John Baker, who represented Jackson County, had opposed the planned revamping. In exchange for Baker's support of his plan, Heflin agreed to place a second circuit court judgeship in Jackson County. Following approval of the plan by the state legislature, Loy's onetime political foe, Governor George Wallace, appointed him to the judgeship.[21]

Also in 1975, Loy Campbell filed a civil suit against Hugh Otis Bynum and Billy Ray McCrary seeking two million dollars in damages. The suit became one of the most complex civil cases in Alabama legal history and is now used as a textbook case for law students. In May 1978 the case went before a Jefferson County jury with Circuit Court Judge Dugan Calloway presiding over the trial. During the trial, Campbell testified that the bombing had changed his life forever.[22] Talking about his young daughter, Ramona, Campbell told the court, "I can't be a real father, can't take part in school events, can't go places with my daughter like a normal dad."[23] Hugh Otis Bynum took the stand and again asserted he had nothing to do with the bombing. On Thursday, 25 May 1978, the jury awarded Campbell two million dollars. However, the case remained in the courts for years.[24]

Roderick Beddow defended Bynum in the civil trial. Reflecting on the case, he said, "The only good thing to come out of the civil trial was that we managed to keep the jury out for four and a half hours." Beddow said that in civil trials, the longer a jury deliberates, the greater the chance they may rule in favor of the defendant or bring back a lesser judgment. Nevertheless, Beddow called the length of deliberation "a shallow victory."[25]

During the course of the civil case, Hugh Otis Bynum, anticipating that he might lose, began to transfer ownership of much of his property and wealth in an effort to avoid paying Campbell, who filed a separate lawsuit challenging the transfers.

On 1 September 1981, the Alabama Supreme Court invalidated the land transfers.[26] Campbell had filed a separate suit claiming that he was entitled to Bynum's share of a trust set up by their father for Bynum and his two sisters. Circuit Court Judge Randall Cole of Fort Payne ruled in Campbell's favor. Bynum's two sisters, Jessie Sue and Lucy, appealed Judge Cole's decision to the Alabama Supreme Court, which ultimately upheld the judge's ruling.[27]

On 21 April 1980, Hugh Otis Bynum was taken to Veterans' Hospital in Montgomery. Warden J. D. White remembers that sometime before his hospitalization, Bynum had been transferred from Staton Prison to Kilby Prison (also in Montgomery) which has a holding facility for seriously ill inmates.[28]

At 3:05 P.M. on Saturday, 10 May 1980, Hugh Otis Bynum, one of the most enigmatic and bizarre characters in Alabama criminal history, died. He was sixty-five years old. Though the exact cause of his death is not known, one can speculate that the scleroderma that had plagued him over the course of his life had finally taken its toll. Like his spirit, his internal organs had hardened and had finally ended his life. During a private ceremony, he was buried beside his father in the family plot in Cedar Hill Cemetery in Scottsboro.[29]

23   *Postscript*

Of all the legal cases with which Bill Baxley has been involved during his career, he says the case of Hugh Otis Bynum was by far the strangest. "I have never known anyone, either before or since, like Hugh Otis Bynum," Baxley said. "Every county in Alabama probably has a character like Billy Ray McCrary, but there has only been one Hugh Otis Bynum."[1] For Baxley and his team of young, idealistic prosecutors, the Bynum case was a dress rehearsal for the more well known trial of Robert Chambliss for the bombing of the Sixteenth Street Baptist Church in Birmingham. The cases were very similar, and the prosecution used much the same style in presenting the evidence to the two juries.

In 1978, Baxley ran for governor of Alabama. In spite of the endorsements of George Wallace and University of Alabama football Coach Paul "Bear" Bryant, Baxley lost the campaign for the Democratic nomination to a former Auburn University football star named Forrest Hood "Fob" James, Jr. Baxley blamed his 1978 loss, in part, on the convictions of Chambliss and Bynum. He said that after prosecuting the Bynum case, "I never got a good vote in Jackson County."[2]

In 1982, Baxley was elected lieutenant governor. In 1986 he ran again for governor. This time he lost the runoff for the Democratic nomination to Charlie Graddick, then the state's attorney general. Baxley contested the result, however, saying Graddick had broken the law when he urged Republicans to vote in the Democratic primary runoff. Baxley hired his onetime enemy Buck Watson to represent him in his suit against Graddick.[3] A panel of federal judges ultimately ruled that Graddick had indeed broken the law, and the Alabama Democratic Party Executive Committee designated Baxley as its nominee. The voters of Alabama, perceiving that the nomination had been unfairly taken from Graddick, revolted and elected Guy Hunt, a little-known farmer from Holly Pond, who became the first Republican governor of Alabama since Reconstruction. Hunt was later removed from office after being convicted of misusing campaign funds.

Following his 1986 defeat, Baxley retired from politics and returned to a private law practice in Birmingham. During an interview for this project, Baxley said he had no intention of ever again being a candidate for political office.

John Yung remained as a prosecutor for Attorney General Charlie Graddick. In May 1980 he prosecuted J. B. Stoner of Marietta, Georgia, for the 1958 bombing of the Bethel Baptist Church in Birmingham. Stoner was convicted and sentenced to ten years in prison. After Stoner's conviction, Yung resigned from the attorney general's office and went to work for the state bar association. He retired in 1990 and presently lives in Montgomery.[4]

Bill Bowen was elected a judge on the Alabama Criminal Court of Appeals in 1976. When he defeated the incumbent, Judge Aubrey Cates, it was one of the great political upsets in Alabama history. Bill Baxley took an active role in Bowen's campaign. Judge Cates had earned a notorious reputation for overturning cases because of such trivial errors as misspelled words in legal briefs. Baxley became convinced that Cates was a bad judge. He held a series of news conferences throughout the state with local district attorneys who went over the details of decisions that Cates had overturned. Baxley's involvement had a profound impact on the campaign.[5]

Donald Valeska is still a prosecutor with the Alabama attorney general's office. In 1993, he prosecuted Peggy Lowe. Lowe was accused of assisting her twin sister, Betty Wilson, in the contract murder of Betty's husband, Jack Wilson, a prominent eye doctor in Huntsville. Betty Wilson was convicted of the murder, but a Montgomery jury acquitted Lowe, who was defended by attorney Buck Watson. During an interview for this project, Valeska said he remains convinced that Peggy Lowe is guilty.[6]

Roderick Beddow and Al Bowen continue to practice law as partners in Birmingham. Beddow said he still believes Hugh Otis Bynum was innocent. He blames Billy Ray McCrary and Charles X. Hale for the bombing and points to the testimony of Lilah McCrary as proof that the two men hatched the plot at her home the night before the explosion. He called the jewelry salesman, John Poarch, "a joke" and said he will never understand why the court allowed the man's testimony.[7]

In the twenty years since the Bynum trial, Billy Ray McCrary has continued to have legal problems. As of this writing, he is out of prison and living in Jackson County.

Linda Darlene Sullivan married a guard at the federal prison in Lexington, Kentucky. She returned briefly to Scottsboro in 1984 and worked as a waitress in a nightclub there. Her present whereabouts are unknown by the author.[8]

John Poarch continued to have contact with Loy Campbell after the Bynum trial. Shortly after the trial, he approached Judge Campbell about the possibility of producing a film about the case. Campbell declined to take part in the project, however. Poarch is a used car salesman in Toney, Alabama, just outside of Huntsville.[9]

Charles Xavier Hale remains in prison. Though conceivably he could still stand trial for the bombing of Loy Campbell, the case is officially listed as "inactive."[10]

County Investigator George Tubbs died in June 1994 after a long battle with cancer. Because of his illness, he was unable to

Circuit Court Judge Loy Campbell. In 1975, Campbell was appointed by Governor George C. Wallace to fill a newly created judgeship for Jackson County.
(Photo by Byron Woodfin)

contribute to this project. A few years before his death, he resigned from the Jackson County Sheriff's Department and went back to work as a carpenter.

John East is retired and lives with his wife Jewell in Phenix City, Alabama. An avid baseball fan, he and his wife make annual trips to Florida to watch the Atlanta Braves during spring training. He maintains that the Hugh Otis Bynum case was the most fascinating and bizarre case in which he was ever involved.[11]

Following the Bynum case, East continued to work for Bill Baxley. In 1977, East played a small part in the investigation and trial of Robert Chambliss. On 17 November 1977, Baxley delivered an emotional and dramatic closing argument to the Chambliss jury. Baxley began his statement by telling the jurors, "Today is Denise McNair's birthday." Denise McNair was one of the four black girls killed when the bomb exploded at the church shortly before the start of Sunday school. Baxley ended his statement by pleading for the jurors to "give Denise McNair a birthday present." It was East who learned only moments before Baxley was to begin his closing argument that 17 November was indeed the girl's birthdate.[12]

W. R. "Bob" Collins died on 21 February 1995, shortly before the completion of this book.

Loy Campbell continues to dispense justice as a circuit court judge in Scottsboro. He has never been challenged for reelection. His daughter Ramona graduated from the University of Alabama and is now the director of a youth home in north Alabama. Campbell's brother Bunk continues to practice law in Scottsboro, while his brother John Paul holds a doctorate and is a dean at Northeast Alabama State Community College at Powell's Crossroads on Sand Mountain. Campbell's mother, Dot, is still living.

John T. Reid remained mayor of Scottsboro until 1976, when he lost his bid for a sixth term. He died in 1987.

Hugh Otis Bynum's sister, Lucy Scott Bynum, died on 13 April 1983. She was sixty-six years old. Bynum's remaining sister, Jessie Sue Bynum, still lives in Scottsboro. She recently donated several acres of land to the city of Scottsboro for the expansion of its recreational facilities. The park is to be called Bynum Field.

R. I. "Bob" Gentry retired as Jackson County probate judge in January 1995 after holding the office for thirty-six years. He now devotes his time to his antique business.

Judge John B. Tally retired from the bench in 1983, two years before his death. The mystery of the attempted bombing of Judge Tally has never been solved, and the attempt never has been linked officially to the bombing of Loy Campbell.

J. T. "Jay" Black is retired and spends much of his time in Florida.

William C. Sullivan is still a circuit court judge in Talladega. He is currently the longest-serving circuit judge in Alabama.

Keith Smith is presently the chief of the Scottsboro Police Department.

Notes

1. First Monday

1.   Robert I. Gentry, interview by author, Scottsboro, Ala., 13 December 1993.

2.   Ron Wilson, "Bynum: His Life and Times," *Scottsboro Daily Sentinel,* 1 April 1975; "Bynum Holdings Included Mule-Trading Business," *Huntsville Times,* 15 December 1974; Virginia Brock, "Hugh Otis Bynum, Jr.—A Series of Events Drastically Altered His Life," *Gadsden Times,* 5 January 1975.

3.   Brock, "Hugh Otis Bynum."

4.   Hugh Otis Bynum, Jr., testimony, *State of Alabama v. Hugh Otis Bynum, Jr.* (case number 75-CR-116), 28 March 1975, transcript, p. 562.

5.   "No Leads in Bombing," *Huntsville Times,* 5 December 1972.

6.   Guy Hollis, "Horror Mixed with Disbelief Public Reaction to Bombing," *Huntsville Times,* 6 December 1972.

7.   Bill Eastering, "Auburn Shocked Tide and Cotton Bowl Man," *Huntsville Times,* 3 December 1972.

8.   Hollis, "Horror Mixed with Disbelief."

2. Currents of Change

1.   W. Jerry Gist, *The Story of Scottsboro, Alabama* (Nashville, Tenn.: Rich Printing, 1968), 43–50.

2.   Ibid.

3.   "Nine Negro Men Rape Two White Girls, Charge," *Jackson County Sentinel,* 26 March 1931.

4.   Ibid.

5.   Gist, *Story of Scottsboro,* 183–243.

6.   Ibid.

7.   Alabama Department of Economic and Community Affairs, *Alabama Municipal Data Book* (Montgomery: Alabama Department of Economic and Community Affairs, 1993), 72.

3. The Enigma

1.   Ron Wilson, "Bynum: His Life and Times," *Scottsboro Daily Sentinel,* 1 April 1975; "Bynum Holdings Included Mule-Trading Business," *Huntsville Times,* 15 December 1974; Virginia Brock, "Hugh Otis Bynum, Jr.—A Series of Events Drastically Altered His Life," *Gadsden Times,* 5 January 1975.

2.   Brock, "Hugh Otis Bynum."

3.   Ibid.

4.   Ibid.

5.   Ibid.

6. Ibid.

7. Ibid.

8. Robert I. Gentry, interview by author, Scottsboro, Ala., 13 December 1993.

9. Brock, "Hugh Otis Bynum"; "Mrs. H. O. Bynum, Sr., Dies in Scottsboro," *Jackson County Sentinel,* 17 October 1950.

10. Brock, "Hugh Otis Bynum"; "Mrs. H. O. Bynum, Sr., Dies in Scottsboro."

11. Jackson County (Ala.) Circuit Court Criminal Index, 20 March 1951, 11 December 1950, 19 March 1952.

12. Wilson, "Bynum: His Life and Times"; Loy Campbell, interview by author, Langston, Ala., 4 June 1994.

13. John East, interview by author, tape recording, Phenix City, Ala., 28 February 1994; Peggy Roberson, "Bynum Following Old Habits as Jury Works," *Birmingham News,* 30 March 1975, Dixie edition; Archie F. Stewart, interview by author, Scottsboro, Ala., 15 July 1994; Wilson, "Bynum: His Life and Times."

14. Ray Webb, telephone interview by author, Scottsboro, Ala., 7 September 1994; Wilson, "Bynum: His Life and Times"; Campbell interview; East interview; Roberson, "Bynum Following Old Habits."

15. Brock, "Hugh Otis Bynum."

16. Hugh Otis Bynum, Jr., testimony, *State of Alabama v. Hugh Otis Bynum, Jr.* (case number 75-CR-116), 28 March 1975, transcript, p. 602.

17. Brock, "Hugh Otis Bynum"; Wilson, "Bynum: His Life and Times."

18. Wilson, "Bynum: His Life and Times."

19. Brock, "Hugh Otis Bynum."

4. "Not So Damn Good"

1. "Buildings Burn Following Thursday Afternoon Shooting," *Scottsboro Daily Sentinel,* 25 September 1970; "H. O. Bynum Found Guilty of Assault and Fined $500," *Scottsboro Daily Sentinel,* 28 April 1971.

2. "Second Day of Bynum Trial Begins Tuesday," *Scottsboro Daily Sentinel,* 27 April 1971.

3. Ibid.

4. "Buildings Burn Following Thursday Afternoon Shooting."

5. "H. O. Bynum Found Guilty"; Hugh Otis Bynum, Jr., testimony, *State of Alabama v. Hugh Otis Bynum, Jr.* (case number 75-CR-116), 28 March 1975, transcript, p. 631.

6. "Buildings Burn Following Thursday Afternoon Shooting."

7. John East, interview by author, Phenix City, Ala., 28 February 1994; Archie F. Stewart, interview by author, Scottsboro, Ala., 15 July 1994; Peggy Roberson, "Bynum Following Old Habits as Jury Works," *Birmingham News,* 30 March 1975, Dixie edition; Ron Wilson, "Bynum: His Life and Times," *Scottsboro Daily Sentinel,* 1 April 1975.

8. "Buildings Burn Following Thursday Afternoon Shooting"; testimony of Porter Dawson, *State of Alabama v. Hugh Otis Bynum, Jr.* (case number 75-CR-116), 25–31 March 1975, transcript, p. 36; Billy Ray McCrary testimony, p. 78; Hugh Otis Bynum, Jr., testimony, p. 622; Harold Wilson testimony, p. 408.

9. Billy Ray McCrary testimony, p. 78; Wilson testimony, p. 408; Bynum testimony, p. 622.

10. Bynum testimony, p. 622; W. R. Collins testimony, p. 139.

11. Ibid.

12. Bynum testimony, p. 622; Billy Ray McCrary testimony, p. 78; Wilson testimony, p. 408.

13. Stuart Stephenson, "Municipal Programs and Profiles," *Alabama Municipal Journal*, Montgomery, Ala., April 1974, pp. 18, 19, 29.

14. Bynum testimony, pp. 629–30.

15. Ibid., p. 628.

16. Ibid.

17. Jackson County Sheriff's Department, arrest records, 19 August 1969; "Not Guilty Verdict Returned in Cases," *Scottsboro Daily Sentinel*, 8 April 1971.

18. Loy Campbell, interview by author, Langston, Ala., 4 June 1994.

19. Roderick Beddow, Jr., telephone interview by author, Birmingham, Ala., 22 August 1994; "Second Day of Bynum Trial Begins Tuesday"; Loy Campbell testimony, p. 317.

20. Campbell testimony, p. 324; Campbell interview.

21. Campbell interview.

22. Campbell interview; Jackson County Circuit Court docket, spring term, 1971; "Not Guilty Verdict Returned in Cases."

23. Bynum testimony, p. 624; Campbell testimony, p. 317.

24. Bynum testimony, p. 624; Campbell testimony, p. 317.

25. "Second Day of Bynum Trial Begins Tuesday."

26. Ibid.

27. "H. O. Bynum Found Guilty."

28. Ibid.

29. Campbell interview.

30. "H. O. Bynum Found Guilty."

31. Campbell testimony, p. 321.

5. Threads of Skin

1. Robert I. Gentry, interview by author, Scottsboro, Ala., 13 December 1993; "No Leads in Bombing," *Huntsville Times*, 5 December 1972.

2. Gentry interview; "No Leads in Bombing."

3. Dr. Durwood Hodges testimony, *State of Alabama v. Hugh Otis Bynum, Jr.* (case number 75-CR-116), 24 March 1975, transcript, pp. 69–70.

4. Unless otherwise noted, this and other material concerning the personal history of Loy Campbell is taken from Loy Campbell, interview by author, Langston, Ala., 4 June 1994.

5.   "Demo Committee Official Figures Now Complete," *Scottsboro Sentinel-Age*, 6 May 1962.

6.   "Sargent Has Filed a Contest Count," *Scottsboro Sentinel-Age*, 2 September 1962.

7.   "Campbell Named to Single Rep Seat," *Scottsboro Sentinel-Age*, 30 September 1962.

8.   Campbell interview.

9.   Gentry interview; Campbell interview.

10.   Donald Barrett testimony, p. 38.

11.   Ibid.

12.   Porter Dawson testimony, pp. 12–13.

13.   Barrett testimony, p. 38.

14.   Ibid., p. 42.

15.   Ibid., p. 43.

16.   Norman Farrior testimony, pp. 723–24.

6. No More Races

1.   "Reward Offered in Bombing Case," *Scottsboro Daily Sentinel*, 7 December 1972; Tallulah Bush, interview by author, Scottsboro, Ala., 1 February 1994. Bush was charge nurse at the time of Campbell's hospitalization in Scottsboro and was present when the investigators questioned him.

2.   Bush interview.

3.   Ibid.

4.   Loy Campbell, interview by author, Langston, Ala., 4 June 1994.

5.   "Reward Offered in Bombing Case," *Scottsboro Daily Sentinel*, 7 December 1972; "Bomb Victim Is Improved," *Huntsville Times*, 6 December 1972; Donald G. Valeska II, telephone interview by author, Montgomery, Ala., 10 June 1994; William J. Baxley II, interview by author, Birmingham, Ala., 14 January 1994.

6.   Frank Sikora, *Until Justice Rolls Down: The Birmingham Church Bombing Case* (Tuscaloosa: University of Alabama Press, 1991).

7.   Peggy Morgan, "Loy Campbell Returns to Law Office," *Scottsboro Daily Sentinel*, 2 May 1973.

8.   Donald Barrett testimony, *State of Alabama v. Hugh Otis Bynum, Jr.* (case number 75-CR-116), transcript, p. 64; Billy Ray McCrary testimony, p. 191.

9.   Billy Ray McCrary testimony; Jackson County (Ala.) Sheriff's Department arrest records; Scottsboro (Ala.) Police Department arrest records.

10.   Billy Ray McCrary testimony; Virgil McCrary testimony, pp. 179–81; Jackson County (Ala.) Sheriff's Department arrest records; Scottsboro (Ala.) Police Department arrest records.

11.   Billy Ray McCrary testimony, pp. 252–53; Claire T. Dean testimony, p. 544; "Official Counts Completed by Demo Committee," *Scottsboro Sentinel-Age*, 3 June 1962.

12.   Dean testimony, p. 544; Billy Ray McCrary testimony, p. 253.

13. Baxley interview; John East, interview by author, tape recording, Phenix City, Ala., 28 February 1994.

14. East interview.

15. Billy Ray McCrary testimony, p. 191.

16. Loy Campbell testimony, p. 329; Billy Ray McCrary testimony, p. 190.

17. Billy Ray McCrary testimony, p. 272.

18. Barrett testimony, p. 64.

19. Ibid.

20. Lilah McCrary testimony, p. 568.

21. Barrett testimony, p. 58.

22. Billy Ray McCrary testimony, p. 82.

23. Wendell Britt testimony, p. 133.

24. Ron Wilson, "Charles Hale—Elusive 'Mystery Man,' " *Scottsboro Daily Sentinel,* 6 April 1975; "Two Men Being Held," *Scottsboro Daily Sentinel,* 14 August 1969; Scottsboro (Ala.) Police Department arrest records.

25. Wilson, "Charles Hale—Elusive 'Mystery Man.' "

26. Linda Darlene Sullivan, interview by Donald Barrett and John East, tape recording, Orlando, Fla., 24 September 1974; Billy Ray McCrary testimony, p. 219.

27. Sullivan interview; Sullivan testimony, p. 381.

28. Barrett testimony, p. 52.

29. Barrett testimony, p. 55; Jimmy Evett testimony, p. 108.

30. Barrett testimony, p. 43.

31. "Campbell Moved from Local Hospital," *Scottsboro Daily Sentinel,* 10 December 1972; Campbell interview; Dr. Durwood Hodges testimony, p. 70.

32. Campbell interview; Campbell testimony, p. 320; Peggy Morgan, "Campbell Returns to Law Office," *Scottsboro Daily Sentinel,* 2 May 1973.

33. Campbell interview.

34. Ibid.

35. Ibid.

36. "Bynum, McCrary Ordered to Pay Campbell $2 Mil. [*sic*]," *Scottsboro Daily Sentinel,* 26 May 1978.

37. United Press International, "Wallace Stands to Address Lawmakers," *Scottsboro Daily Sentinel,* 2 May 1973.

38. Campbell interview.

39. Ibid.

40. Robert I. Gentry, interview by author, Scottsboro, Ala., 13 December 1993.

41. Obituary of Grover McCrary, *Scottsboro Daily Sentinel,* 17 December 1972; Billy Ray McCrary testimony, p. 76; Virgil McCrary testimony, p. 172.

42. Virgil McCrary testimony, pp. 172–73.

43.   Hugh Otis Bynum, Jr., testimony, p. 615; Billy Ray McCrary testimony.

44.   Bynum testimony, p. 616; Lonnie Grider testimony, p. 300; Annie Ruth McCrary testimony, p. 184.

45.   Bynum testimony, p. 611.

46.   Campbell testimony, p. 321.

7. **What's Going On Up There?**

1.   Ron Wilson, "Bomb Found in Local Judge's Car," *Scottsboro Daily Sentinel*, 15 September 1974.

2.   Ibid.

3.   Ron Wilson, "Tally Bomb Was 'Explosive,' " *Scottsboro Daily Sentinel*, 18 September 1974.

4.   Ibid.

5.   Ibid.

6.   William J. Baxley II, interview by author, Birmingham, Ala., 14 January 1994; John East, interview by author, tape recording, Phenix City, Ala., 28 February 1994.

7.   East interview.

8.   Ibid.

9.   East interview; Linda Darlene Sullivan, interview by Donald Barrett and John East, tape recording, Orlando, Fla., 24 September 1974; Linda Darlene Sullivan testimony, *State of Alabama v. Hugh Otis Bynum, Jr.* (case number 75-CR-116), 26 March 1975, transcript, pp. 358–59, 387.

10.   East interview; Ron Wilson, "Charles Hale—Elusive 'Mystery Man,' " *Scottsboro Daily Sentinel*, 6 April 1975.

11.   East interview.

12.   East interview; Sullivan testimony, p. 369; Wilson, "Charles Hale—Elusive 'Mystery Man.' "

13.   Keith Smith, interview by author, Scottsboro, Ala., 8 February 1994.

14.   East interview; Wilson, "Charles Hale—Elusive 'Mystery Man.' "

15.   Smith interview.

16.   Wilson, "Charles Hale—Elusive 'Mystery Man.' "

17.   Wilson, "Charles Hale—Elusive 'Mystery Man' "; Smith interview.

18.   Smith interview.

19.   Smith interview; Sullivan testimony, pp. 380–81.

20.   Smith interview; Sullivan testimony, pp. 380–81.

21.   Loy Campbell, interview by author, Langston, Ala., 4 June 1994.

22.   Campbell interview; Sullivan interview.

23.   East interview; Baxley interview.

24.   East interview; Donald Barrett testimony, p. 45.

8. **A Woman Scorned**

1.   This and other excerpts and quotations relating to the conversation of Linda Darlene Sullivan, Donald Barrett, and John East, un-

less otherwise noted, are taken from Linda Darlene Sullivan, interview by Donald Barrett and John East, tape recording, Orlando, Fla., 24 September 1974.

2. The oft-quoted saying comes from a play by the English dramatist William Congreve (1660–1729). The original line reads, "Heaven has no rage like love to hatred turned, nor hell a fury like a woman scorned." *The Mourning Bride* (1697), act 3, scene 8.

3. John East, interview by author, Phenix City, Alabama, 28 February 1994.

4. East interview; Sullivan interview.

5. Scottsboro (Ala.) City Police Department arrest records.

6. East interview.

7. Donald Barrett testimony, *State of Alabama v. Hugh Otis Bynum, Jr.* (case number 75-CR-116), 24 March 1975, transcript, pp. 46–47; East interview.

8. Barrett testimony, p. 45.

9. Ibid.

10. Linda Darlene Sullivan testimony, p. 358; East interview.

11. Sullivan interview; East interview.

12. East interview.

13. Ibid.

14. Loy Campbell, interview by author, Langston, Ala., 4 June 1994.

15. Ibid.

16. Campbell interview; William J. Baxley II, interview by author, Birmingham, Ala., 14 January 1994; East interview.

17. Hugh Otis Bynum, Jr., testimony, p. 600; Isaac Roberts testimony, p. 401.

18. Barrett testimony, p. 492.

19. Bill Baxley, closing argument, *State of Alabama v. Hugh Otis Bynum, Jr.* (case number 75-CR-116), 29 March 1975, tape recording; Bynum testimony, p. 622.

20. Barrett testimony, p. 488.

21. W. R. Collins testimony, p. 157.

22. "County Man Killed after Liquor Sale," *Scottsboro Daily Sentinel,* 27 June 1974.

23. "County Two Jailed on VPL Charge," *Scottsboro Daily Sentinel,* 27 November 1974; Jackson County (Ala.) Sheriff's Department arrest records.

24. Baxley interview; East interview.

9. First One to the Table

1. William J. Baxley II, interview by author, Birmingham, Ala., 14 January 1994.

2. Ibid.

3. Baxley interview; John East, interview by author, tape recording, Phenix City, Ala., 28 February 1994.

4. Baxley interview.

5.   Ibid.

6.   Baxley interview; Frank Sikora, *Until Justice Rolls Down: The Bir-mingham Church Bombing Case* (Tuscaloosa: University of Ala-bama Press, 1991).

7.   Bill Baxley, closing argument, *State of Alabama v. Hugh Otis Bynum, Jr.* (case number 75-CR-116), 29 March 1975, tape record-ing.

8.   Baxley interview; East interview.

9.   Baxley interview; East interview; Billy Ray McCrary testimony, *State of Alabama v. Hugh Otis Bynum, Jr.* (case number 75-CR-116), 24–31 March 1975, transcript, p. 239.

10.   Baxley interview.

11.   Baxley interview; East interview.

12.   Baxley closing argument; Baxley interview.

13.   Baxley closing argument; Billy Ray McCrary testimony, p. 239.

14.   East interview; Billy Ray McCrary testimony, pp. 76–77.

15.   Baxley interview.

16.   Hugh Otis Bynum, Jr., testimony, p. 632; Billy Ray McCrary testi-mony, p. 78; Harold Wilson testimony, p. 407.

17.   Baxley closing argument; Baxley interview; Billy Ray McCrary tes-timony, p. 241.

18.   Baxley closing argument; Baxley interview; Billy Ray McCrary tes-timony, p. 241.

19.   Billy Ray McCrary testimony, p. 284.

20.   Baxley closing argument.

21.   Baxley closing argument; Baxley interview; Billy Ray McCrary tes-timony, p. 287.

22.   Baxley closing argument; Billy Ray McCrary testimony, p. 283; Harold Wilson testimony, p. 413.

10. "It's About Four, Isn't It, Hugh?"

1.   Harold Wilson testimony, *State of Alabama v. Hugh Otis Bynum, Jr.* (case number 75-CR-116), 25 March 1975, transcript, p. 413.

2.   Wilson testimony, p. 404; Troy Ferguson testimony, p. 352.

3.   W. R. Collins testimony, p. 160; Wilson testimony, p. 404; Ron Wilson, "No Bail for Bynum, Judge Orders," *Scottsboro Daily Senti-nel,* 18 December 1974.

4.   Wilson testimony, p. 404; Ferguson testimony, p. 352.

5.   William J. Baxley II, interview by author, Birmingham, Ala., 14 January 1994.

6.   Ibid.

7.   This and other excerpts and quotations relating to the conversa-tion of Hugh Otis Bynum, Jr., Billy Ray McCrary, and Harold Wilson, unless otherwise noted, are taken from Hugh Otis Bynum, Jr., testimony, Billy Ray McCrary testimony, and Harold Wilson testimony, *State of Alabama v. Hugh Otis Bynum, Jr.* (case number 75-CR-116), 24–31 March 1975, transcript.

8.   Donald G. Valeska II, telephone interview by author, Montgomery, Ala., 10 June 1994.

9.   Collins testimony, pp. 355–56.

10.   Baxley, closing argument, *State of Alabama v. Hugh Otis Bynum, Jr.* (case number 75-CR-116), tape recording, 29 March 1975.

11.   Ibid.

12.   Donald Barrett testimony, pp. 491–92.

13.   Collins testimony, p. 146.

14.   Baxley interview.

15.   John East, interview by author, tape recording, Phenix City, Ala., 28 February 1994.

16.   Baxley interview.

11. Terrorize Scottsboro

1.   Roderick Beddow, Jr., telephone interview by author, Birmingham, Ala., 22 August 1994. In 1971, the law firm was known as Beddow, Embry, and Beddow. In 1975, the firm reincorporated under the title of Beddow, Vowell, and Fullan; William J. Baxley II, interview by author, Birmingham, Ala., 14 January 1994.

2.   Ron Wilson, "State Court Hears Bynum Case Today," *Scottsboro Daily Sentinel*, 11 December 1974; Guy Hollis, "Bombing Arrests Don't Ease Tension," *Huntsville Times*, 8 December 1974.

3.   Robert I. Gentry, interview by author, Scottsboro, Ala., 13 December 1993.

4.   Ibid.

5.   Ibid.

6.   Gentry interview; Guy Hollis, "Bond Refused in Scottsboro Bombing Case," *Huntsville Times*, 10 December 1974.

7.   John East, interview by author, Phenix City, Ala., 28 February 1994.

8.   Ibid.

9.   Baxley interview; East interview.

10.   East interview; Donald G. Valeska II, telephone interview by author, Montgomery, Ala., 10 June 1994.

11.   Ibid.

12.   Donald Barrett testimony, *State of Alabama v. Hugh Otis Bynum, Jr.* (case number 75-CR-116), 24–31 March 1975, transcript, p. 488; East interview.

13.   Baxley interview; East interview.

14.   East interview; Valeska interview.

15.   Baxley interview; East interview; Valeska interview.

16.   Gentry interview.

17.   Hollis, "Bond Refused in Scottsboro Bombing Case"; "Judge Delays Hearing in Bombing Case," *Scottsboro Daily Sentinel*, 10 December 1974.

18.   "Judge Delays Hearing in Bombing Case."

19.   Hollis, "Bond Refused in Scottsboro Bombing Case."

20. "Judge Delays Hearing in Bombing Case."

21. Hollis, "Bond Refused in Scottsboro Bombing Case."

22. Ibid.

23. Ibid.

24. Hollis, "Bond Refused in Scottsboro Bombing Case"; Baxley interview.

25. Wilson, "State Court Hears Bynum Case Today."

26. Guy Hollis, "Bynum Bond Appeal Denied," *Huntsville Times,* 12 December 1974; Ron Wilson, "State Court Refuses Bond," *Scottsboro Daily Sentinel,* 12 December 1974.

27. Hollis, "Bynum Bond Appeal Denied"; Wilson, "State Court Refuses Bond."

28. Hollis, "Bynum Bond Appeal Denied"; Wilson, "State Court Refuses Bond."

29. Fred Casteel testimony, p. 542; Tom Sisk testimony, p. 498; Virginia Brock, "Hugh Otis Bynum, Jr.—A Series of Events Drastically Altered His Life," *Gadsden Times,* 5 January 1975; East interview.

30. Ron Wilson, "No Bail for Bynum, Judge Orders," *Scottsboro Daily Sentinel,* 18 December 1974.

31. Ibid.

32. Ibid.

33. Bill Baxley, closing argument, *State of Alabama v. Hugh Otis Bynum, Jr.* (case number 75-CR-116), 29 March 1975, tape recording; Wilson, "No Bail for Bynum, Judge Orders."

34. Wilson, "No Bail for Bynum, Judge Orders."

35. Baxley interview.

36. Ron Wilson, "Bynum Appeal Planned," *Scottsboro Daily Sentinel,* 19 December 1974.

37. Ron Wilson, "State Court Refuses Bynum Bond," *Scottsboro Daily Sentinel,* 22 December 1974.

38. East interview.

39. East interview; Billy Ray McCrary testimony, p. 97.

40. East interview.

41. Ibid.

42. Ibid.

43. Wilson, "State Court Refuses Bynum Bond."

44. Ibid.

45. Ibid.

46. "No Bond For Bynum—Again," *Scottsboro Daily Sentinel,* 29 December 1974.

47. "Supreme Court Denies Bynum Bond," *Scottsboro Daily Sentinel,* 8 January 1975.

48. "No Link Seen in Gunshot, Bombing," *Scottsboro Daily Sentinel,* 8 January 1975.

49. Baxley interview; Peggy Ferguson, "Tally Steps Down; Sullivan Appointed," *Scottsboro Daily Sentinel,* 31 January 1975.

50. "Bond Set for Bynum," *Scottsboro Daily Sentinel,* 4 February 1975.

51. "Bynum Released on Bond," *Scottsboro Daily Sentinel,* 5 February 1975.

52. "Trial Date Set for Bynum," *Scottsboro Daily Sentinel,* 13 February 1975.

53. "Bynum in Court; Motions Answered," *Scottsboro Daily Sentinel,* 27 February 1975.

54. Baxley interview; East interview.

55. Ron Wilson, "Bynum Facing Second Charge," 14 March 1975.

12. The Voir Dire

1. "32 Die in Jackson," *Jackson County Sentinel,* 17 March 1932.

2. William J. Baxley II, interview by author, Birmingham, Ala., 10 May 1994.

3. John A. Yung IV, telephone interview by author, Montgomery, Ala., 25 August 1994.

4. Ibid.

5. William M. Bowen, Jr., telephone interview by author, Montgomery, Ala., 18 August 1994; Baxley interview.

6. Baxley interview; Donald G. Valeska II, telephone interview by author, Montgomery, Ala., 10 June 1994.

7. Bill Baxley, closing argument, *State of Alabama v. Hugh Otis Bynum, Jr.* (case number 75-CR-116), 29 March 1975, tape recording.

8. Roderick Beddow, Jr., telephone interview by author, Birmingham, Ala., 22 August 1994.

9. Baxley closing argument.

10. Billy Ray McCrary testimony, *State of Alabama v. Hugh Otis Bynum, Jr.* (case number 75-CR-116), 24–31 March 1975, transcript; Baxley interview.

11. Baxley interview; Valeska interview; John East, interview by author, tape recording, Phenix City, Ala., 28 February 1994.

12. Baxley interview.

13. John East testimony, p. 734.

14. East interview.

15. East interview; Archie F. Stewart, interview by author, Scottsboro, Ala., 15 July 1994.

16. East interview.

17. East interview; Stewart interview.

18. East interview; Peggy Roberson, "Bynum Following Old Habits as Jury Works," *Birmingham News,* Dixie edition, 30 March 1975.

19. East interview.

20. Ron Wilson, "Madness: Manslaughter; Bynum Witness Appears," *Scottsboro Daily Sentinel,* 21 March 1975.

21. Linda Darlene Sullivan testimony, p. 376.

22. Kathryn Johnson, "Three Dead, 50 Hurt in Atlanta Tornado," *Huntsville (Alabama) Times,* 24 March 1975.

23. Baxley interview; Valeska interview; Ron Wilson, "Bynum—His Life and Times," *Scottsboro Daily Sentinel*, 1 April 1975; Larry Smith, "Bynum on Trial for Campbell Bombing," *Jackson County Advertiser*, 27 March 1975.

24. Baxley interview.

25. Smith, "Bynum on Trial for Campbell Bombing."

26. Archie D. Farmer, interview by author, Rosalie, Ala., 16 July 1994.

13. A Crazy Motive

1. Peggy Roberson, "His Chief Witness 'Just as Guilty as Anyone': Baxley," *Birmingham News*, 25 March 1975.

2. Guy Hollis, "State May Call Surprise Witness in Bynum Case," *Huntsville Times*, 25 March 1975.

3. Roberson, "His Chief Witness 'Just as Guilty as Anyone.' "

4. Hollis, "State May Call Surprise Witness."

5. Roberson, "His Chief Witness 'Just as Guilty as Anyone.' "

6. Ron Wilson, "Witnesses Take Stand in case against Bynum," *Scottsboro Daily Sentinel*, 25 March 1975.

7. Roberson, "His Chief Witness 'Just as Guilty as Anyone.' "

8. John East, interview by author, tape recording, Phenix City, Ala., 28 February 1994.

9. The testimony of Irene Glass and quotations of other trial testimony, unless otherwise noted, are taken from *State of Alabama v. Hugh Otis Bynum, Jr.* (case number 75-CR-116), 24–31 March 1975, transcript.

10. East interview.

11. Ibid.

12. William J. Baxley II, interview by author, Birmingham, Ala., 10 May 1994; Loy Campbell, interview by author, Langston, Ala., 4 June 1994; East interview.

13. Campbell interview.

14. Bill Baxley closing argument, *State of Alabama v. Hugh Otis Bynum, Jr.* (case number 75-CR-116), 29 March 1975, tape recording.

14. He Will Bleed to Death

1. William J. Baxley II, interview by author, Birmingham, Ala., 10 May 1994; Ron Wilson, "McCrary Testifies in Bynum Case," *Scottsboro Daily Sentinel*, 26 March 1975.

2. Excerpts from the testimony of Billy Ray McCrary and quotations of other trial testimony, unless otherwise noted, are taken from *State of Alabama v. Hugh Otis Bynum, Jr.*, (case number 75-CR-116), 24–31 March 1975, transcript.

3. John East, interview by author, tape recording, Phenix City, Ala., 28 February 1994.

4. Baxley interview; East interview; Loy Campbell, interview by author, Langston, Ala., 4 June 1994.

5. Campbell interview.

6. Herman A. Watson, Jr., telephone interview by author, Huntsville, Ala., 23 May 1994.
7. Ibid.
8. Baxley interview; Watson interview.
9. Baxley interview; East interview.
10. Baxley interview.

15. Like a Child That Has Seen a New Toy

1. Excerpts from the testimony of Billy Ray McCrary and quotations of other trial testimony, unless otherwise noted, are from *State of Alabama v. Hugh Otis Bynum, Jr.* (case number 75-CR-116), 24–31 March 1975, transcript.
2. William J. Baxley II, interview by author, Birmingham, Ala., 10 May 1994.
3. Herman A. Watson, Jr., telephone interview by author, Huntsville, Ala., 23 May 1994.
4. Baxley interview; John East, interview by author, tape recording, Phenix City, Ala., 28 February 1994.
5. Baxley interview.
6. "State Witness Given Jail 'Poker' Money, Says Jackson Deputy," *Huntsville Times,* 27 March 1975.
7. East interview.
8. East interview; John Poarch testimony, pp. 692–93.
9. Baxley interview.
10. Ibid.

16. We Have a Job to Do

1. Ron Wilson, "Hale's Girlfriend Testifies in Court," *Scottsboro Daily Sentinel,* 27 March 1975.
2. Loy Campbell, interview by author, Langston, Ala., 4 June 1994.
3. Excerpts from the testimony of Linda Darlene Sullivan and quotations of other trial testimony, unless otherwise noted, are taken from *State of Alabama v. Hugh Otis Bynum, Jr.* (case number 75-CR-116), 24–31 March 1975, transcript.
4. Campbell interview.
5. William J. Baxley II, interview by author, Birmingham, Ala., 10 May 1994; Campbell interview; John East, interview by author, tape recording, Phenix City, Ala., 28 February 1994.
6. Campbell interview.
7. Ibid.

17. Truth and Veracity

1. This and other excerpts and quotations of trial testimony, unless otherwise noted, are taken from *State of Alabama v. Hugh Otis Bynum, Jr.* (case number 75-CR-116), 24–31 March, 1975, transcript.

18. I Wouldn't Do a Thing Like That

1. Guy Hollis, "Bynum Jury Quits without a Verdict," *Huntsville Times,* 30 March 1975; Archie D. Farmer, interview by author, Rosalie, Ala., 16 July 1994.

2. Excerpts from the testimony of Lilah McCrary and quotations of other trial testimony, unless otherwise noted, are taken from *State of Alabama v. Hugh Otis Bynum, Jr.* (case number 75-CR-116), 24–31 March 1975, transcript.

3. Roderick Beddow, Jr., telephone interview by author, Birmingham, Ala., 22 August 1994.

4. Guy Hollis, "Bynum Denies Charges," *Huntsville Times,* 27 March 1975.

5. Ron Wilson, "Jury Deciding Bynum's Fate," *Scottsboro Daily Sentinel,* 30 March 1975.

6. John East, interview by author, tape recording, Phenix City, Ala., 28 February 1994.

7. Ibid.

19. Putting On a Front

1. William J. Baxley II, interview by author, Birmingham, Ala., 10 May 1994; Guy Hollis, "Bynum Case Slated for Deliberation," *Huntsville Times,* 29 March 1975.

2. Roderick Beddow, Jr., telephone interview by author, Birmingham, Ala., 22 August 1994.

3. John East, interview by author, tape recording, Phenix City, Ala., 28 February 1994; Oliver Laney testimony, *State of Alabama v. Hugh Otis Bynum, Jr.* (case number 75-CR-116), motion for a new trial, 7 July 1975, transcript.

4. Excerpts from the testimony of John Poarch and quotations of other trial testimony, unless otherwise noted, are taken from *State of Alabama v. Hugh Otis Bynum, Jr.* (case number 75-CR-116), 24–31 March 1975, transcript.

5. Hollis, "Bynum Case Slated for Deliberation."

6. East interview.

7. Ibid.

8. East interview; Beddow interview.

20. Lay Down with Dogs

1. Bill Baxley, closing argument, *State of Alabama v. Hugh Otis Bynum, Jr.* (case number 75-CR-116), 29 March 1975, tape recording.

2. John Yung, closing argument, *State of Alabama v. Hugh Otis Bynum, Jr.* (case number 75-CR-116), 29 March 1975, transcript.

3. Ibid.

4. William J. Baxley II, interview by author, Birmingham, Ala., 10 May 1994; William M. Bowen, Jr., telephone interview by author, Montgomery, Ala., 18 August 1994; John East, interview by author, tape recording, Phenix City, Ala., 28 February 1994; John Yung, telephone interview by author, Montgomery, Ala., 25 August 1994.

5. Yung interview.

6. Baxley interview.

7. Yung interview.

8. Ron Wilson, "Jury Deciding Bynum's Fate," *Scottsboro Daily Sentinel*, 30 March 1975; Baxley closing argument.

9. Wilson, "Jury Deciding Bynum's Fate"; Baxley closing argument.

10. Baxley closing argument; Roderick Beddow, Jr., telephone interview by author, Birmingham, Ala., 22 August 1994.

11. Baxley closing argument.

12. Baxley closing argument; Wilson, "Jury Deciding Bynum's Fate."

13. Baxley closing argument.

14. Wilson, "Jury Deciding Bynum's Fate"; Baxley closing argument; Peggy Roberson, "Bynum Following Old Habits as Jury Works," *Birmingham News*, 30 March 1975.

15. Wilson, "Jury Deciding Bynum's Fate."

16. Ibid.

17. East interview; Bowen interview.

18. Baxley closing argument.

19. Tallulah Bush, interview by author, Scottsboro, Ala., 1 February 1994.

21. The Verdict

1. Judge William C. Sullivan, oral instructions to the jury, *State of Alabama v. Hugh Otis Bynum, Jr.* (case number 75-CR-116), 29 March 1975, transcript.

2. Ibid.

3. Ibid.

4. William J. Baxley II, interview by author, Birmingham, Ala., 10 May 1994; John East, interview by author, tape recording, Phenix City, Ala., 28 February 1994.

5. Baxley interview; Frank Sikora, *Until Justice Rolls Down: The Birmingham Church Bombing Case* (Tuscaloosa: University of Alabama Press, 1991), 49.

6. Archie D. Farmer, interview by author, Rosalie, Ala., 16 July 1994.

7. Ibid.

8. Ibid.

9. Ibid.

10. Ibid.

11. Farmer interview; *State of Alabama v. Hugh Otis Bynum, Jr.*, 29 March 1975, transcript, pp. 769–70.

12. Farmer interview.

13. Ibid.

14. *State of Alabama v. Hugh Otis Bynum, Jr.*, transcript, p. 77.

15. Farmer interview.

16. *State of Alabama v. Hugh Otis Bynum, Jr.*, transcript, p. 770–71; Guy Hollis, "Bynum Jury Quits without a Verdict," *Huntsville Times*, 30 March 1975.

17. Farmer interview.

18. Ibid.

19. Ibid.

20. East interview; Roderick Beddow, Jr., telephone interview by author, Birmingham, Ala., 22 August 1994.

21. Robert G. Campbell testimony, motion for new trial, *State of Alabama v. Hugh Otis Bynum, Jr.*, 7 July 1975, transcript, p. 817.

22. Farmer interview.

23. Farmer interview; Loy Campbell, interview by author, Langston, Ala., 7 July 1994; John C. Graham, "The Mountains Laugh Because He Walked upon Them: A Remembrance of My Daddy," unpublished typescript, 1990, pp. 27–28.

24. William M. Bowen, Jr., telephone interview by author, Montgomery, Ala., 18 August 1994.

25. Farmer interview.

26. Guy Hollis, "Bynum Found Guilty, Given 20-Year Term," *Huntsville Times*, 31 March 1975.

27. Ibid.

28. Donald G. Valeska II, telephone interview by author, Montgomery, Ala., 10 June 1994.

22. Aftermath

1. Jackson County Circuit Court records, Scottsboro, Ala.

2. James Westmoreland, John Graham, Grady Roberts, Roy Shaw, James Bell, Homer Johnson, Gaylon Stone, Wesley Allen, and John Wann testimony, *State of Alabama v. Hugh Otis Bynum, Jr.* (case number 75-CR-116), motion for new trial, 7 July 1975, transcript; Roderick Beddow, Jr., telephone interview by author, Birmingham, Ala., 22 August 1994.

3. Jackson County Circuit Court records, Scottsboro, Ala.

4. Ibid.

5. Beddow interview.

6. Larry Smith, "McCrary Remains Jailed," *Scottsboro Daily Sentinel*, 22 June 1975.

7. Ibid.

8. Larry Smith, "Decision Expected on McCrary Hearing," *Scottsboro Daily Sentinel*, 1 July 1975.

9. "McCrary Probation Revoked by Judge," *Scottsboro Daily Sentinel*, 9 July 1975.

10. Jackson County (Ala.) Circuit Court records, Scottsboro, Ala.

11. "Wisconsin Authorities Arrest Hale," *Scottsboro Daily Sentinel*, 17 November 1976.

12. Ibid.

13. William J. Baxley II, interview by author, Birmingham, Ala., 10 May 1994; John East, interview by author, tape recording, Phenix City, Ala., 28 February 1994.

14. East interview; Loy Campbell, interview by author, Langston, Ala., 10 June 1994.

15.   Campbell interview.

16.   Ibid.

17.   Jackson County (Ala.) Circuit Court records, Scottsboro, Ala.

18.   Baxley interview; Roderick Beddow, Jr., telephone interview by author, Birmingham, Ala., 22 August 1994; Frank Sikora, *Until Justice Rolls Down: The Birmingham Church Bombing Case* (Tuscaloosa: University of Alabama Press, 1991).

19.   Beddow interview.

20.   J. D. White, telephone interview by author, Montgomery, Ala., 1 August 1994; Campbell interview.

21.   Campbell interview.

22.   Associated Press, "Campbell Says Bombing Changed Life for Worse," *Scottsboro Daily Sentinel*, 25 May 1978.

23.   Ibid.

24.   Associated Press, "Bynum, McCrary Ordered to Pay Campbell $2 Mil.," *Scottsboro Daily Sentinel*, 26 May 1978.

25.   Beddow interview.

26.   Associated Press, "Campbell Court Suit Reviewed," *Scottsboro Daily Sentinel*, 16 October 1981.

27.   Ibid.

28.   White interview; "Bynum Dies in Hospital," *Scottsboro Daily Sentinel*, 11 May 1980.

29.   "Bynum Dies in Hospital."

23. Postscript

1.   William J. Baxley II, interview by author, Birmingham, Ala., 10 May 1994.

2.   Baxley interview; Frank Sikora, *Until Justice Rolls Down: The Birmingham Church Bombing Case* (Tuscaloosa: University of Alabama Press, 1991), 156.

3.   Herman A. Watson, Jr., telephone interview by author, Huntsville, Ala., 23 May 1994.

4.   Sikora, *Until Justice Rolls Down*, 156; John A. Yung IV, telephone interview by author, Montgomery, Ala., 25 August 1994.

5.   Baxley interview; William M. Bowen, Jr., telephone interview by author, Montgomery, Ala., 18 August 1994.

6.   Donald G. Valeska II, telephone interview by author, Montgomery, Ala., 10 June 1994.

7.   Roderick Beddow, Jr., telephone interview by author, Birmingham, Ala., 22 August 1994.

8.   Loy Campbell, interview by author, Langston, Ala., 10 June 1994.

9.   Ibid.

10.   Ibid.

11.   John East, interview by author, tape recording, Phenix City, Ala., 28 February 1994.

12.   East interview; Sikora, *Until Justice Rolls Down*, 152–53.

Index

Collins, Sheriff W. R. "Bob," 30, 32, 42, 51, 63, 68, 70, 76, 77, 87, 104, 112, 113, 114, 115, 122, 123, 124, 128, 134, 137, 141, 150, 154, 156, 165–66, 173–74, 177, 184, 187, 195, 206; friendship with Hugh Otis Bynum, 24–25; testimony, 116–18; sent to interview Charles X. Hale, 199–200
Cordell, Jimmy, 29
Cornelison, C. E. "Eb," 90, 151, 158
Cotten, Ed, 61, 155
Cotten, Minnie, 105
Cumberland Mountain, 8, 16
Cumberland School of Law, 96

Daily Sentinel, 128
Da Nang, South Vietnam, 194
Dante, 182
Dawson, Joe, 103
Dawson, Porter: testimony, 106–8
Dean, C. T., 42
Dean, William G., 45
Decatur, Ala., 13, 14
DeKalb County, Ala., 29, 33, 159
DeKalb County High School, 33
Dickerson, Howard Luther, 100
Dixon, E. Jennings, 71
Dolberry, John T., 42
Dothan, Ala., 65, 78, 91, 191
Downtown Merchants Association, 6
Draper Penitentiary, 57
Dresden, Germany, 13
Dutton, Ala., 103

East, Jewell, 205
East, John, 54–55, 67, 77, 87–88, 90–91, 99–100, 105, 106, 118–19, 129, 138, 164, 176, 177–78, 194, 205–6; background, 50–51; interviews Linda Darlene Sullivan, 56–65; search of Hugh Otis Bynum house, 80–81; meets John Poarch in Huntsville, 134–35
Eau Claire County, Wisc., 199
Embry, T. Eric, 90
Evett, Jimmy Dewayne, 44, 45, 108; testimony, 115

Fabius, Ala., 103
Farmer, Adrienne, 193
Farmer, Archie Douglas "Doug," 103, 191–95, 197

Farrior, Norman, 39, 176, 181, 188
Faulkner, James, 90
Fayette County, Ala., 39
Federal Bureau of Investigation (FBI), 40, 41, 51, 53
Ferguson, Troy, 70; testimony, 133–34
First Monday Trade Day, 31, 64, 80, 106, 112, 114, 130, 145, 150, 154, 157, 167, 176, 179, 181; history of, 3–6
Flat Rock, Ala., 29, 103
Florida, 52, 53, 60, 62, 63, 65, 66, 80, 139, 140, 168, 187, 199, 200, 205, 206
Fort McClellan, Anniston, Ala., 49
Fort Oglethorpe, Ga., 53
Fort Payne, Ala., 29, 33, 34, 72, 119, 137, 138, 146
Foster, Harold, 19, 63, 100, 194
Foster, Dr. Tommy, 105
Franklin, Tenn., 10
Freedom Riders, 14
Fullan, James M., Jr., 27, 79; at preliminary hearing, 82–86
Fyffe, Ala., 33

Gadsden, Ala., 13
Gallion, MacDonald, 66
Gamble, Linda, 6
Gant, Jerry Brent, 48, 100, 163
Gentry, Judge R. I. "Bob," 6, 7, 18, 31, 36, 79–80, 82–83, 206
Georgetown Law Center, 95
Georgia, 8, 52, 65, 66
Gibson, George H., 175, 177
Giles, Jack, 119
Gilliam, Jimmy, 151
Ginsberg, Allen, 14
Glass, Irene: testimony, 105–6
Goodyear Tire and Rubber Company, 9
Graddick, Charlie, 203
Graham, John H., 103, 191, 192, 193, 194–95, 197
Grant, Ala., 155
Grant Post Office, 155
Great Depression, 17–18, 32
Green, Claxton, Jr., 22, 25, 26, 29–30, 116
Grider, Lonnie: testimony, 129–30, 187
Guntersville Lake, 16, 52

McCrary, Joyce (Turner), 89, 121–22, 146, 152, 156. *See also* Turner, Joyce
McCrary, Lilah, 43, 64, 112, 121–23, 124, 145, 151, 152, 180, 184, 186, 204; testimony, 153–56
McCrary, Virgil, 48, 187, 188; testimony, 118
McGee, Darlene, 71
McKnight, Bill, 90–91
McLaughlin, Ray, 150–51
McNair, Denise, 206
McNeese, Bill, 197
Maddox, Hugh, 90
Madison County, Ala., 10, 13
Madison County Sheriff's Department, 177
Malcolm X, 14
Marietta, Ga., 203
Martintown Hill, Ala., 64, 77, 149, 162, 170
Memphis-Charleston Railroad, 10
Merrill, Pelham, 90
Mexico, 140, 159, 167, 187
Micronesia, 96
Miller, Robert, 115–16
Milnes, H. Jack, 148
Mims, Fla., 52, 80
Mink Creek, Ala., 52, 59, 138
Mobile County, Ala., 98
Money, Joe, 34
Montgomery, Ala., 24, 36, 55, 61, 67, 77, 78, 83, 86, 120, 125, 133, 134, 145, 172, 174, 180, 188, 191, 200, 202, 203, 204
Moore, Jamie, 40
Morgan, Robert, 43
Morris, Ernest "Ern," 63
Morrison, Joe, Jr.: testimony, 109–10
Moscow, 13
Mount, Paul, 70, 129, 134–35, 174
Mountain Street, 107, 113

National Association for the Advancement of Colored People, 13
North Carolina, 10
Northeast Alabama State Community College, 206

Oak Street, 107
Old Baptist Institute, 18
Orlando, Fla., 51, 52, 56, 61, 62

Paint Rock, Ala., 13, 95
Parker, Vaughn, 19, 100

Paul, Clarence, 115
Payne, George Hunter, 90, 113, 125, 156, 157
Paynes Drug Store, 5, 39, 157
Peace Corps, 96
Pepper, Ed, 43, 120
Phenix City, Ala., 50, 51, 205
Pisgah, Ala., 6, 57, 100, 103, 136, 191
Poarch, John, 88, 115, 118–19, 139, 147, 176, 177, 178, 180–81, 184, 191, 204; located by Artie Wooten, 128–29; brought to Scottsboro, 134–35; testimony, 169–75
Powell's Crossroads, Ala., 206
Price, Ollie, Jr., 26–28, 104
Price, Victoria, 13
Prohibition, 11
Prosch, Dr. Gus, 40

Reconstruction, 203
Redstone Arsenal, Huntsville, Ala., 103
Reed, Robert, 42, 43, 120, 154
Reid, Mayor John T., 25, 26, 30, 63, 68, 104, 112, 114, 122, 123, 142, 158, 166–67, 184, 206
Revere Copper and Brass, 9
Richards, Lucy, 191
Roberson, Peggy, 178, 194
Roberts, Grady, 103, 191, 192, 193, 197
Roberts, Isaac, 159, 167, 187, 188; testimony, 139–40
Rosalie, Ala., 51

Sage Town, Ala., 10
Saigon, South Vietnam, 194
Salt Peter Cave, Ala., 19
Sand Mountain, 8, 14, 16, 33, 48, 51, 54, 57, 206
Sargent, J. D., 35
Scotland, 10
Scott, Robert Thomas, 6, 9–10, 16
Scottsboro, Ala., 18, 22, 23, 26, 28, 30, 36, 53, 56, 68, 69, 70, 71, 75, 77, 79, 81, 90, 91, 96, 100, 106, 107, 108, 109, 119, 125, 129, 133, 135, 136, 139, 152, 171, 174, 175, 177, 180, 181, 182, 191, 200, 201, 202, 204; history, 8–16; First Monday Trade Day, 3–6; "The Friendly City," 25; jury members from, 103; lawyers, 34, 51, 82,